GREAT
AMERICAN
CIVIL WAR
STORIES

LYONS PRESS CLASSICS

GREAT AMERICAN CIVIL WAR STORIES

EDITED BY

LAMAR UNDERWOOD

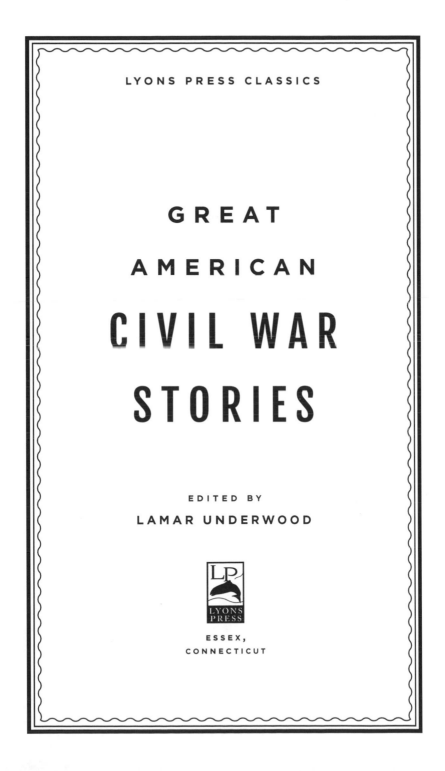

LYONS
PRESS

ESSEX,
CONNECTICUT

An imprint of Globe Pequot, the trade division of
The Rowman & Littlefield Publishing Group, Inc.
4501 Forbes Blvd., Ste. 200
Lanham, MD 20706
www.rowman.com

Distributed by NATIONAL BOOK NETWORK

British Library Cataloguing in Publication Information available

Library of Congress Cataloging-in-Publication Data

Names: Underwood, Lamar, editor.
Title: Great American Civil War stories / edited by Lamar Underwood.
Description: Essex, Connecticut : Lyons Press, [2023] | Series: Great
American stories | Includes bibliographical references.
Identifiers: LCCN 2022028116 (print) | LCCN 2022028117 (ebook) | ISBN
9781493069088 (paperback) | ISBN 9781493069095 (epub)
Subjects: LCSH: United States–History–Civil War, 1861-1865–Anecdotes. |
United States–History–Civil War, 1861-1865–Personal narratives.
Classification: LCC E655 .G767 2023 (print) | LCC E655 (ebook) | DDC
973.7–dc23/eng/20220707
LC record available at https://lccn.loc.gov/2022028116
LC ebook record available at https://lccn.loc.gov/2022028117

♾️™ The paper used in this publication meets the minimum requirements
of American National Standard for Information Sciences—Permanence of
Paper for Printed Library Materials, ANSI/NISO Z39.48-1992.

CONTENTS

INTRODUCTION

Today's reader of the myriad Civil War books available does not seek the facts that once stirred the population, clamoring, more excited with every heartbeat: news! Headlines large and small, telegraphs clicking with activity, voices shouting the names of strange places where a tide of blood was the bounty of both armies, North and South. Bull Run, Antietam, Chancellorsville, Vicksburg, Gettysburg, and countless others, all resulting in casualty lists.

Looking back on events of 175-plus years ago, both scholarly and pleasure-seeking readers are longing to experience a "felt life" that makes them part of the stories lived by others. Reading can transport any of us from easy chairs to the turmoil of exploding shells and bullet volleys so thick they cut cornfields to shreds in minutes, amid orders being shouted by commanders full of doubt, even panic. And always the weather— often cruel and sometimes the deadliest enemy of all.

Back in 1953, when Americans "liked Ike" and TV was burgeoning with growth—with possibilities yet to be discovered—CBS TV launched *You Are There*. Add to the mix leading news anchorman Walter Cronkite with his confidence-building voice, and you have a hit show.

Writers roamed the historic landscape freely, focusing on dramatic events such as Lincoln's Gettysburg Address, Pearl Harbor, even classics from ancient Rome. With actors in costumes and playing the roles that cast one back to the actual events, *You Are There* lived up to its promise, with a five-year run in the black-and-white TV of that time.

In this book your editor and the publishers—admittedly poor substitutes for Walter Cronkite and CBS TV [for consistency with above]—still hope to convince you that there is plenty of *You Are There* magic in the pages ahead. All you have to do is go there and see for yourself.

These are personal accounts of what happened during Pickett's charge at Gettysburg, at wounded Stonewall Jackson's bedside, and in the house where Grant met Lee at Appomattox. Sometimes the prose voices of those days may sound stiff and stilted compared to the free-wheeling voices of today. Nevertheless, they are authentic and alive as the real events unfold.

Often when I find myself looking back on the Civil War books and stories that have come my way, I find myself wondering, How in the world did any of the combat veterans survive the battles? Yet, survive they did. And in their well-earned years of peace that followed the war, many took their pens in hand and wrote about what they had seen and heard. I am very grateful that they did.

As you read today, you might feel more comfortable if Walter Cronkite were reading the text to you. But the *You Are There* magic still lives in the printed words, when given the chance.

—Lamar Underwood

EDITOR'S NOTE

The stories that follow, excerpted from full books, are presented with their original spelling and punctuation largely untouched. Spelling errors will be apparent, such as Pittsburg for Pittsburgh. Also, readers should be aware that in some cases the writers have incorrect dates. In all cases, the numbers of troops in the various encounters have not been validated to historical accuracy. They are given as written and have suspect accuracy in some cases. At the time most of these stories were written, paragraphs sometimes ran on for pages. The editor has inserted paragraph breaks in appropriate spots to provide a break from the monotonous grayness of the long-running original paragraphs.

—Lamar Underwood

1

LINCOLN AT WAR: PROMINENT LETTERS AND PAPERS

BY ABRAHAM LINCOLN

The president was not only a man of clear thinking; he had a sharp wit to deliver his thoughts with great force. The tough going for the Union Army in the early stages of the war sometimes moved Abraham Lincoln to tears and sometimes to anger.

TELEGRAM TO GENERAL G. B. McCLELLAN. WAR DEPARTMENT, WASHINGTON, D.C.

September 15, 1862. 2.45 P.M. MAJOR-GENERAL CLELLAN:

Your despatch of to-day received. God bless you, and all with you. Destroy the rebel army if possible.

A. LINCOLN.

TELEGRAM TO J. K. DUBOIS. WASHINGTON, D.C., September 15, 1862. 3 P.M.

HON. K. DUBOIS, Springfield, Illinois:

I now consider it safe to say that General McClellan has gained a great victory over the great rebel army in Maryland, between Fredericktown and Hagerstown. He is now pursuing the flying foe.

RECORD EXPLAINING THE DISMISSAL OF MAJOR JOHN J. KEY FROM THE MILITARY SERVICE OF THE UNITED STATES. EXECUTIVE MANSION, WASHINGTON, September 26, 1862.

MAJOR JOHN J. KEY:

I am informed that, in answer to the question, "Why was not the rebel army bagged immediately after the battle near Sharps-burg?" propounded to you by Major Levi C. Turner, Judge Advocate, etc., you said: "That is not the game. The object is, that neither army shall get much advantage of the other; that both shall be kept in the field till they are exhausted, when we will make a compromise and save slavery." I shall be very happy if you will, within twenty-four hours from the receipt of this, prove to me by Major Turner that you did not, either literally or in substance, make the answer stated.

[Above delivered to Major Key at 10.25 a.m., September 27.]

At about 11 o'clock A.M., September 27, 1862, Major Key and Major Turner appeared before me. Major Turner says:

"As I remember it, the conversation was: 'Why did we not bag them after the battle of Sharpsburg?' Major Key's reply was: 'That was not the game; that we should tire the rebels out and ourselves; that that was the only way the Union could be preserved, we come together fraternally, and slavery be saved.'"

On cross-examination, Major Turner says he has frequently heard Major Key converse in regard to the present troubles, and never heard him utter a sentiment unfavorable to the maintenance of the Union. He has never uttered anything which he, Major T., would call disloyalty. The particular conversation detailed was a private one.

In my view, it is wholly inadmissible for any gentleman holding a military commission from the United States to utter such sentiments as Major Key is within proved to have done. Therefore, let Major John J. Key be forthwith dismissed from the military service of the United States.

A. LINCOLN.

TO GENERAL G. B. McCLELLAN.
EXECUTIVE MANSION, WASHINGTON, October 13, 1862.

MY DEAR SIR—You remember my speaking to you of what I called your over-cautiousness. Are you not over-cautious when you assume that you cannot do what the enemy is constantly doing? Should you not claim to be at least his equal in prowess, and act upon the claim?

As I understand, you telegraphed General Halleck that you cannot subsist your army at Winchester unless the railroad from Harper's Ferry to that point be put in working order. But the enemy does now subsist his army at Winchester, at a distance nearly twice as great from railroad transportation as you would have to do, without the railroad last named. He now wagons from Culpepper CourtHouse, which is just about twice as far as you would have to do from Harper's Ferry. He is certainly not more than half as well provided with wagons as you are. I certainly should be pleased for you to have the advantage of the railroad from Harper's Ferry to Winchester; but it wastes an the remainder of autumn to give it to you, and, in fact, ignores the question of time, which cannot and must not be ignored.

Again, one of the standard maxims of war, as you know, is "to operate upon the enemy's communications as much as possible, without exposing your own." You seem to act as if this applies against you, but cannot apply in your favor. Change positions with the enemy, and think you not he would break your communication with Richmond within the next twenty-four hours? You dread his going into Pennsylvania. But if he does so in full force, he gives up his communications to you absolutely, and you have nothing to do but to follow and ruin him; if he does so with less than full force, fall upon and beat what is left behind all the easier.

Exclusive of the water line, you are now nearer to Richmond than the enemy is, by the route that you can and he must take. Why can you not reach there before him, unless you admit that he is more than your equal on a march? His route is the arc of a circle, while yours is the chord. The roads are as good on yours as on his.

You know I desired, but did not order, you to cross the Potomac below instead of above the Shenandoah and Blue Ridge. My idea was that this would at once menace the enemy's communications, which I would seize if he would permit. If he should move northward, I would follow him closely, holding his communications. If he should prevent our seizing his communications, and move toward Richmond, I would press closely to him, fight him if a favorable opportunity should present, and at least try to beat him to Richmond on the inside track. I say "try;" if we never try, we shall never succeed. If he makes a stand at Winchester, moving neither north or south, I would fight him there, on the idea that if we cannot beat him when he bears the wastage of coming to us, we never can when we bear the wastage of going to him. This proposition is a simple truth, and is too important to be lost sight of for a moment. In coming to us he tenders us an advantage which we should not waive. We should not so operate as to merely drive him away. As we must beat him somewhere or fail finally, we can do it, if at all, easier near to us than far away. If we cannot beat the enemy where he now is, we never can, he again being within the entrenchments of Richmond.

Recurring to the idea of going to Richmond on the inside track, the facility of supplying from the side away from the enemy is remarkable, as it were, by the different spokes of a wheel extending from the hub toward the rim, and this whether you move directly by the chord or on the inside arc, hugging the Blue Ridge more closely. The chord line, as you see, carries you by Aldie, Hay Market, and Fredericksburg; and you see how turn-pikes, railroads, and finally the Potomac, by Aquia Creek, meet you at all points from WASHINGTON; the same, only the lines lengthened a little, if you press closer to the Blue Ridge part of the way.

The gaps through the Blue Ridge I understand to be about the following distances from Harper's Ferry, to wit: Vestal's, 5 miles; Gregory's, 13; Snicker's, 18; Ashby's, 28; Manassas, 38; Chester, 45; and Thornton's, 53. I should think it preferable to take the route nearest the enemy, disabling him to make an important move without your knowledge, and compelling him to keep his forces together for dread of you. The gaps would enable you to attack if you should wish. For a great part of the way you would be practically between the enemy and both WASHINGTON and Richmond, enabling us to spare you the greatest number of troops from here. When at length running for Richmond ahead of him enables him to move this way, if he does so, turn and attack him in rear. But I think he should be engaged long before such a point is reached. It is all easy if our troops march as well as the enemy, and it is unmanly to say they cannot do it. This letter is in no sense an order.

Yours truly,

A. LINCOLN.

GENERAL McCLELLAN'S TIRED HORSES TELEGRAM
TO GENERAL G. B. McCLELLAN.
WAR DEPARTMENT, WASHINGTON CITY,
October 24 [25?], 1862.

MAJOR-GENERAL McCLELLAN:

I have just read your despatch about sore-tongued and fatigued horses. Will you pardon me for asking what the horses of your army have done since the battle of Antietam that fatigues anything?

A. LINCOLN.

TELEGRAM TO GENERAL G. B. McCLELLAN.

EXECUTIVE MANSION WASHINGTON,

October 26, 1862. 11.30 a.m.

MAJOR-GENERAL McCLELLAN:

Yours, in reply to mine about horses, received. Of course you know the facts better than I; still two considerations remain: Stuart's cavalry outmarched ours, having certainly done more marked service on the Peninsula and everywhere since. Secondly, will not a movement of our army be a relief to the cavalry, compelling the enemy to concentrate instead of foraging in squads everywhere? But I am so rejoiced to learn from your despatch to General Halleck that you begin crossing the river this morning.

A. LINCOLN.

TELEGRAM TO GENERAL G. B. McCLELLAN.

EXECUTIVE MANSION, WASHINGTON,

October 27, 1862. 3.25 p.m. MAJOR-GENERAL McCLELLAN:

Your despatch of 3 P.M. to-day, in regard to filling up old regiments with drafted men, is received, and the request therein shall be complied with as far as practicable.

And now I ask a distinct answer to the question, Is it your purpose not to go into action again until the men now being drafted in the States are incorporated into the old regiments?

A. LINCOLN

TELEGRAM TO GENERAL G. B. McCLELLAN.
EXECUTIVE MANSION, WASHINGTON D.C,
October 29, 1863. MAJOR-GENERAL McCLELLAN:

Your despatches of night before last, yesterday, and last night all received. I am much pleased with the movement of the army. When you get entirely across the river let me know. What do you know of the enemy?

A. LINCOLN.

ORDER RELIEVING GENERAL G. B. McCLELLAN
AND MAKING OTHER CHANGES.
EXECUTIVE MANSION, WASHINGTON, D.C,
November 5, 1862.

By direction of the President, it is ordered that Major-General McClellan be relieved from the command of the Army of the Potomac, and that Major-General Burnside take the command of that army. Also that Major-General Hunter take command of the corps in said army which is now commanded by General Burnside. That Major-General Fitz. John Porter be relieved from command of the corps he now commands in said army, and that Major-General Hooker take command of said corps.

The general-in-chief is authorized, in [his] discretion, to issue an order substantially as the above forthwith, or so soon as he may deem proper.

A. LINCOLN.

DELAYING TACTICS OF GENERALS TO
GENERAL N. P. BANKS.
EXECUTIVE MANSION, WASHINGTON,
November 22, 1862.

MY DEAR GENERAL BANKS:—Early last week you left me in high hope with your assurance that you would be off with your expedition at the end of that week, or early in this. It is now the end of this, and I have just been overwhelmed and confounded with the sight of a requisition made by you which, I am assured, cannot be filled and got off within an hour short of two months. I enclose you a copy of the requisition, in some hope that it is not genuine—that you have never seen it. My dear General, this expanding and piling up of impedimenta has been, so far, almost our ruin, and will be our final ruin if it is not abandoned. If you had the articles of this requisition upon the wharf, with the necessary animals to make them of any use, and forage for the animals, you could not get vessels together in two weeks to carry the whole, to say nothing of your twenty thousand men; and, having the vessels, you could not put the cargoes aboard in two weeks more. And, after all, where you are going you have no use for them. When you parted with me you had no such ideas in your mind. I know you had not, or you could not have expected to be off so soon as you said. You must get back to something like the plan you had then, or your expedition is a failure before you start. You must be off before Congress meets. You would be better off anywhere, and especially where you are going, for not having a thousand wagons doing nothing but hauling forage to feed the animals that draw them, and taking at least two thousand men to care for the wagons and animals, who otherwise might be two thousand good soldiers. Now, dear General, do not think this is an ill-natured letter; it is the very reverse. The simple publication of this requisition would ruin you.

Very truly your friend,

A. LINCOLN.

CONGRATULATIONS TO THE ARMY OF THE
POTOMAC EXECUTIVE MANSION, WASHINGTON,
December 22, 1862.

TO THE ARMY OF THE POTOMAC:

I have just read your general's report of the battle of Fredericksburg. Although you were not successful, the attempt was not an error, nor the failure other than accident. The courage with which you, in an open field, maintained the contest against an intrenched foe, and the consummate skill and success with which you crossed and recrossed the river in the face of the enemy, show that you possess all the qualities of a great army, which will yet give victory to the cause of the country and of popular government.

Condoling with the mourners for the dead, and sympathizing with the severely wounded, I congratulate you that the number of both is comparatively so small.

I tender to you, officers and soldiers, the thanks of the nation.

A. LINCOLN.

LETTER OF CONDOLENCE
TO MISS FANNY McCULLOUGH.
EXECUTIVE MANSION, WASHINGTON,
December, 23, 1862.

DEAR FANNY:—It is with deep regret that I learn of the death of your kind and brave father, and especially that it is affecting your young heart beyond what is common in such cases. In this sad world of ours sorrow comes to all, and to the young it comes with bittered agony because it takes them unawares.

The older have learned ever to expect it. I am anxious to afford some alleviation of your present distress, perfect relief is not possible, except with time. You cannot now realize that you will ever feel better. Is not this so? And yet it is a mistake. You are sure to be happy again. To know this, which is certainly true, will make you some less miserable now. I have had experience enough to know what I say, and you need only to believe it to feel better at once. The memory of your dear father, instead of an agony, will yet be a sad, sweet feeling in your heart, of a purer and holier sort than you have known before.

Please present my kind regards to your afflicted mother. Your sincere friend,

A. LINCOLN.

ORDER RELIEVING GENERAL A. E. BURNSIDE AND MAKING OTHER CHANGES.

(General Orders No.20.)

WAR DEPARTMENT, ADJUTANT-GENERAL'S OFFICE, WASHINGTON, D.C. JANUARY 25, 1863.

The President of the United States has directed:

1st. That Major-General A. E. Burnside, at his own request, be relieved from the command of the Army of the Potomac.

2d. That Major-General E. V. Sumner, at his own request, be relieved from duty in the Army of the Potomac.

3d. That Major-General W. B. Franklin be relieved from duty in the Army of the Potomac.

4th. That Major-General J. Hooker be assigned to the command of the Army of the Potomac.

II. The officers relieved as above will report in person to the adjutant-general of the army.

By order of the Secretary of War: D. TOWNSEND, Assistant Adjutant-General

TO GENERAL J. HOOKER.

EXECUTIVE MANSION, WASHINGTON, D. C.,

January 26, 1863. MAJOR-GENERAL HOOKER.

GENERAL:—I have placed you at the head of the Army of the Potomac. Of course I have done this upon what appear to me to be sufficient reasons, and yet I think it best for you to know that there are some things in regard to which I am not quite satisfied with you. I believe you to be a brave and skillful soldier, which of course I like. I also believe you do not mix politics with your profession, in which you are right. You have confidence in yourself, which is a valuable if not an indispensable quality. You are ambitious, which within reasonable bounds does good rather than harm; but I think that during General Burnside's command of the army you have taken counsel of your ambition and thwarted him as much as you could, in which you did a great wrong to the country and to a most meritorious and honorable brother officer. I have heard, in such a way as to believe it, of your recently saying that both the army and the government needed a dictator. Of course it was not for this, but in spite of it, that I have given you the command. Only those generals who gain successes can set up dictators. What I now ask of you is military success, and I will risk the dictatorship. The government will support you to the utmost of its ability, which is neither more nor less than it has done and will do for all commanders. I much fear that the spirit that you have aided to infuse into the army, of criticizing their commander and withholding confidence from him, will now turn upon you. I shall assist you as far as I can to put it down. Neither you nor Napoleon, if he were alive again, could get any good out of an army while such a spirit prevails in it. And now beware of rashness. Beware of rashness, but with energy and sleepless vigilance go forward and give us victories.

Yours very truly,

A. LINCOLN.

TELEGRAM TO GENERAL S. HOOKER.
WASHINGTON, D. C., April 15, 1863. 10.15 P.M.
MAJOR-GENERAL HOOKER:

It is now 10.15 P.M. An hour ago I received your letter of this morning, and a few moments later your despatch of this evening. The latter gives me considerable uneasiness. The rain and mud of course were to be calculated upon. General S. is not moving rapidly enough to make the expedition come to anything. He has now been out three days, two of which were unusually fair weather, and all three without hindrance from the enemy, and yet he is not twenty-five miles from where he started. To reach his point he still has sixty to go, another river (the Rapidan) to cross, and will be hindered by the enemy. By arithmetic, how many days will it take him to do it? I do not know that any better can be done, but I greatly fear it is another failure already. Write me often. I am very anxious.

Yours truly,

A. LINCOLN.

TELEGRAM TO GENERAL HOOKER.
WASHINGTON, D.C., May 6, 1863. 2.25. P.M. MAJOR-GEN-
ERAL HOOKER:

We have through General Dix the contents of Richmond papers of the 5th. General Dix's despatch in full is going to you by Captain Fox of the navy. The substance is General Lee's despatch of the 3d (Sunday), claiming that he had beaten you and that you were then retreating across the Rappahannock, distinctly stating that two of Longstreet's divisions fought you on Saturday, and that General [E. F.] Paxton was killed, Stonewall Jackson severely wounded, and Generals Heth and A. P. Hill slightly wounded. The Richmond papers also stated, upon what authority not mentioned, that our cavalry have been at Ashland, Hanover Court-House, and other points, destroying several locomotives and a good deal of other property, and all the railroad bridges to within five miles of Richmond.

A. LINCOLN.

TELEGRAM TO GENERAL HOOKER
WASHINGTON, D.C., May 6, 1863. 12.30 P.M.

Just as I telegraphed you contents of Richmond papers showing that our cavalry has not failed, I received General Butterfield's of 11 A.M. yesterday. This, with the great rain of yesterday and last night securing your right flank, I think puts a new face upon your case; but you must be the judge.

A. LINCOLN.

TELEGRAM TO COLONEL R. INGALLS. WASHINGTON, D. C., May 6, 1863. 1.45 P.M. COLONEL INGALLS:

News has gone to General Hooker which may change his plans. Act in view of such contingency.

A. LINCOLN.

TO GENERAL J. HOOKER.
HEADQUARTERS ARMY OF THE POTOMAC, May 7, 1863.
MAJOR-GENERAL HOOKER.

MY DEAR SIR:—The recent movement of your army is ended without effecting its object, except, perhaps, some important breakings of the enemy's communications. What next? If possible, I would be very glad of another movement early enough to give us some benefit from the fact of the enemy's communication being broken; but neither for this reason nor any other do I wish anything done in desperation or rashness. An early movement would also help to supersede the bad moral effect of there certain, which is said to be considerably injurious. Have you already in your mind a plan wholly or partially formed? If you have, prosecute it without interference from me. If you have not, please inform me, so that I, incompetent as I may be, can try and assist in the formation of some plan for the army.

Yours as ever,

A. LINCOLN.

TELEGRAM TO GENERAL J. HOOKER. WASHINGTON, D. C. May 8, 1863. 4 P.M. MAJOR-GENERAL HOOKER·

The news is here of the capture by our forces of Grand Gulf—a large and very important thing. General Willich, an exchanged prisoner just from Richmond, has talked with me this morning. He was there when our cavalry cut the roads in that vicinity. He says there was not a sound pair of legs in Richmond, and that our men, had they known it, could have safely gone in and burned everything and brought in Jeff Davis. We captured and paroled 300 or 400 men. He says as he came to City Point there was an army three miles long (Longstreet's, he thought) moving toward Richmond.

Muroy has captured a despatch of General Lee, in which he says his loss was fearful in his last battle with you.

A. LINCOLN.

TO GENERAL J. HOOKER.

EXECUTIVE MANSION, WASHINGTON, D.C. May 14, 1863.

MAJOR-GENERAL HOOKER, Commanding.

MY DEAR SIR:—When I wrote on the 7th, I had an impression that possibly by an early movement you could get some advantage from the supposed facts that the enemy's communications were disturbed and that he was somewhat deranged in position. That idea has now passed away, the enemy having reestablished his communications, regained his positions, and actually received reinforcements. It does not now appear probable to me that you can gain anything by an early renewal of the attempt to cross the Rappahannock. I therefore shall not complain if you do no more for a time than to keep the enemy at bay and out of other mischief by menaces and occasional cavalry raids, if practicable, and to put your own army in good condition again. Still, if in your own clear judgment you can renew the attack successfully, I do not mean to restrain you. Bearing upon this last point, I must tell you that I have some painful intimations that some of your corps and division commanders are not giving you their entire confidence. This would be ruinous, if true, and you should therefore, first of all, ascertain the real facts beyond all possibility of doubt.

Yours truly,

A. LINCOLN.

TELEGRAM TO GENERAL HOOKER.

WASHINGTON, D.C. JUNE 5, 1863 MAJOR-GENERAL HOOKER:

Yours of to-day was received an hour ago. So much of professional military skill is requisite to answer it that I have turned the task over to General Halleck. He promises to perform it with his utmost care. I have but one idea which I think worth suggesting to you, and that is, in case you find Lee coming to the north of the Rappahannock, I would by no means cross to the south of it. If he should leave a rear force at Fredericksburg, tempting you to fall upon it, it would fight in entrenchments and have you at advantage, and so, man for man, worst you at that point, While his main force would in some way be getting an advantage of you northward. In one word, I would not take any risk of being entangled up on the river like an ox jumped half over a fence and liable to be torn by dogs front and rear without a fair chance to gore one way or to kick the other.

If Lee would come to my side of the river I would keep on the same side and fight him, or act on the defensive, according as might be my estimate of his strength relatively to my own. But these are mere suggestions, which I desire to be controlled by the judgment of yourself and General Halleck.

A. LINCOLN.

TELEGRAM TO GENERAL HOOKER.
WASHINGTON, D. C. June 10, 1863 MAJOR-GENERAL HOOKER:

Your long despatch of to-day is just received. If left to me, I would not go south of the Rappahannock upon Lee's moving north of it. If you had Richmond invested to-day you would not be able to take it in twenty days; meanwhile your communications, and with them your army, would be ruined. I think Lee's army, and not Richmond, is your true objective point. If he comes towards the upper Potomac, follow on his flank, and on the inside track, shortening your lines while he lengthens his. Fight him, too, when opportunity offers. If he stay where he is, fret him and fret him.

A. LINCOLN.

RESPONSE TO A "BESIEGED" GENERAL TELEGRAM TO GENERAL TYLER.

WAR DEPARTMENT, June 14, 1863.

GENERAL TYLER, Martinsburg:

If you are besieged, how do you despatch me? Why did you not leave before being besieged?

A. LINCOLN.

TELEGRAM TO GENERAL HOOKER.

WASHINGTON, D.C., June 14, 1863.3.50 P.M.,

MAJOR-GENERAL HOOKER:

So far as we can make out here, the enemy have Muroy surrounded at Winchester, and Tyler at Martinsburg. If they could hold out a few days, could you help them? If the head of Lee's army is at Martinsburg and the tail of it on the plank-road between Fredericksburg and Chancellorsville, the animal must be very slim somewhere; could you not break him?

A. LINCOLN.

TELEGRAM TO GENERAL HOOKER.

WASHINGTON, June 16, 1863.10 P.M.

MAJOR-GENERAL HOOKER:

To remove all misunderstanding, I now place you in the strict military relation to General Halleck of a commander of one of the armies to the general-in-chief of all the armies. I have not intended differently, but as it seems to be differently understood I shall direct him to give you orders and you to obey them.

A. LINCOLN.

TELEGRAM TO GENERAL COUCH. WAR DEPARTMENT, June 24, 1863.

MAJOR-GENERAL COUCH, Harrisburg, Pa.:

Have you any reports of the enemy moving into Pennsylvania? And if any, what?

A. LINCOLN.

ANNOUNCEMENT OF NEWS FROM GETTYSBURG. WASHINGTON, D.C. July 4, 10.30 A.M.

The President announces to the country that news from the Army of the Potomac, up to 10 P.M. of the 3d, is such as to cover that army with the highest honor, to promise a great success to the cause of the Union, and to claim the condolence of all for the many gallant fallen; and that for this he especially desires that on this day He whose will, not ours, should ever be done be everywhere remembered and reverenced with profoundest gratitude.

A. LINCOLN

TELEGRAM TO GENERAL FRENCH. [Cipher] WAR DEPARTMENT, WASHINGTON, D. C., July 5, 1863.

MAJOR-GENERAL FRENCH, Fredericktown, Md.:

I see your despatch about destruction of pontoons. Cannot the enemy ford the river?

A. LINCOLN.

CONTINUED FAILURE TO PURSUE ENEMY TELEGRAM
TO GENERAL H. W. HALLECK.
SOLDIERS' HOME, WASHINGTON, JULY 6 1863.7 P.M.,
MAJOR-GENERAL HALLECK:

I left the telegraph office a good deal dissatisfied. You know I did not like the phrase—in Orders, No. 68, I believe—"Drive the invaders from our soil." Since that, I see a despatch from General French, saying the enemy is crossing his wounded over the river in flats, without saying why he does not stop it, or even intimating a thought that it ought to be stopped. Still later, another despatch from General Pleasonton, by direction of General Meade, to General French, stating that the main army is halted because it is believed the rebels are concentrating "on the road towards Hagerstown, beyond Fairfield," and is not to move until it is ascertained that the rebels intend to evacuate Cumberland Valley.

These things appear to me to be connected with a purpose to cover Baltimore and Washington and to get the enemy across the river again without a further collision, and they do not appear connected with a purpose to prevent his crossing and to destroy him. I do fear the former purpose is acted upon and the latter rejected.

If you are satisfied the latter purpose is entertained, and is judiciously pursued, I am content. If you are not so satisfied, please look to it.

Yours truly,

A. LINCOLN.

TELEGRAM FROM GENERAL HALLECK TO
GENERAL G. C. MEADE. WASHINGTON, D. C., July 8, 1863.

MAJOR-GENERAL MEADE, Frederick, Md.:

There is reliable information that the enemy is crossing at Williamsport. The opportunity to attack his divided forces should not be lost. The President is urgent and anxious that your army should move against him by forced marches.

H. W. HALLECK, General-in-Chief

TELEGRAM TO F. F. LOWE.

WAR DEPARTMENT, WASHINGTON, D.C., July 8, 1863.

HON. F. F. LOWE, San Francisco, Cal.:

There is no doubt that General Meade, now commanding the Army of the Potomac, beat Lee at Gettysburg, Pa., at the end of a three days' battle, and that the latter is now crossing the Potomac at Williamsport over the swollen stream and with poor means of crossing, and closely pressed by Meade. We also have despatches rendering it entirely certain that Vicksburg surrendered to General Grant on the glorious old 4th.

A. LINCOLN.

TO GENERAL GRANT.

EXECUTIVE MANSION, WASHINGTON, July 13, 1863.

MAJOR-GENERAL GRANT:

MY DEAR GENERAL:—I do not remember that you and I ever met personally. I write this now as a grateful acknowledgment of the almost inestimable service you have done the Country. I write to say a word further. When you first reached the vicinity of Vicksburg, I thought you should do what you finally did—march the troops across the neck, run the batteries with the transports, and thus go below; and I never had any faith except a general hope that you knew better than I, that the Yazoo Pass expedition and the like could succeed. When you dropped below, and took Port Gibson, Grand Gulf, and vicinity, I thought you should go down the river and join General Banks; and when you turned northward, east of the Big Black, I feared it was a mistake. I now wish to make the personal acknowledgment that you were right and I was wrong.

Yours very truly,

A. LINCOLN.

TO GENERAL H. W. HALLECK. EXECUTIVE MANSION, July 29, 1863 MAJOR-GENERAL HALLECK:

Seeing General Meade's despatch of yesterday to yourself causes me to fear that he supposes the Government here is demanding of him to bring on a general engagement with Lee as soon as possible. I am claiming no such thing of him. In fact, my judgment is against it; which judgment, of course, I will yield if yours and his are the contrary. If he could not safely engage Lee at Williamsport, it seems absurd to suppose he can safely engage him now, when he has scarcely more than two thirds of the force he had at Williamsport, while it must be that Lee has been reinforced. True, I desired General Meade to pursue Lee across the Potomac, hoping, as has proved true, that he would thereby clear the Baltimore and Ohio Railroad, and get some advantages by harassing him on his retreat. These being past, I am unwilling he should now get into a general engagement on the impression that we here are pressing him, and I shall be glad for you to so inform him, unless your own judgment is against it.

Yours truly,

A. LINCOLN.

H. W. HALLECK, General-in-Chief.

MILITARY STRATEGY

TO GENERAL H. W. HALLECK

EXECUTIVE MANSION, WASHINGTON, D.C., September 19, 1863. MAJOR-GENERAL HALLECK:

By General Meade's despatch to you of yesterday it appears that he desires your views and those of the government as to whether he shall advance upon the enemy. I am not prepared to order, or even advise, an advance in this case, wherein I know so little of particulars, and wherein he, in the field, thinks the risk is so great and the promise of advantage so small.

And yet the case presents matter for very serious consideration in another aspect. These two armies confront each other across a small river, substantially midway between the two capitals, each defending its own capital, and menacing the other. General Meade estimates the enemy's infantry in front of him at not less than 40,000. Suppose we add fifty per cent to this for cavalry, artillery, and extra-duty men stretching as far as Richmond, making the whole force of the enemy 60,000.

General Meade, as shown by the returns, has with him, and between him and Washington, of the same classes, of well men, over 90,000. Neither can bring the whole of his men into a battle; but each can bring as large a percentage in as the other. For a battle, then, General Meade has three men to General Lee's two. Yet, it having been determined that choosing ground and standing on the defensive gives so great advantage that the three cannot safely attack the two, the three are left simply standing on the defensive also.

If the enemy's 60,000 are sufficient to keep our 90,000 away from Richmond, why, by the same rule, may not 40,000 of ours keep their 60,000 away from Washington, leaving us 50,000 to put to some other use? Having practically come to the mere defensive, it seems to be no economy at all to employ twice as many men for that object as are needed. With no object, certainly, to mislead myself, I can perceive no fault in this statement, unless we admit we are not the equal of the enemy, man for man. I hope you will consider it.

To avoid misunderstanding, let me say that to attempt to fight the enemy slowly back into his entrenchments at Richmond, and then to capture him, is an idea I have been trying to repudiate for quite a year.

My judgment is so clear against it that I would scarcely allow the attempt to be made if the general in command should desire to make it. My last attempt upon Richmond was to get McClellan, when he was nearer there than the enemy was, to run in ahead of him. Since then I have constantly desired the Army of the Potomac to make Lee's army, and not Richmond, its objective point. If our army cannot fall upon the enemy and hurt him where he is, it is plain to me it can gain nothing by attempting to follow him over a succession of intrenched lines into a fortified city.

Yours truly,

A. LINCOLN.

2

WALT WHITMAN'S TRIBUTE TO LINCOLN AND OTHER CIVIL WAR POEMS

BY WALT WHITMAN

Although they never met, Whitman saw Abraham Lincoln several times, between 1861 and 1865, sometimes at close quarters. The first time was when Lincoln stopped in New York City in 1861 on his way to Washington. Whitman (1819–1892) noticed the president-elect's "striking appearance" and "unpretentious dignity" and trusted Lincoln's "supernatural tact" and "idiomatic Western genius." He admired the president, writing in October 1863, "I love the President personally." Whitman considered himself and Lincoln to be "afloat in the same stream" and "rooted in the same ground." Whitman and Lincoln shared similar views on slavery and the Union, and similarities have been noted in their literary styles and inspirations. Whitman later declared that "Lincoln gets almost nearer me than anybody else."

Lincoln's death on April 15, 1865, greatly moved Whitman, who wrote several poems in tribute to the fallen president. "O Captain! My Captain!," "When Lilacs Last in the Dooryard Bloom'd," "Hush'd Be the Camps To-Day," and "This Dust Was Once the Man" were all written on Lincoln's death. While these poems do not specifically mention Lincoln, they turn the assassination of the president into a sort of martyrdom.

"O Captain! My Captain!" was used as a centerpiece in the movie Dead Poets Society, with Robin Williams playing a teacher and his students reading the poem aloud.

O CAPTAIN! MY CAPTAIN!

O Captain! My Captain! our fearful trip is done;
The ship has weather'd every rack, the prize we sought is won;
The port is near, the bells I hear, the people all exulting,
While follow eyes the steady keel, the vessel grim and daring:
But O heart! heart! heart!
O the bleeding drops of red,
Where on the deck my Captain lies,
Fallen cold and dead.

O Captain! My Captain! rise up and hear the bells;

Rise up—for you the flag is flung—for you the bugle trills;

For you bouquets and ribbon'd wreaths—for you the shores a-crowding;

For you they call, the swaying mass, their eager faces turning;

Here captain! dear father!

This arm beneath your head;

It is some dream that on the deck,

You've fallen cold and dead.

My Captain does not answer, his lips are pale and still;

My father does not feel my arm, he has no pulse nor will;

The ship is anchor'd safe and sound, its voyage closed and done;

From fearful trip, the victor ship, comes in with object won;

Exult, O shores, and ring, O bells!

But I, with mournful tread,

Walk the deck my captain lies,

Fallen cold and dead.

The following poems are from Walt Whitman's collection of poetry entitled *Drum-Taps*.

BEAT! BEAT! DRUMS!

Beat! beat! drums!—blow! bugles! blow!

Through the windows—through doors—burst like a ruthless force,

Into the solemn church, and scatter the congregation,

Into the school where the scholar is studying;

Leave not the bridegroom quiet—no happiness must he have now with his bride,

Nor the peaceful farmer any peace, ploughing his field or gathering

his grain,
So fierce you whirr and pound you drums—so shrill you bugles blow.

Beat! beat! drums!—blow! bugles! blow!
Over the traffic of cities—over the rumble of wheels in the streets;
Are beds prepared for sleepers at night in the houses? no sleepers
must sleep in those beds,
No bargainers' bargains by day—no brokers or speculators—would they
continue?
Would the talkers be talking? would the singer attempt to sing?
Would the lawyer rise in the court to state his case before the
judge?
Then rattle quicker, heavier drums—you bugles wilder blow.

Beat! beat! drums!—blow! bugles! blow!
Make no parley—stop for no expostulation,
Mind not the timid—mind not the weeper or prayer,
Mind not the old man beseeching the young man,
Let not the child's voice be heard, nor the mother's entreaties,
Make even the trestles to shake the dead where they lie awaiting the
hearses,
So strong you thump O terrible drums—so loud you bugles blow.

COME UP FROM THE FIELDS FATHER.

Come up from the fields father, here's a letter from our Pete,
And come to the front door mother, here's a letter from thy dear son.

Lo, 'tis autumn,

Lo, where the trees, deeper green, yellower and redder,

Cool and sweeten Ohio's villages with leaves fluttering in the
moderate wind,

Where apples ripe in the orchards hang and grapes on the trellis'd
vines,

(Smell you the smell of the grapes on the vines?

Smell you the buckwheat where the bees were lately buzzing?)

Above all, lo, the sky so calm, so transparent after the rain, and
with wondrous clouds,

Below too, all calm, all vital and beautiful, and the farm prospers
well.

Down in the fields all prospers well,

But now from the fields come father, come at the daughter's call,

And come to the entry mother, to the front door come right away.

Fast as she can she hurries, something ominous, her steps trembling,

She does not tarry to smooth her hair nor adjust her cap.

Open the envelope quickly,

O this is not our son's writing, yet his name is sign'd,

O a strange hand writes for our dear son, O stricken mother's soul!

All swims before her eyes, flashes with black, she catches the main
words only,

Sentences broken, gunshot wound in the breast, cavalry skirmish,
taken to hospital,

At present low, but will soon be better.

Ah now the single figure to me,
Amid all teeming and wealthy Ohio with all its cities and farms,
Sickly white in the face and dull in the head, very faint,
By the jamb of a door leans.

Grieve not so, dear mother, (the just-grown daughter speaks through
her sobs,
The little sisters huddle around speechless and dismay'd,)
See, dearest mother, the letter says Pete will soon be better.

Alas poor boy, he will never be better, (nor may-be needs to be
better, that brave and simple soul,)
While they stand at home at the door he is dead already,
The only son is dead.

But the mother needs to be better,
She with thin form presently drest in black,
By day her meals untouch'd, then at night fitfully sleeping, often
waking,
In the midnight waking, weeping, longing with one deep longing,
O that she might withdraw unnoticed, silent from life escape and
withdraw,
To follow, to seek, to be with her dear dead son.

THE WOUND-DRESSER (AN EXCERPT)

Bearing the bandages, water and sponge,
Straight and swift to my wounded I go,
Where they lie on the ground after the battle brought in,
Where their priceless blood reddens the grass the ground,

Or to the rows of the hospital tent, or under the roof'd hospital,

To the long rows of cots up and down each side I return,

To each and all one after another I draw near, not one do I miss,

An attendant follows holding a tray, he carries a refuse pail,

Soon to be fill'd with clotted rags and blood, emptied, and fill'd

again.

I onward go, I stop,

With hinged knees and steady hand to dress wounds,

I am firm with each, the pangs are sharp yet unavoidable,

One turns to me his appealing eyes—poor boy! I never knew you,

Yet I think I could not refuse this moment to die for you, if that

would save you.

On, on I go, (open doors of time! open hospital doors!)

The crush'd head I dress, (poor crazed hand tear not the bandage

away,)

The neck of the cavalry-man with the bullet through and through I

examine,

Hard the breathing rattles, quite glazed already the eye, yet life

struggles hard,

(Come sweet death! be persuaded O beautiful death!

In mercy come quickly.)

From the stump of the arm, the amputated hand,

I undo the clotted lint, remove the slough, wash off the matter and

blood,

Back on his pillow the soldier bends with curv'd neck and

side-falling head,

His eyes are closed, his face is pale, he dares not look on the

bloody stump,

And has not yet look'd on it.
I dress a wound in the side, deep, deep,
But a day or two more, for see the frame all wasted and sinking,
And the yellow-blue countenance see.

I dress the perforated shoulder, the foot with the bullet-wound,
Cleanse the one with a gnawing and putrid gangrene, so sickening, so
offensive,
While the attendant stands behind aside me holding the tray and pail.

I am faithful, I do not give out,
The fractur'd thigh, the knee, the wound in the abdomen,
These and more I dress with impassive hand, (yet deep in my breast a fire, a
burning flame.)

Thus in silence in dreams' projections,
Returning, resuming, I thread my way through the hospitals,
The hurt and wounded I pacify with soothing hand,
I sit by the restless all the dark night, some are so young,
Some suffer so much, I recall the experience sweet and sad,
(Many a soldier's loving arms about this neck have cross'd and
rested,
Many a soldier's kiss dwells on these bearded lips.)

3

FACING PICKETT'S CHARGE

BY FRANK ARETAS HASKELL

In his 1948 novel Intruder in the Dust, *William Faulkner wrote about the promise the afternoon of July 3, 1863, held for the Southern cause, the moment before the Confederate attack that became known as Pickett's Charge.*

For every Southern boy fourteen years old, not once but whenever he wants it, there is the instant when it's still not yet two o'clock on that July afternoon in 1863, the brigades are in position behind the rail fence, the guns are laid and ready in the woods and the furled flags are already loosened to break out and Pickett himself with his long oiled ringlets and his hat in one hand probably and his sword in the other looking up the hill waiting for Longstreet to give the word and it's all in the balance, it hasn't happened yet, it hasn't even begun yet, it not only hasn't begun yet but there is still time for it not to begin against that position and those circumstances.

Those words of a Nobel Prize winner launch our chapter on the afternoon that doomed the Southern Confederacy. This account of Pickett's Charge reverses the usual Southern viewpoint and takes us onto Cemetery Hill, where the Union Army is ready to battle Robert E. Lee's forces for the third straight day. The story is from the pen of Frank Aretas Haskell, a colonel of the Thirty-Sixth Wisconsin Infantry and aide-de-camp to General John Gibbon, a prominent figure in the Union defense. Haskell, a Dartmouth graduate, survived the war and went on to write The Battle of Gettysburg, *published in 1908.*

It is the opinion of many of our Generals that the Rebels will not give us battle to-day—that he had enough yesterday—that he will be heading towards the Potomac at the earliest practicable moment, if he has not already done so; but the better, and controlling judgment is, that he will make another grand effort to pierce or turn our lines—that he will either mass and attack the left again, as yesterday, or direct his operations against the left of our center, the position of the Second Corps, and try to sever our line. I infer that Gen. Meade was of the opinion that the attack to-day would be upon the left—this from the disposition he ordered, I know that Gen. Hancock anticipated the attack upon the center.

The dispositions to-day upon the left are as follows:

The Second and Third Divisions of the Second Corps are in the position of yesterday; then on the left come Doubleday's—the Third Division and Col. Stannard's brigade of the First Corps; then Colwell's—the First Division of the Second Corps; then the Third Corps, temporarily under the command of Hancock, since Sickles' wound. The Third Corps is upon the same ground in part, and on the identical line where it first formed yesterday morning, and where, had it stayed instead of moving out to the front, we should have many more men to-day, and should not have been upon the brink of disaster yesterday. On the left of the Third Corps is the Fifth Corps, with a short front and deep line; then comes the Sixth Corps, all but one brigade, which is sent over to the Twelfth. The Sixth, a splendid Corps, almost intact in the fight of yesterday, is the extreme left of our line, which terminates to the south of Round Top, and runs along its western base, in the woods, and thence to the Cemetery. This Corps is burning to pay off the old scores made on the 4th of May, there back of Fredericksburg. Note well the position of the Second and Third Divisions of the Second Corps—it will become important.

There are nearly six thousand men and officers in these two Divisions here upon the field—the losses were quite heavy yesterday, some regiments are detached to other parts of the field—so all told there are less than six thousand men now in the two Divisions, who occupy a line of about a thousand yards. The most of the way along this line upon the crest was a stone fence, constructed of small, rough stones, a good deal of the way badly pulled down, but the men had improved it and patched it with rails from the neighboring fences, and with earth, so as to render it in many places a very passable breastwork against musketry and flying fragments of shells.

These works are so low as to compel the men to kneel or lie down generally to obtain cover. Near the right of the Second Division, and just by the little group of trees that I have mentioned there, this stone fence made a right angle, and extended thence to the front, about twenty or thirty yards, where with another less than a right angle it followed along the crest again.

The lines were conformed to these breastworks and to the nature of the ground upon the crest, so as to occupy the most favorable places, to be covered, and still be able to deliver effective fire upon the enemy should he come there. In some places a second line was so posted as to be able to deliver its fire over the heads of the first line behind the works; but such formation was not practicable all of the way. But all the force of these two divisions was in line, in position, without reserves, and in such a manner that every man of them could have fired his piece at the same instant.

The division flags, that of the Second Division, being a white trefoil upon a square blue field, and of the Third Division a blue trefoil upon a white rectangular field, waved behind the divisions at the points where the Generals of Division were supposed to be; the brigade flags, similar to these but with a triangular field, were behind the brigades; and the national flags of the regiments were in the lines of their regiments. To the left of the Second Division, and advanced something over a hundred yards, were posted a part of Stannard's Brigade two regiments or more, behind a small bush-crowned crest that ran in a direction oblique to the general line. These were well covered by the crest, and wholly concealed by the bushes, so that an advancing enemy would be close upon them before they could be seen. Other troops of Doubleday's Division were strongly posted in rear of these in the general line.

I could not help wishing all the morning that this line of the two divisions of the Second Corps was stronger; it was so far as numbers constitute strength, the weakest part of our whole line of battle. What if, I thought, the enemy should make an assault here to-day, with two or three heavy lines—a great overwhelming mass; would he not sweep through that thin six thousand?

But I was not General Meade, who alone had power to send other troops there; and he was satisfied with that part of the line as it was. He was early on horseback this morning, and rode along the whole line, looking to it himself, and with glass in hand sweeping the woods and fields in the direction of the enemy, to see if aught of him could be discovered. His manner was calm and serious, but earnest. There was no arrogance of hope, or timidity of fear discernible in his face; but you would have supposed he would do his duty conscientiously and well, and would be willing to abide the result. You would have seen this in his face. He was well pleased with the left of the line to-day, it was so strong with good troops. He had no apprehension for the right where the fight now was going on, on account of the admirable position of our forces there. He was not of the opinion that the enemy would attack the center, our artillery had such sweep there, and this was not the favorite point of attack with the Rebel. Besides, should he attack the center, the General thought he could reinforce it in good season. I heard Gen. Meade speak of these matters to Hancock and some others, at about nine o'clock in the morning, while they were up by the line, near the Second Corps.

No further changes of importance except those mentioned, were made in the disposition of the troops this morning, except to replace some of the batteries that were disabled yesterday by others from the artillery reserve, and to brace up the lines well with guns wherever there were eligible places, from the same source. The line is all in good order again, and we are ready for general battle.

Save the operations upon the right, the enemy so far as we could see, was very quiet all the morning. Occasionally the outposts would fire a little, and then cease. Movements would be discovered which would indicate the attempt on the part of the enemy to post a battery. Our Parrotts would send a few shells to the spot, then silence would follow.

At one of these times a painful accident happened to us, this morning. First Lieut. Henry Ropes, 20th Mass., in Gen. Gibbon's Division, a most estimable gentleman and officer, intelligent, educated, refined, one of the noble souls that came to the country's defense, while lying at his post with his regiment, in front of one of the Batteries, which fired over the Infantry, was instantly killed by a badly made shell, which, or some portion of it, fell but a few yards in front of the muzzle of the gun. The same accident killed or wounded several others. The loss of Ropes would have pained us at any time, and in any manner; in this manner his death was doubly painful.

Between ten and eleven o'clock, over in a peach orchard in front of the position of Sickles yesterday, some little show of the enemy's infantry was discovered; a few shells scattered the gray-backs; they again appeared, and it becoming apparent that they were only posting a skirmish line, no further molestation was offered them. A little after this some of the enemy's flags could be discerned over near the same quarter, above the top and behind a small crest of a ridge. There seemed to be two or three of them—possibly they were guidons—and they moved too fast to be carried on foot. Possibly, we thought, the enemy is posting some batteries there. We knew in about two hours from this time better about the matter. Eleven o'clock came. The noise of battle has ceased upon the right; not a sound of a gun or musket can be heard on all the field; the sky is bright, with only the white fleecy clouds floating over from the West. The July sun streams down its fire upon the bright iron of the muskets in stacks upon the crest, and the dazzling brass of the Napoleons. The army lolls and longs for the shade, of which some get a hand's breadth, from a shelter tent stuck upon a ramrod. The silence and sultriness of a July noon are supreme.

Now it so happened that just about this time of day a very original and interesting thought occurred to Gen. Gibbon and several of his staff; that it would be a very good thing, and a very good time, to have something to eat. When I announce to you that I had not tasted a mouthful of food since yesterday noon, and that all I had had to drink since that time, but the most miserable muddy warm water, was a little drink of whiskey that Major Biddle, General Meade's aide-de-camp, gave me last evening, and a cup of strong coffee that I gulped down as I was first mounting this morning, and further, that, save the four or five hours in the night, there was scarcely a moment since that time but that I was in the saddle, you may have some notion of the reason of my assent to this extraordinary proposition. Nor will I mention the doubts I had as to the feasibility of the execution of this very novel proposal, except to say that I knew this morning that our larder was low; not to put too fine a point upon it, that we had nothing but some potatoes and sugar and coffee in the world. And I may as well say here, that of such, in scant proportion, would have been our repast, had it not been for the riding of miles by two persons, one an officer, to procure supplies; and they only succeeded in getting some few chickens, some butter, and one huge loaf of bread, which last was bought of a soldier, because he had grown faint in carrying it, and was afterwards rescued with much difficulty and after a long race from a four-footed hog, which had got hold of and had actually eaten a part of it. "There is a divinity," etc.

Suffice it, this very ingenious and unheard of contemplated proceeding, first announced by the General, was accepted and at once undertaken by his staff. Of the absolute quality of what we had to eat, I could not pretend to judge, but I think an unprejudiced person would have said of the bread that it was good; so of the potatoes before they were boiled. Of the chickens he would have questioned their age, but they were large and in good *running* order. The toast was good, and the butter. There were those who, when coffee was given them, called for tea, and vice versa, and were so ungracious as to suggest that the water that was used in both might have come from near a barn. Of course it did not. We all came down to the little peach orchard where we had stayed last night, and, wonderful to see and tell, ever mindful of our needs, had it all ready, had our faithful John. There was an enormous pan of stewed chickens, and the potatoes, and toast, all hot, and the bread and the butter, and tea and coffee. There was satisfaction derived from just naming them all over. We called John an angel, and he snickered and said he "knowed" we'd come. General Hancock is of course invited to partake, and without delay we commence operations. Stools are not very numerous, two in all, and these the two Generals have by common consent. Our table was the top of a mess chest. By this the Generals sat. The rest of us sat upon the ground, cross-legged, like the picture of a smoking Turk, and held our plates upon our laps. How delicious was the stewed chicken. I had a cucumber pickle in my saddle bags, the last of a lunch left there two or three days ago, which George brought, and I had half of it. We were just well at it when General Meade rode down to us from the line, accompanied by one of his staff, and by General Gibbon's invitation, they dismounted and joined us. For the General commanding the Army of the Potomac George, by an effort worthy of the person and the occasion, finds an empty cracker box for a seat. The staff officer must sit upon the ground with the rest of us. Soon Generals Newton and Pleasonton, each with an aide, arrive. By an almost superhuman effort a roll of blankets is found, which, upon a pinch, is long enough to seat these Generals both, and room is made for them.

The aides sit with us. And, fortunate to relate, there was enough cooked for us all, and from General Meade to the youngest second lieutenant we all had a most hearty and well relished dinner. Of the "past" we were "secure." The Generals ate, and after, lighted cigars, and under the flickering shade of a very small tree, discoursed of the incidents of yesterday's battle and of the probabilities of to-day. General Newton humorously spoke of General Gibbon as "this young North Carolinian," and how he was becoming arrogant and above his position, because he commanded a corps. General Gibbon retorted by saying that General Newton had not been long enough in such a command, only since yesterday, to enable him to judge of such things. General Meade still thought that the enemy would attack his left again to-day towards evening; but he was ready for them. General Hancock thought that the attack would be upon the position of the Second Corps. It was mentioned that General Hancock would again assume command of the Second Corps from that time, so that General Gibbon would again return to the Second Division.

General Meade spoke of the Provost Guards, that they were good men, and that it would be better to-day to have them in the works than to stop stragglers and skulkers, as these latter would be good for but little even in the works; and so he gave the order that all the Provost Guards should at once temporarily rejoin their regiments. Then General Gibbon called up Captain Farrel, First Minnesota, who commanded the provost guard of his division, and directed him for that day to join the regiment. "Very well, sir," said the Captain, as he touched his hat and turned away. He was a quiet, excellent gentleman and thorough soldier. I knew him well and esteemed him. I never saw him again. He was killed in two or three hours from that time, and over half of his splendid company were either killed or wounded.

And so the time passed on, each General now and then dispatching some order or message by an officer or orderly, until about half-past twelve, when all the Generals, one by one, first General Meade, rode off their several ways, and General Gibbon and his staff alone remained.

We dozed in the heat, and lolled upon the ground, with half open eyes. Our horses were hitched to the trees munching some oats. A great lull rests upon all the field. Time was heavy, and for want of something better to do, I yawned, and looked at my watch. It was five minutes before one o'clock. I returned my watch to its pocket, and thought possibly that I might go to sleep, and stretched myself upon the ground accordingly. *Ex uno disce omnes.* My attitude and purpose were those of the General and the rest of the staff.

What sound was that? There was no mistaking it. The distinct sharp sound of one of the enemy's guns, square over to the front, caused us to open our eyes and turn them in that direction, when we saw directly above the crest the smoke of the bursting shell, and heard its noise. In an instant, before a word was spoken, as if that was the signal gun for general work, loud, startling, booming, the report of gun after gun in rapid succession smote our ears and their shells plunged down and exploded all around us.

We sprang to our feet. In briefest time the whole Rebel line to the West was pouring out its thunder and its iron upon our devoted crest. The wildest confusion for a few moments obtained sway among us. The shells came bursting all about. The servants ran terror-stricken for dear life and disappeared. The horses, hitched to the trees or held by the slack hands of orderlies, neighed out in fright, and broke away and plunged riderless through the fields. The General at the first had snatched his sword, and started on foot for the front. I called for my horse; nobody responded. I found him tied to a tree, near by, eating oats, with an air of the greatest composure, which under the circumstances, even then struck me as exceedingly ridiculous.

He alone, of all beasts or men near was cool. I am not sure but that I learned a lesson then from a horse. Anxious alone for his oats, while I put on the bridle and adjusted the halter, he delayed me by keeping his head down, so I had time to see one of the horses of our mess wagon struck and torn by a shell. The pair plunge—the driver has lost the reins—horses, driver and wagon go into a heap by a tree. Two mules close at hand, packed with boxes of ammunition, are knocked all to pieces by a shell. General Gibbon's groom has just mounted his horse and is starting to take the General's horse to him, when the flying iron meets him and tears open his breast. He drops dead and the horses gallop away. No more than a minute since the first shot was fired, and I am mounted and riding after the General. The mighty din that now rises to heaven and shakes the earth is not all of it the voice of the rebellion; for our guns, the guardian lions of the crest, quick to awake when danger comes, have opened their fiery jaws and begun to roar—the great hoarse roar of battle.

I overtake the General half way up to the line. Before we reach the crest his horse is brought by an orderly. Leaving our horses just behind a sharp declivity of the ridge, on foot we go up among the batteries. How the long streams of fire spout from the guns, how the rifled shells hiss, how the smoke deepens and rolls. But where is the infantry? Has it vanished in smoke? Is this a nightmare or a juggler's devilish trick? All too real. The men of the infantry have seized their arms, and behind their works, behind every rock, in every ditch, wherever there is any shelter, they hug the ground, silent, quiet, unterrified, little harmed. The enemy's guns now in action are in position at their front of the woods along the second ridge that I have before mentioned and towards their right, behind a small crest in the open field, where we saw the flags this morning. Their line is some two miles long, concave on the side towards us, and their range is from one thousand to eighteen hundred yards. A hundred and twenty-five rebel guns, we estimate, are now active, firing twenty-four pound, twenty, twelve and ten-pound projectiles, solid shot and shells, spherical, conical, spiral. The enemy's fire is chiefly concentrated upon the position of the Second Corps.

From the Cemetery to Round Top, with over a hundred guns, and to all parts of the enemy's line, our batteries reply, of twenty and ten-pound Parrotts, ten-pound rifled ordnance, and twelve-pound Napoleons, using projectiles as various in shape and name as those of the enemy. Captain Hazard commanding the artillery brigade of the Second Corps was vigilant among the batteries of his command, and they were all doing well. All was going on satisfactorily. We had nothing to do, therefore, but to be observers of the grand spectacle of battle.

Captain Wessels, Judge Advocate of the Division, now joined us, and we sat down behind the crest, close to the left of Cushing's Battery, to bide our time, to see, to be ready to act when the time should come, which might be at any moment. Who can describe such a conflict as is raging around us? To say that it was like a summer storm, with the crash of thunder, the glare of lightning, the shrieking of the wind, and the clatter of hailstones, would be weak. The thunder and lightning of these two hundred and fifty guns and their shells, whose smoke darkens the sky, are incessant, all pervading, in the air above our heads, on the ground at our feet, remote, near, deafening, ear-piercing, astounding; and these hailstones are massy iron, charged with exploding fire. And there is little of human interest in a storm; it is an absorbing element of this. You may see flame and smoke, and hurrying men, and human passion at a great conflagration; but they are all earthly and nothing more. These guns are great infuriate demons, not of the earth, whose mouths blaze with smoky tongues of living fire, and whose murky breath, sulphur-laden, rolls around them and along the ground, the smoke of Hades. These grimy men, rushing, shouting, their souls in frenzy, plying the dusky globes and the igniting spark, are in their league, and but their willing ministers.

We thought that at the second Bull Run, at the Antietam and at Fredericksburg on the 11th of December, we had heard heavy cannonading; they were but holiday salutes compared with this. Besides the great ceaseless roar of the guns, which was but the background of the others, a million various minor sounds engaged the ear. The projectiles shriek long and sharp. They hiss, they scream, they growl, they sputter; all sounds of life and rage; and each has its different note, and all are discordant. Was ever such a chorus of sound before? We note the effect of the enemies' fire among the batteries and along the crest. We see the solid shot strike axle, or pole, or wheel, and the tough iron and heart of oak snap and fly like straws.

The great oaks there by Woodruff's guns heave down their massy branches with a crash, as if the lightning smote them. The shells swoop down among the battery horses standing there apart. A half a dozen horses start, they tumble, their legs stiffen, their vitals and blood smear the ground. And these shot and shells have no respect for men either. We see the poor fellows hobbling back from the crest, or unable to do so, pale and weak, lying on the ground with the mangled stump of an arm or leg, dripping their life-blood away; or with a cheek torn open, or a shoulder mashed. And many, alas! hear not the roar as they stretch upon the ground with upturned faces and open eyes, though a shell should burst at their very ears. Their ears and their bodies this instant are only mud. We saw them but a moment since there among the flame, with brawny arms and muscles of iron wielding the rammer and pushing home the cannon's plethoric load.

Strange freaks these round shot play! We saw a man coming up from the rear with his full knapsack on, and some canteens of water held by the straps in his hands. He was walking slowly and with apparent unconcern, though the iron hailed around him. A shot struck the knapsack, and it, and its contents flew thirty yards in every direction, the knapsack disappearing like an egg, thrown spitefully against a rock. The soldier stopped and turned about in puzzled surprise, put up one hand to his back to assure himself that the knapsack was not there, and then walked slowly on again unharmed, with not even his coat torn. Near us was a man crouching behind a small disintegrated stone, which was about the size of a common water bucket. He was bent up, with his face to the ground, in the attitude of a Pagan worshipper before his idol. It looked so absurd to see him thus, that I went and said to him, "Do not lie there like a toad. Why not go to your regiment and be a man?" He turned up his face with a stupid, terrified look upon me, and then without a word turned his nose again to the ground. An orderly that was with me at the time, told me a few moments later, that a shot struck the stone, smashing it in a thousand fragments, but did not touch the man, though his head was not six inches from the stone.

All the projectiles that came near us were not so harmless. Not ten yards away from us a shell burst among some small bushes, where sat three or four orderlies holding horses. Two of the men and one horse were killed. Only a few yards off a shell exploded over an open limber box in Cushing's battery, and at the same instant, another shell over a neighboring box. In both the boxes the ammunition blew up with an explosion that shook the ground, throwing fire and splinters and shells far into the air and all around, and destroying several men. We watched the shells bursting in the air, as they came hissing in all directions. Their flash was a bright gleam of lightning radiating from a point, giving place in the thousandth part of a second to a small, white, puffy cloud, like a fleece of the lightest, whitest wool. These clouds were very numerous.

We could not often see the shell before it burst; but sometimes, as we faced towards the enemy, and looked above our heads, the approach would be heralded by a prolonged hiss, which always seemed to me to be a line of something tangible, terminating in a black globe, distinct to the eye, as the sound had been to the ear. The shell would seem to stop, and hang suspended in the air an instant, and then vanish in fire and smoke and noise. We saw the missiles tear and plow the ground. All in rear of the crest for a thousand yards, as well as among the batteries, was the field of their blind fury. Ambulances, passing down the Taneytown road with wounded men, were struck. The hospitals near this road were riddled. The house which was General Meade's headquarters was shot through several times, and a great many horses of officers and orderlies were lying dead around it.

Riderless horses, galloping madly through the fields, were brought up, or down rather, by these invisible horse-tamers, and they would not run any more. Mules with ammunition, pigs wallowing about, cows in the pastures, whatever was animate or inanimate, in all this broad range, were no exception to their blind havoc. The percussion shells would strike, and thunder, and scatter the earth and their whistling fragments; the Whitworth bolts would pound and ricochet, and bowl far away sputtering, with the sound of a mass of hot iron plunged in water; and the great solid shot would smite the unresisting ground with a sounding "thud," as the strong boxer crashes his iron fist into the jaws of his unguarded adversary. Such were some of the sights and sounds of this great iron battle of missiles. Our artillerymen upon the crest budged not an inch, nor intermitted, but, though caisson and limber were smashed, and guns dismantled, and men and horses killed, there amidst smoke and sweat, they gave back, without grudge, or loss of time in the sending, in kind whatever the enemy sent, globe, and cone, and bolt, hollow or solid, an iron greeting to the rebellion, the compliments of the wrathful Republic.

An hour has droned its flight since first the war began. There is no sign of weariness or abatement on either side. So long it seemed, that the din and crashing around began to appear the normal condition of nature there, and fighting man's element. The General proposed to go among the men and over to the front of the batteries, so at about two o'clock he and I started. We went along the lines of the infantry as they lay there flat upon the earth, a little to the front of the batteries. They were suffering little, and were quiet and cool. How glad we were that the enemy were no better gunners, and that they cut the shell fuses too long. To the question asked the men, "What do you think of this?" the replies would be, "O, this is bully," "We are getting to like it," "O, we don't mind this." And so they lay under the heaviest cannonade that ever shook the continent, and among them a thousand times more jokes than heads were cracked.

We went down in front of the line some two hundred yards, and as the smoke had a tendency to settle upon a higher plain than where we were, we could see near the ground distinctly all over the fields, as well back to the crest where were our own guns as to the opposite ridge where were those of the enemy. No infantry was in sight, save the skirmishers, and they stood silent and motionless—a row of gray posts through the field on one side confronted by another of blue. Under the grateful shade of some elm trees, where we could see much of the field, we made seats of the ground and sat down. Here all the more repulsive features of the fight were unseen, by reason of the smoke. Man had arranged the scenes, and for a time had taken part in the great drama; but at last, as the plot thickened, conscious of his littleness and inadequacy to the mighty part, he had stepped aside and given place to more powerful actors.

So it seemed; for we could see no men about the batteries. On either crest we could see the great flaky streams of fire, and they seemed numberless, of the opposing guns, and their white banks of swift, convolving smoke; but the sound of the discharges was drowned in the universal ocean of sound. Over all the valley the smoke, a sulphury arch, stretched its lurid span; and through it always, shrieking on their unseen courses, thickly flew a myriad iron deaths. With our grim horizon on all sides round toothed thick with battery flame, under that dissonant canopy of warring shells, we sat and heard in silence. What other expression had we that was not mean, for such an awful universe of battle?

A shell struck our breastwork of rails up in sight of us, and a moment afterwards we saw the men bearing some of their wounded companions away from the same spot; and directly two men came from there down toward where we were and sought to get shelter in an excavation near by, where many dead horses, killed in yesterday's fight, had been thrown. General Gibbon said to these men, more in a tone of kindly expostulation than of command: "My men, do not leave your ranks to try to get shelter here. All these matters are in the hands of God, and nothing that you can do will make you safer in one place than in another." The men went quietly back to the line at once. The General then said to me: "I am not a member of any church, but I have always had a strong religious feeling; and so in all these battles I have always believed that I was in the hands of God, and that I should be unharmed or not, according to his will. For this reason, I think it is, I am always ready to go where duty calls, no matter how great the danger."

Half-past two o'clock, an hour and a half since the commencement, and still the cannonade did not in the least abate; but soon thereafter some signs of weariness and a little slacking of fire began to be apparent upon both sides. First we saw Brown's battery retire from the line, too feeble for further battle. Its position was a little to the front of the line. Its commander was wounded, and many of its men were so, or worse; some of its guns had been disabled, many of its horses killed; its ammunition was nearly expended. Other batteries in similar case had been withdrawn before to be replaced by fresh ones, and some were withdrawn afterwards. Soon after the battery named had gone the General and I started to return, passing towards the left of the division, and crossing the ground where the guns had stood. The stricken horses were numerous, and the dead and wounded men lay about, and as we passed these latter, their low, piteous call for water would invariably come to us, if they had yet any voice left.

I found canteens of water near—no difficult matter where a battle has been—and held them to livid lips, and even in the faintness of death the eagerness to drink told of their terrible torture of thirst. But we must pass on. Our infantry was still unshaken, and in all the cannonade suffered very little. The batteries had been handled much more severely. I am unable to give any figures. A great number of horses had been killed, in some batteries more than half of all. Guns had been dismounted. A great many caissons, limbers and carriages had been destroyed, and usually from ten to twenty-five men to each battery had been struck, at least along our part of the crest. Altogether the fire of the enemy had injured us much, both in the modes that I have stated, and also by exhausting our ammunition and fouling our guns, so as to render our batteries unfit for further immediate use. The scenes that met our eyes on all hands among the batteries were fearful. All things must end, and the great cannonade was no exception to the general law of earth. In the number of guns active at one time, and in the duration and rapidity of their fire, this artillery engagement, up to this time, must stand alone and pre-eminent in this war. It has not been often, or many times, surpassed in the battles of the world. Two hundred and fifty guns, at least, rapidly fired for two mortal hours. Cipher out the number of tons of gunpowder and iron that made these two hours hideous.

Of the injury of our fire upon the enemy, except the facts that ours was the superior position, if not better served and constructed artillery, and that the enemy's artillery hereafter during the battle was almost silent, we know little. Of course, during the fight we often saw the enemy's caissons explode, and the trees rent by our shot crashing about his ears, but we can from these alone infer but little of general results. At three o'clock almost precisely the last shot hummed, and bounded and fell, and the cannonade was over. The purpose of General Lee in all this fire of his guns—we know it now, we did not at the time so well—was to disable our artillery and break up our infantry upon the position of the Second Corps, so as to render them less an impediment to the sweep of his own brigades and divisions over our crest and through our lines.

He probably supposed our infantry was massed behind the crest and the batteries; and hence his fire was so high, and his fuses to the shells were cut so long, too long. The Rebel General failed in some of his plans in this behalf, as many generals have failed before and will again. The artillery fight over, men began to breathe more freely, and to ask, What next, I wonder? The battery men were among their guns, some leaning to rest and wipe the sweat from their sooty faces, some were handling ammunition boxes and replenishing those that were empty. Some batteries from the artillery reserve were moving up to take the places of the disabled ones; the smoke was clearing from the crests. There was a pause between acts, with the curtain down, soon to rise upon the great final act, and catastrophe of Gettysburg. We have passed by the left of the Second Division, coming from the First; when we crossed the crest the enemy was not in sight, and all was still—we walked slowly along in the rear of the troops, by the ridge cut off now from a view of the enemy in his position, and were returning to the spot where we had left our horses.

General Gibbon had just said that he inclined to the belief that the enemy was falling back, and that the cannonade was only one of his noisy modes of covering the movement. I said that I thought that fifteen minutes would show that, by all his bowling, the Rebel did not mean retreat. We were near our horses when we noticed Brigadier General Hunt, Chief of Artillery of the Army, near Woodruff's Battery, swiftly moving about on horseback, and apparently in a rapid manner giving some orders about the guns. Thought we, what could this mean? In a moment afterwards we met Captain Wessels and the orderlies who had our horses; they were on foot leading the horses. Captain Wessels was pale, and he said, excited: "General, they say the enemy's infantry is advancing." We sprang into our saddles, a score of bounds brought us upon the all-seeing crest. To say that men grew pale and held their breath at what we and they there saw, would not be true. Might not six thousand men be brave and without shade of fear, and yet, before a hostile eighteen thousand, armed, and not five minutes' march away, turn ashy white?

None on that crest now need be told that *the enemy is advancing.* Every eye could see his legions, an overwhelming resistless tide of an ocean of armed men sweeping upon us! Regiment after regiment and brigade after brigade move from the woods and rapidly take their places in the lines forming the assault. Pickett's proud division, with some additional troops, hold their right; Pettigrew's (Worth's) their left. The first line at short interval is followed by a second, and that a third succeeds; and columns between support the lines. More than half a mile their front extends; more than a thousand yards the dull gray masses deploy, man touching man, rank pressing rank, and line supporting line. The red flags wave, their horsemen gallop up and down; the arms of eighteen thousand men, barrel and bayonet, gleam in the sun, a sloping forest of flashing steel. Right on they move, as with one soul, in perfect order, without impediment of ditch, or wall or stream, over ridge and slope, through orchard and meadow, and cornfield, magnificent, grim, irresistible.

All was orderly and still upon our crest; no noise and no confusion. The men had little need of commands, for the survivors of a dozen battles knew well enough what this array in front portended, and, already in their places, they would be prepared to act when the right time should come. The click of the locks as each man raised the hammer to feel with his fingers that the cap was on the nipple; the sharp jar as a musket touched a stone upon the wall when thrust in aiming over it, and the clicking of the iron axles as the guns were rolled up by hand a little further to the front, were quite all the sounds that could be heard. Cap-boxes were slid around to the front of the body; cartridge boxes opened, officers opened their pistol-holsters. Such preparations, little more was needed.

The trefoil flags, colors of the brigades and divisions moved to their places in rear; but along the lines in front the grand old ensign that first waved in battle at Saratoga in 1777, and which these people coming would rob of half its stars, stood up, and the west wind kissed it as the sergeants sloped its lance towards the enemy. I believe that not one above whom it then waved but blessed his God that he was loyal to it, and whose heart did not swell with pride towards it, as the emblem of the Republic before that treason's flaunting rag in front.

General Gibbon rode down the lines, cool and calm, and in an unimpassioned voice he said to the men, "Do not hurry, men, and fire too fast, let them come up close before you fire, and then aim low and steadily." The coolness of their General was reflected in the faces of his men. Five minutes has elapsed since first the enemy have emerged from the woods—no great space of time surely, if measured by the usual standard by which men estimate duration—but it was long enough for us to note and weigh some of the elements of mighty moment that surrounded us; the disparity of numbers between the assailants and the assailed; that few as were our numbers we could not be supported or reinforced until support would not be needed or would be too late; that upon the ability of the two trefoil divisions to hold the crest and repel the assault depended not only their own safety or destruction, but also the honor of the Army of the Potomac and defeat or victory at Gettysburg.

Should these advancing men pierce our line and become the entering wedge, driven home, that would sever our army asunder, what hope would there be afterwards, and where the blood-earned fruits of yesterday? It was long enough for the Rebel storm to drift across more than half the space that had at first separated it from us. None, or all, of these considerations either depressed or elevated us. They might have done the former, had we been timid; the latter had we been confident and vain. But, we were there waiting, and ready to do our duty—that done, results could not dishonor us.

Our skirmishers open a spattering fire along the front, and, fighting, retire upon the main line—the first drops, the heralds of the storm, sounding on our windows. Then the thunders of our guns, first Arnold's then Cushing's and Woodruff's and the rest, shake and reverberate again through the air, and their sounding shells smite the enemy. The General said I had better go and tell General Meade of this advance. To gallop to General Meade's headquarters, to learn there that he had changed them to another part of the field, to dispatch to him by the Signal Corps in General Gibbon's name the message, "The enemy is advancing his infantry in force upon my front," and to be again upon the crest, were but the work of a minute.

All our available guns are now active, and from the fire of shells, as the range grows shorter and shorter, they change to shrapnel, and from shrapnel to canister; but in spite of shells, and shrapnel and canister, without wavering or halt, the hardy lines of the enemy continue to move on. The Rebel guns make no reply to ours, and no charging shout rings out to-day, as is the Rebel wont; but the courage of these silent men amid our shots seems not to need the stimulus of other noise. The enemy's right flank sweeps near Stannard's bushy crest, and his concealed Vermonters rake it with a well-delivered fire of musketry. The gray lines do not halt or reply, but withdrawing a little from that extreme, they still move on. And so across all that broad open ground they have come, nearer and nearer, nearly half the way, with our guns bellowing in their faces, until now a hundred yards, no more, divide our ready left from their advancing right. The eager men there are impatient to begin. Let them. First, Harrow's breastworks flame; then Hall's; then Webb's. As if our bullets were the fire coals that touched off their muskets, the enemy in front halts, and his countless level barrels blaze back upon us.

The Second Division is struggling in battle. The rattling storm soon spreads to the right, and the blue trefoils are vieing with the white. All along each hostile front, a thousand yards, with narrowest space between, the volleys blaze and roll; as thick the sound as when a summer hail-storm pelts the city roofs; as thick the fire as when the incessant lightning fringes a summer cloud. When the Rebel infantry had opened fire our batteries soon became silent, and this without their fault, for they were foul by long previous use. They were the targets of the concentrated Rebel bullets, and some of them had expended all their canister. But they were not silent before Rhorty was killed, Woodruff had fallen mortally wounded, and Cushing, firing almost his last canister, had dropped dead among his guns shot through the head by a bullet. The conflict is left to the infantry alone.

Unable to find my general when I had returned to the crest after transmitting his message to General Meade, and while riding in the search having witnessed the development of the fight, from the first fire upon the left by the main lines until all of the two divisions were furiously engaged, I gave up hunting as useless—I was convinced General Gibbon could not be on the field; I left him mounted; I could easily have found him now had he so remained—but now, save myself, there was not a mounted officer near the engaged lines—and was riding towards the right of the Second Division, with purpose to stop there, as the most eligible position to watch the further progress of the battle, there to be ready to take part according to my own notions whenever and wherever occasion was presented. The conflict was tremendous, but I had seen no wavering in all our line. Wondering how long the Rebel ranks, deep though they were, could stand our sheltered volleys, I had come near my destination, when—great heaven! were my senses mad? The larger portion of Webb's brigade—my God, it was true—there by the group of trees and the angles of the wall, was breaking from the cover of their works, and, without orders or reason, with no hand lifted to check them, was falling back, a fear-stricken flock of confusion!

The fate of Gettysburg hung upon a spider's single thread! A great magnificent passion came on me at the instant, not one that overpowers and confounds, but one that blanches the face and sublimes every sense and faculty. My sword, that had always hung idle by my side, the sign of rank only in every battle, I drew, bright and gleaming, the symbol of command. Was not that a fit occasion, and these fugitives the men on whom to try the temper of the Solinzen steel? All rules and proprieties were forgotten; all considerations of person, and danger and safety despised; for, as I met the tide of these rabbits, the damned red flags of the rebellion began to thicken and flaunt along the wall they had just deserted, and one was already waving over one of the guns of the dead Cushing. I ordered these men to "halt," and "face about" and "fire," and they heard my voice and gathered my meaning, and obeyed my commands. On some unpatriotic backs of those not quick of comprehension, the flat of my sabre fell not lightly, and at its touch their love of country returned, and, with a look at me as if I were the destroying angel, as I might have become theirs, they again faced the enemy.

General Webb soon came to my assistance. He was on foot, but he was active, and did all that one could do to repair the breach, or to avert its calamity. The men that had fallen back, facing the enemy, soon regained confidence in themselves, and became steady. This portion of the wall was lost to us, and the enemy had gained the cover of the reverse side, where he now stormed with fire. But Webb's men, with their bodies in part protected by the abruptness of the crest, now sent back in the enemies' faces as fierce a storm. Some scores of venturesome Rebels, that in their first push at the wall had dared to cross at the further angle, and those that had desecrated Cushing's guns, were promptly shot down, and speedy death met him who should raise his body to cross it again. At this point little could be seen of the enemy, by reason of his cover and the smoke, except the flash of his muskets and his waving flags. These red flags were accumulating at the wall every moment, and they maddened us as the same color does the bull.

Webb's men are falling fast, and he is among them to direct and encourage; but, however well they may now do, with that walled enemy in front, with more than a dozen flags to Webb's three, it soon becomes apparent that in not many minutes they will be overpowered, or that there will be none alive for the enemy to overpower. Webb, has but three regiments, all small, the 69th, 71st and 72d Pennsylvania—the 106th Pennsylvania, except two companies, is not here to-day—and he must have speedy assistance, or this crest will be lost. Oh, where is Gibbon? where is Hancock?—some general—anybody with the power and the will to support that wasting, melting line? No general came, and no succor! I thought of Hayes upon the right, but from the smoke and war along his front, it was evident that he had enough upon his hands, if he stayed the in-rolling tide of the Rebels there. Doubleday upon the left was too far off and too slow, and on another occasion I had begged him to send his idle regiments to support another line battling with thrice its numbers, and this "Old Sumpter Hero" had declined. As a last resort I resolved to see if Hall and Harrow could not send some of their commands to reinforce Webb.

I galloped to the left in the execution of my purpose, and as I attained the rear of Hall's line, from the nature of the ground and the position of the enemy it was easy to discover the reason and the manner of this gathering of Rebel flags in front of Webb. The enemy, emboldened by his success in gaining our line by the group of trees and the angle of the wall, was concentrating all his right against and was further pressing that point. There was the stress of his assault; there would he drive his fiery wedge to split our line. In front of Harrow's and Hall's Brigades he had been able to advance no nearer than when he first halted to deliver fire, and these commands had not yielded an inch. To effect the concentration before Webb, the enemy would march the regiment on his extreme right of each of his lines by the left flank to the rear of the troops, still halted and facing to the front, and so continuing to draw in his right, when they were all massed in the position desired, he would again face them to the front, and advance to the storming. This was the way he made the wall before Webb's line blaze red with his battle flags, and such was the purpose there of his thick-crowding battalions. Not a moment must be lost.

Colonel Hall I found just in rear of his line, sword in hand, cool, vigilant, noting all that passed and directing the battle of his brigade. The fire was constantly diminishing now in his front, in the manner and by the movement of the enemy that I have mentioned, drifting to the right. "How is it going?" Colonel Hall asked me, as I rode up. "Well, but Webb is hotly pressed and must have support, or he will be overpowered. Can you assist him?" "Yes." "You cannot be too quick." "I will move my brigade at once." "Good." He gave the order, and in briefest time I saw five friendly colors hurrying to the aid of the imperilled three; and each color represented true, battle-tried men, that had not turned back from Rebel fire that day nor yesterday, though their ranks were sadly thinned, to Webb's brigade, pressed back as it had been from the wall, the distance was not great from Hall's right.

The regiments marched by the right flank. Col. Hall superintended the movement in person. Col. Devereux coolly commanded the 19th Massachusetts. His major, Rice, had already been wounded and carried off. Lieut. Col. Macy, of the 20th Mass., had just had his left hand shot off, and so Capt. Abbott gallantly led over this fine regiment. The 42d New York followed their excellent Colonel Mallon. Lieut. Col. Steele, 7th Mich., had just been killed, and his regiment, and the handful of the 59th N. Y., followed their colors. The movement, as it did, attracting the enemy's fire, and executed in haste, as it must be, was difficult; but in reasonable time, and in order that is serviceable, if not regular, Hall's men are fighting gallantly side by side with Webb's before the all important point. I did not stop to see all this movement of Hall's, but from him I went at once further to the left, to the 1st brigade. Gen'l

Harrow I did not see, but his fighting men would answer my purpose as well. The 19th Me., the 15th Mass., the 32d N. Y. and the shattered old thunderbolt, the 1st Minn.—poor Farrell was dying then upon the ground where he had fallen,—all men that I could find I took over to the right at the *double quick.*

As we were moving to, and near the other brigade of the division, from my position on horseback I could see that the enemy's right, under Hall's fire, was beginning to stagger and to break. "See," I said to the men, "See the *chivalry!* See the gray-backs run!" The men saw, and as they swept to their places by the side of Hall and opened fire, they roared, and this in a manner that said more plainly than words— for the deaf could have seen it in their faces, and the blind could have heard it in their voices—*the crest is safe!*

The whole Division concentrated, and changes of position, and new phases, as well on our part as on that of the enemy, having as indicated occurred, for the purpose of showing the exact present posture of affairs, some further description is necessary. Before the 2d Division the enemy is massed, the main bulk of his force covered by the ground that slopes to his rear, with his front at the stone wall. Between his front and us extends the very apex of the crest. All there are left of the White Trefoil Division—yesterday morning there were three thousand eight hundred, this morning there were less than three thousand—at this moment there are somewhat over two thousand;— twelve regiments in three brigades are below or behind the crest, in such a position that by the exposure of the head and upper part of the body above the crest they can deliver their fire in the enemy's faces along the top of the wall. By reason of the disorganization incidental in Webb's brigade to his men's having broken and fallen back, as mentioned, in the two other brigades to their rapid and difficult change of position under fire, and in all the division in part to severe and continuous battle, formation of companies and regiments in regular ranks is lost; but commands, companies, regiments and brigades are blended and intermixed—an irregular extended mass—men enough, if in order, to form a line of four or five ranks along the whole front of the division. The twelve flags of the regiments wave defiantly at intervals along the front; at the stone wall, at unequal distances from ours of forty, fifty or sixty yards, stream nearly double this number of the battle flags of the enemy.

These changes accomplished on either side, and the concentration complete, although no cessation or abatement in the general din of conflict since the commencement had at any time been appreciable, now it was as if a new battle, deadlier, stormier than before, had sprung from the body of the old—a young Phoenix of combat, whose eyes stream lightning, shaking his arrowy wings over the yet glowing ashes of his progenitor. The jostling, swaying lines on either side boil, and roar, and dash their flamy spray, two hostile billows of a fiery ocean. Thick flashes stream from the wall, thick volleys answer from the crest. No threats or expostulation now, only example and encouragement. All depths of passion are stirred, and all combatives fire, down to their deep foundations. Individuality is drowned in a sea of clamor, and timid men, breathing the breath of the multitude, are brave. The frequent dead and wounded lie where they stagger and fall—there is no humanity for them now, and none can be spared to care for them. The men do not cheer or shout; they growl, and over that uneasy sea, heard with the roar of musketry, sweeps the muttered thunder of a storm of growls. Webb, Hall, Devereux, Mallon, Abbott among the men where all are heroes, are doing deeds of note. Now the loyal wave rolls up as if it would overleap its barrier, the crest. Pistols flash with the muskets. My "Forward to the wall" is answered by the Rebel counter-command, "Steady, men!" and the wave swings back.

Again it surges, and again it sinks. These men of Pennsylvania, on the soil of their own homesteads, the first and only to flee the wall, must be the first to storm it. "Major—, *lead* your men over the crest, they will follow." "By the tactics I understand my place is in rear of the men." "Your pardon, sir; I see *your* place is in rear of the men. I thought you were fit to lead." "Capt. Sapler, come on with your men." "Let me first stop this fire in the rear, or we shall be hit by our own men." "Never mind the fire in the rear; let us take care of this in front first." "Sergeant, forward with your color. Let the Rebels see it close to their eyes once before they die." The color sergeant of the 72d Pa., grasping the stump of the severed lance in both his hands, waved the flag above his head and rushed towards the wall. "Will you see your color storm the wall alone?" One man only starts to follow. Almost half way to the wall, down go color bearer and color to the ground—the gallant sergeant is dead. The line springs—the crest of the solid ground with a great roar, heaves forward its maddened load, men, arms, smoke, fire, a fighting mass. It rolls to the wall—flash meets flash, the wall is crossed—a moment ensues of thrusts, yells, blows, shots, and undistinguishable conflict, followed by a shout universal that makes the welkin ring again, and the last and bloodiest fight of the great battle of Gettysburg is ended and won.

Many things cannot be described by pen or pencil—such a fight is one. Some hints and incidents may be given, but a description or picture never. From what is told the imagination may for itself construct the scene; otherwise he who never saw can have no adequate idea of what such a battle is.

When the vortex of battle passion had subsided, hopes, fears, rage, joy, of which the maddest and the noisiest was the last, and we were calm enough to look about us, we saw that, as with us, the fight with the Third Division was ended, and that in that division was a repetition of the scenes immediately about us. In that moment the judgment almost refused to credit the senses. Are these abject wretches about us, whom our men are now disarming and driving together in flocks, the jaunty men of Pickett's Division, whose steady lines and flashing arms but a few moment's since came sweeping up the slope to destroy us? Are these red cloths that our men toss about in derision the "fiery Southern crosses," thrice ardent, the battle flags of the rebellion that waved defiance at the wall? We know, but so sudden has been the transition, we yet can scarce believe.

Just as the fight was over, and the first outburst of victory had a little subsided, when all in front of the crest was noise and confusion—prisoners being collected, small parties in pursuit of them far down into the fields, flags waving, officers giving quick, sharp commands to their men—I stood apart for a few moments upon the crest, by that group of trees which ought to be historic forever, a spectator of the thrilling scene around. Some few musket shots were still heard in the Third Division; and the enemy's guns, almost silent since the advance of his infantry until the moment of his defeat, were dropping a few sullen shells among friend and foe upon the crest. Rebellion fosters such humanity.

Near me, saddest sight of the many of such a field and not in keeping with all this noise, were mingled alone the thick dead of Maine and Minnesota, and Michigan and Massachusetts, and the Empire and Keystone States, who, not yet cold, with the blood still oozing from their death-wounds, had given their lives to the country upon that stormy field. So mingled upon that crest let their honored graves be. Look with me about us. These dead have been avenged already. Where the long lines of the enemy's thousands so proudly advanced, see how thick the silent men of gray are scattered. It is not an hour since these legions were sweeping along so grandly; now sixteen hundred of that fiery mass are strewn among the trampled grass, dead as the clods they load; more than seven thousand, probably eight thousand, are wounded, some there with the dead, in our hands, some fugitive far towards the woods, among them Generals Pettigrew, Garnett, Kemper and Armstead, the last three mortally, and the last one in our hands. "Tell General Hancock," he said to Lieutenant Mitchell, Hancock's aide-de-camp, to whom he handed his watch, "that I know I did my country a great wrong when I took up arms against her, for which I am sorry, but for which I cannot live to atone."

Four thousand, not wounded, are prisoners of war. More in number of the captured than the captors. Our men are still "gathering them in." Some hold up their hands or a handkerchief in sign of submission; some have hugged the ground to escape our bullets and so are taken; few made resistance after the first moment of our crossing the wall; some yield submissively with good grace, some with grim, dogged aspect, showing that but for the other alternative they could not submit to this. Colonels, and all less grades of officers, in the usual proportion are among them, and all are being stripped of their arms. Such of them as escaped wounds and capture are fleeing routed and panic stricken, and disappearing in the woods. Small arms, more thousands than we can count, are in our hands, scattered over the field. And these defiant battle-flags, some inscribed with "First Manassas," the numerous battles of the Peninsula, "Second Manassas," "South Mountain," "Sharpsburg," (our Antietam), "Fredericksburg," "Chancellorsville," and many more names, our men have, and are showing about, *over thirty of them.*

Such was really the closing scene of the grand drama of Gettysburg. After repeated assaults upon the right and the left, where, and in all of which repulse had been his only success, this persistent and presuming enemy forms his chosen troops, the flower of his army, for a grand assault upon our center. The manner and result of such assault have been told—a loss to the enemy of from twelve thousand to fourteen thousand, killed, wounded and prisoners, and of over thirty battle-flags. This was accomplished by not over six thousand men, with a loss on our part of not over two thousand five hundred killed and wounded.

[Editor's note: As his troops came running back down Cemetery Hill in panic and retreat after suffering horrific losses, General Robert E. Lee both rode and walked up the hill to meet the survivors. His calls to them have been recorded by many sources, with these as the major most-quoted:

"All will come right in the end. We'll talk it over afterward, but meanwhile every good man must rally. We want all good and true men just now."

"All this has been my fault. It is I who have lost this fight, and you must help me out of it in the best way you can."

"This has been a sad day for us, a sad day. But we can't expect always to gain victories."]

4

CATASTROPHE AT CHANCELLORSVILLE: THE DEATH OF STONEWALL JACKSON

BY COLONEL

G. F. R. HENDERSON

The Battle of Chancellorsville was fought from April 30 to May 6, 1863, in Spotsylvania County, Virginia, near the village of Chancellorsville. Two related battles were fought nearby on May 3 in the vicinity of Fredericksburg. The campaign pitted Union Army major general Joseph Hooker's Army of the Potomac against an army less than half its size, General Robert E. Lee's Confederate Army of Northern Virginia.

Chancellorsville is known as Lee's "perfect battle" because his risky decision to divide his army in the presence of a much larger enemy force resulted in a significant Confederate victory. The victory, a product of Lee's audacity and Hooker's timid decision-making, was tempered by heavy casualties, including Lieutenant General Thomas J. "Stonewall" Jackson. Jackson was hit by friendly fire, requiring his left arm to be amputated. He died of pneumonia eight days later, a loss that Lee likened to losing his right arm.

This account of the battle and the loss of Jackson was written by Confederate Colonel G. F. R. Henderson and is from his book Stonewall Jackson and the American Civil War.

To the Federal headquarters confusion and dismay had come, indeed, with appalling suddenness. Late in the afternoon Hooker was sitting with two aides-de-camp in the verandah of the Chancellor House. There were few troops in sight. The Third Corps and Pleasonton's cavalry had long since disappeared in the forest. The Twelfth Army Corps, with the exception of two brigades, was already advancing against Anderson; and only the trains and some artillery remained within the intrenchments at Hazel Grove. All was going well. A desultory firing broke out at intervals to the eastward, but it was not sustained; and three miles to the south, where, as Hooker believed, in pursuit of Jackson, Sickles and Pleasonton were, the reports of their cannon, growing fainter and fainter as they pushed further south, betokened no more than a lively skirmish. The quiet of the Wilderness, save for those distant sounds, was undisturbed, and men and animals, free from every care, were enjoying the calm of the summer evening. It was about half-past six. Suddenly the cannonade swelled to a heavier roar, and the sound came from a new direction. All were listening intently, speculating on what this might mean, when a staff-officer, who had stepped out to the front of the house and was looking down the plank road with his glass, exclaimed: "My God, here they come!" Hooker sprang upon his horse; and riding rapidly down the road, met the stragglers of the Eleventh Corps—men, wagons, and ambulances, an ever-increasing crowd—rushing in blind terror from the forest, flying they knew not whither. The whole of the right wing, they said, overwhelmed by superior numbers, was falling back on Chancellorsville, and Stonewall Jackson was in hot pursuit.

The situation had changed in the twinkling of an eye. Just now congratulating himself on the complete success of his manœuvres, on the retreat of his enemies, on the flight of Jackson and the helplessness of Lee, Hooker saw his strong intrenchments taken in reverse, his army scattered, his reserves far distant, and the most dreaded of his opponents, followed by his victorious veterans, within a few hundred yards of his headquarters. His weak point had been found, and there were no troops at hand wherewith to restore the fight. The centre was held only by the two brigades of the Twelfth Corps at the Fairview Cemetery. The works at Hazel Grove were untenanted, save by a few batteries and a handful of infantry. The Second and Fifth Corps on the left were fully occupied by McLaws, for Lee, at the first sound of Jackson's guns, had ordered a vigorous attack up the pike and the plank road. Sickles, with 20,000 men, was far away, isolated and perhaps surrounded, and the line of retreat, the road to United States Ford, was absolutely unprotected.

Messengers were dispatched in hot haste to recall Sickles and Pleasonton to Hazel Grove. Berry's division, forming the reserve north-east of the Chancellor House, was summoned to Fairview, and Hays' brigade of the Second Corps ordered to support it. But what could three small brigades, hurried into position and unprotected by intrenchments, avail against 25,000 Southerners, led by Stonewall Jackson, and animated by their easy victory? If Berry and Hays could stand fast against the rush of fugitives, it was all that could be expected; and as the uproar in the dark woods swelled to a deeper volume, and the yells of the Confederates, mingled with the crash of the musketry, were borne to his ears, Hooker must have felt that all was lost. To make matters worse, as Pleasonton, hurrying back with his cavalry, arrived at Hazel Grove, the trains of the Third Army Corps, fired on by the Confederate skirmishers, dashed wildly across the clearing, swept through the parked artillery, and, breaking through the forest, increased the fearful tumult which reigned round Chancellorsville.

The gunners, however, with a courage beyond all praise, stood staunchly to their pieces; and soon a long line of artillery, for which two regiments of the Third Army Corps, coming up rapidly from the south, formed a sufficient escort, was established on this commanding hill. Other batteries, hitherto held in reserve, took post on the high ground at Fairview, a mile to the north-east, and, although Berry's infantry were not yet in position, and the stream of broken troops was still pouring past, a strong front of fifty guns opposed the Confederate advance.

But it was not the artillery that saved Hooker from irretrievable disaster. As they followed the remnants of the Eleventh Army Corps, the progress of Rodes and Colston had been far less rapid than when they stormed forward past the Wilderness Church. A regiment of Federal cavalry, riding to Howard's aid by a track from Hazel Grove to the plank road, was quickly swept aside; but the deep darkness of the forest, the efforts of the officers to re-form the ranks, the barriers opposed by the tangled undergrowth, the difficulty of keeping the direction, brought a large portion of the troops to a standstill. At the junction of the White House road the order to halt was given, and although a number of men, pushing impetuously forward, seized a line of log breastworks which ran north-west through the timber below the Fairview heights, the pursuit was stayed in the midst of the dense thickets.

8.15 p.m. At this moment, shortly after eight o'clock, Jackson was at Dowdall's Tavern. The reports from the front informed him that his first and second lines had halted; General Rodes, who had galloped up the plank road to reconnoitre, sent in word that there were no Federal troops to be seen between his line and the Fairview heights; and Colonel Cobb, of the 44th Virginia, brought the news that the strong intrenchments, less than a mile from Chancellorsville, had been occupied without resistance.

There was a lull in the battle; the firing had died away, and the excited troops, with a clamour that was heard in the Federal lines, sought their companies and regiments by the dim light of the rising moon. But deeming that nothing was done while aught remained to do, Jackson was already planning a further movement. Sending instructions to A. P. Hill to relieve Rodes and Colston, and to prepare for a night attack, he rode forward, almost unattended, amongst his rallying troops, and lent his aid to the efforts of the regimental officers. Intent on bringing up the two divisions in close support of Hill, he passed from one regiment to another. Turning to Colonel Cobb, he said to him; "Find General Rodes, and tell him to occupy the barricade at once," and then added: "I need your help for a time; this disorder must be corrected. As you go along the right, tell the troops from me to get into line and preserve their order."

It was long, however, before the men could be assembled, and the delay was increased by an unfortunate incident. Jackson's chief of artillery, pressing forward up the plank road to within a thousand yards of Chancellorsville, opened fire with three guns upon the enemy's position. This audacious proceeding evoked a quick reply. Such Federal guns as could be brought to bear were at once turned upon the road, and although the damage done was small, A. P. Hill's brigades, just coming up into line, were for the moment checked; under the hail of shell and canister the artillery horses became unmanageable, the drivers lost their nerve, and as they rushed to the rear some of the infantry joined them, and a stampede was only prevented by the personal efforts of Jackson, Colston, and their staff-officers. Colonel Crutchfield was then ordered to cease firing; the Federals did the same; and A. P. Hill's brigades, that of General Lane leading, advanced to the deserted breastworks, while two brigades, one from Rodes' division and one from Colston's, were ordered to guard the roads from Hazel Grove.

8.45 p.m. These arrangements made, Jackson proceeded to join his advanced line. At the point where the track to the White House and United States ford strikes the plank road he met General Lane, seeking his instructions for the attack. They were sufficiently brief: "Push right ahead, Lane; right ahead!" As Lane galloped off to his command, General Hill and some of his staff came up, and Jackson gave Hill his orders. "Press them; cut them off from the United States Ford, Hill; press them." General Hill replied that he was entirely unacquainted with the topography of the country, and asked for an officer to act as guide. Jackson directed Captain Boswell, his chief engineer, to accompany General Hill, and then, turning to the front, rode up the plank road, passing quickly through the ranks of the 18th North

Carolina of Lane's brigade. Two or three hundred yards eastward the general halted, for the ringing of axes and the words of command were distinctly audible in the enemy's lines.

While the Confederates were re-forming, Hooker's reserves had reached the front, and Berry's regiments, on the Fairview heights, using their bayonets and tin-plates for intrenching tools, piling up the earth with their hands, and hacking down the brushwood with their knives, were endeavouring in desperate haste to provide some shelter, however slight, against the rush that they knew was about to come.

After a few minutes, becoming impatient for the advance of Hill's division, Jackson turned and retraced his steps towards his own lines. "General," said an officer who was with him, "you should not expose yourself so much." "There is no danger, sir, the enemy is routed. Go back and tell General Hill to press on."

Once more, when he was only sixty or eighty yards from where the 18th North Carolina were standing in the trees, he drew rein and listened—the whole party, generals, staff-officers, and couriers, hidden in the deep shadows of the silent woods. At this moment a single rifle-shot rang out with startling suddenness.

A detachment of Federal infantry, groping their way through the thickets, had approached the Southern lines.

The skirmishers on both sides were now engaged, and the lines of battle in rear became keenly on the alert. Some mounted officers galloped hastily back to their commands. The sound startled the Confederate soldiers, and an officer of the 18th North Carolina, seeing a group of strange horsemen riding towards him through the darkness—for Jackson, hearing the firing, had turned back to his own lines—gave the order to fire.

The volley was fearfully effective. Men and horses fell dead and dying on the narrow track. Jackson himself received three bullets, one in the right hand, and two in the left arm, cutting the main artery, and crushing the bone below the shoulder, and as the reins dropped upon his neck, "Little Sorrel," frantic with terror, plunged into the wood and rushed towards the Federal lines. An overhanging bough struck his rider violently in the face, tore off his cap and nearly unhorsed him; but recovering his seat, he managed to seize the bridle with his bleeding hand, and turned into the road. Here Captain Wilbourn, one of his staff-officers, succeeded in catching the reins; and, as the horse stopped, Jackson leaned forward and fell into his arms. Captain Hotchkiss, who had just returned from a reconnaissance, rode off to find Dr. McGuire, while Captain Wilbourn, with a small penknife, ripped up the sleeve of the wounded arm. As he was doing so, General Hill, who had himself been exposed to the fire of the North Carolinians, reached the scene, and, throwing himself from his horse, pulled off Jackson's gauntlets, which were full of blood, and bandaged the shattered arm with a handkerchief. "General," he said, "are you much hurt?" "I think I am," was the reply, "and all my wounds are from my own men. I believe my right arm is broken."

To all questions put to him he answered in a perfectly calm and self-possessed tone, and, although he spoke no word of complaint, he was manifestly growing weaker. It seemed impossible to move him, and yet it was absolutely necessary that he should be carried to the rear. He was still in front of his own lines, and, even as Hill was speaking, two of the enemy's skirmishers, emerging from the thicket, halted within a few paces of the little group. Hill, turning quietly to his escort, said, "Take charge of those men," and two orderlies, springing forward, seized the rifles of the astonished Federals. Lieutenant Morrison, Jackson's aide-de-camp, who had gone down the road to recon-

noitre, now reported that he had seen a section of artillery unlimbering close at hand. Hill gave orders that the general should be at once
removed, and that no one should tell the men that he was wounded.
Jackson, lying on Hill's breast, opened his eyes, and said, "Tell them
simply that you have a wounded Confederate officer." Lieutenants
Smith and Morrison, and Captain Leigh of Hill's staff, now lifted him
to his feet, and with their aid he walked a few steps through the trees.
But hardly had they gained the road when the Federal batteries, along
their whole front, opened a terrible fire of grape and canister. The
storm of bullets, tearing through the foliage, was fortunately directed
too high, and the three young officers, laying the general down by the
roadside, endeavoured to shield him by lying between him and the
deadly hail. The earth round them was torn up by the shot, covering
them with dust; boughs fell from the trees, and fire flashed from the
flints and gravel of the roadway. Once Jackson attempted to rise; but
Smith threw his arm over him, holding him down, and saying, "General, you must be still—it will cost you your life to rise."

After a few minutes, however, the enemy's gunners, changing
from canister to shell, mercifully increased their range; and again, as
the Confederate infantry came hurrying to the front, their wounded
leader, supported by strong arms, was lifted to his feet. Anxious that
the men should not recognise him, Jackson turned aside into the
wood, and slowly and painfully dragged himself through the undergrowth. As he passed along, General Fender, whose brigade was then
pushing forward, asked Smith who it was that was wounded. "A Confederate officer" was the reply; but as they came nearer Fender, despite
the darkness, saw that it was Jackson.

Springing from his horse, he hurriedly expressed his regret, and
added that his lines were so much disorganised by the enemy's artillery
that he feared it would be necessary to fall back. "At this moment," says

an eye-witness, "the scene was a fearful one. The air seemed to be alive with the shriek of shells and the whistling of bullets; horses riderless and mad with fright dashed in every direction; hundreds left the ranks and hurried to the rear, and the groans of the wounded and dying mingled with the wild shouts of others to be led again to the assault. Almost fainting as he was from loss of blood, desperately wounded, and in the midst of this awful uproar, Jackson's heart was unshaken. The words of Fender seemed to rouse him to life. Pushing aside those who supported him, he raised himself to his full height, and answered feebly, but distinctly enough to be heard above the din, 'You must hold your ground, General Fender; you must hold out to the last, sir.'"

His strength was now completely gone, and he asked to be allowed to lie down. His staff-officers, however, refused assent. The shells were still crashing through the forest, and a litter having been brought up by Captain Leigh, he was carried slowly towards Dowdall's Tavern. But before they were free of the tangled wood, one of the stretcher-bearers, struck by a shot in the arm, let go the handle. Jackson fell violently to the ground on his wounded side. His agony must have been intense, and for the first time he was heard to groan.

Smith sprang to his side, and as he raised his head a bright beam of moonlight made its way through the thick foliage, and rested upon his white and lacerated face. The aide-de-camp was startled by its great pallor and stillness, and cried out, "General, are you seriously hurt?" "No, Mr. Smith, don't trouble yourself about me," he replied quietly, and added some words about winning the battle first, and attending to the wounded afterwards. He was again placed upon the litter, and carried a few hundred yards, still followed by the Federal shells, to where his medical director was waiting with an ambulance.

Dr. McGuire knelt down beside him and said, "I hope you are not badly hurt, General?" He replied very calmly but feebly, "I am badly injured, doctor, I fear I am dying." After a pause he went on, "I am glad you have come. I think the wound in my shoulder is still bleeding." The bandages were readjusted and he was lifted into the ambulance, where Colonel Crutchfield, who had also been seriously wounded, was already lying. Whisky and morphia were administered, and by the light of pine torches, carried by a few soldiers, he was slowly driven through the fields where Hooker's right had so lately fled before his impetuous onset. All was done that could ease his sufferings, but some jolting of the ambulance over the rough road was unavoidable; "and yet," writes Dr. McGuire, "his uniform politeness did not forsake him even in these most trying circumstances. His complete control, too, over his mind, enfeebled as it was by loss of blood and pain, was wonderful. His suffering was intense; his hands were cold, his skin clammy. But not a groan escaped him—not a sign of suffering, except the light corrugation of the brow, the fixed, rigid face, the thin lips, so tightly compressed that the impression of the teeth could be seen through them. Except these, he controlled by his iron will all evidence of emotion, and, more difficult than this even, he controlled that disposition to restlessness which many of us have observed upon the battle-field as attending great loss of blood. Nor was he forgetful of others. He expressed very feelingly his sympathy for Crutchfield, and once, when the latter groaned aloud, he directed the ambulance to stop, and requested me to see if something could not be done for his relief.

"After reaching the hospital, he was carried to a tent, and placed in bed, covered with blankets, and another drink of whisky and water given him. Two hours and a half elapsed before sufficient reaction took place to warrant an examination, and at two o'clock on Sunday morning I informed him that chloroform would be given him; I told him also that amputation would probably be required, and asked, if it was found necessary, whether it should be done at once. He replied promptly, 'Yes, certainly, Dr. McGuire, do for me whatever you think best.'

"Chloroform was then administered, and the left arm amputated about two inches below the shoulder. Throughout the whole of the operation, and until all the dressings were applied, he continued insensible. About half-past three, Colonel (then Major) Pendleton arrived at the hospital. He stated that General Hill had been wounded, and that the troops were in great disorder. General Stuart was in command, and had sent him to see the general. At first I declined to permit an interview, but Pendleton urged that the safety of the army and success of the cause depended upon his seeing him. When he entered the tent the general said, 'Well, Major, I am glad to see you; I thought you were killed.' Pendleton briefly explained the position of affairs, gave Stuart's message, and asked what should be done. Jackson was at once interested, and asked in his quick way several questions. When they were answered, he remained silent, evidently trying to think; he contracted his brow, set his mouth, and for some moments lay obviously endeavouring to concentrate his thoughts. For a moment we believed he had succeeded, for his nostrils dilated, and his eye flashed with its old fire, but it was only for a moment: his face relaxed again, and presently he answered, very feebly and sadly: 'I don't know—I can't tell; say to General Stuart he must do what he thinks best.' Soon after this he slept."

So, leaving behind him, struggling vainly against the oppression of his mortal hurt, the one man who could have completed the Confederate victory, Pendleton rode wearily through the night. Jackson's fall, at so critical a moment, just as the final blow was to be delivered, had proved a terrible disaster. Hill, who alone knew his intention of moving to the White House, had been wounded by a fragment of shell as he rode back to lead his troops. Boswell, who had been ordered to point out the road, had been killed by the same volley which struck down his chief, and the subordinate generals, without instructions and without guides, with their men in disorder, and the enemy's artillery playing fiercely on the forest, had hesitated to advance. Hill, remaining in a litter near the line of battle, had sent for Stuart. The cavalry commander, however, was at some distance from the field. Late in the evening, finding it impossible to employ his command at the front, he had been detached by Jackson, a regiment of infantry supporting him, to take and hold Ely's Ford. He had already arrived within view of a Federal camp established at that point, and was preparing to charge the enemy, under cover of the night, when Hill's messenger recalled him.

When Stuart reached the front he found the troops still halted, Rodes and Colston reforming on the open fields near Dowdall's Tavern, the Light Division deployed within the forest, and the generals anxious for their own security.

So far the attack had been completely successful, but Lee's lack of strength prevented the full accomplishment of his design. Had Longstreet been present, with Pickett and Hood to lead his splendid infantry, the Third Corps and the Twelfth would have been so hardly pressed that Chancellorsville, Hazel Grove, and the White House would have fallen an easy prize to Jackson's bayonets. Anderson, with four small brigades, was powerless to hold the force confronting him, and marching rapidly northwards, Sickles had reached Hazel Grove before Jackson fell. Here Pleasonton, with his batteries, was still in position, and Hooker had not yet lost his head. As soon as Birney's and Whipple's divisions had come up, forming in columns of brigades behind the guns, Sickles was ordered to assail the enemy's right flank and check his advance. Just before midnight the attack was made, in two lines of battle, supported by strong columns. The night was very clear and still; the moon, nearly full, threw enough light into the woods to facilitate the advance, and the tracks leading north-west served as lines of direction.

The attack, however, although gallantly made, gained no material advantage. The preliminary movements were plainly audible to the Confederates, and Lane's brigade, most of which was now south of the plank road, had made every preparation to receive it. Against troops lying down in the woods the Federal artillery, although fifty or sixty guns were in action, made but small impression; and the dangers of a night attack, made upon troops who are expecting it, and whose *moral* is unaffected, were forcibly illustrated. The confusion in the forest was very great; a portion of the assailing force, losing direction, fell foul of Berry's division at the foot of the Fairview heights, which had not been informed of the movement, and at least two regiments, fired into from front and rear, broke up in panic. Some part of the log breastworks which Jackson's advanced line had occupied were recaptured; but not a single one of the assailants, except as prisoners, reached the plank road. And yet the attack was an exceedingly well-timed stroke, and as such, although the losses were heavy, had a very considerable effect on the issue of the day's fighting. It showed, or seemed to show, that the Federals were still in good heart, that they were rapidly concentrating, and that the Confederates might be met by vigorous counter-strokes. "The fact," said Stuart in his official dispatch, "that the attack was made, and at night, made me apprehensive of a repetition of it."

So, while Jackson slept through the hours of darkness that should have seen the consummation of his enterprise, his soldiers lay beside their arms; and the Federals, digging, felling, and building, constructed a new line of parapet, protected by abattis, and strengthened by a long array of guns, on the slopes of Fairview and Hazel Grove. The respite which the fall of the Confederate leader had brought them was not neglected; the fast-spreading panic was stayed; the First Army Corps, rapidly crossing the Rappahannock, secured the road to the White House, and Averell's division of cavalry reached Ely's Ford.

May 3 On the left, between Chancellorsville and the river, where a young Federal colonel, named Miles, handled his troops with conspicuous skill, Lee's continuous attacks had been successfully repulsed, and at dawn on the morning of May 3 the situation of the Union army was far from unpromising. A gap of nearly two miles intervened between the Confederate wings, and within this gap, on the commanding heights of Hazel Grove and Fairview, the Federals were strongly intrenched. An opportunity for dealing a crushing counterblow—for holding one portion of Lee's army in check while the other was overwhelmed—appeared to present itself. The only question was whether the *moral* of the general and the men could be depended upon.

In Stuart, however, Hooker had to deal with a soldier who was no unworthy successor of Stonewall Jackson. Reluctantly abandoning the idea of a night attack, the cavalry general, fully alive to the exigencies of the situation, had determined to reduce the interval between himself and Lee; and during the night the artillery was brought up to the front, and the batteries deployed wherever they could find room. Just before the darkness began to lift, orders were received from Lee that the assault was to be made as early as possible; and the right wing, swinging round in order to come abreast of the centre, became hotly engaged. Away to the south-east, across the hills held by the Federals, came the responding thunder of Lee's guns; and 40,000 infantry, advancing through the woods against front and flank, enveloped in a circle of fire a stronghold which was held by over 60,000 muskets.

It is unnecessary to describe minutely the events of the morning. The Federal troops, such as were brought into action, fought well; but Jackson's tremendous attack had already defeated Hooker. Before Sickles made his night attack from Hazel Grove he had sent orders for

Sedgwick to move at once, occupy Fredericksburg, seize the heights, and march westward by the plank road; and, at the same time, he had instructed his engineers to select and fortify a position about a mile in rear of Chancellorsville. So, when Stuart pressed forward, not only had this new position been occupied by the First and Fifth Army Corps, but the troops hitherto in possession of Hazel Grove were already evacuating their intrenchments.

These dispositions sufficiently attest the demoralisation of the Federal commander. As the historian of the Army of the Potomac puts it: "The movement to be executed by Sedgwick was precisely one of those movements which, according as they are wrought out, may be either the height of wisdom or the height of folly. Its successful accomplishment certainly promised very brilliant results. It is easy to see how seriously Lee's safety would be compromised if, while engaged with Hooker in front, he should suddenly find a powerful force assailing his rear, and grasping already his direct line of communication with Richmond. But if, on the other hand, Lee should be able by any slackness on the part of his opponent to engage him in front with a part of his force, while he should turn swiftly round to assail the isolated moving column, it is obvious that he would be able to repulse or destroy that column, and then by a vigorous return, meet or attack his antagonist's main body. In the successful execution of this plan not only was Sedgwick bound to the most energetic action, but Hooker also was engaged by every consideration of honour and duty to so act as to make the dangerous task he had assigned to Sedgwick possible."

But so far from aiding his subordinate by a heavy counter-attack on Lee's front, Hooker deliberately abandoned the Hazel Grove salient, which, keeping asunder the Confederate wings, strongly facilitated such a manœuvre; and more than this, he divided his own army into two portions, of which the rear, occupying the new position, was actually forbidden to reinforce the front.

It is possible that Hooker contemplated an early retreat of his whole force to the second position. If so, Lee and Stuart were too quick for him. The cavalry commander, as soon as it became light, and the hills and undulations of the Wilderness emerged from the shadows, immediately recognised the importance of Hazel Grove. The hill was quickly seized; thirty pieces of artillery, established on the crest, enfiladed the Federal batteries, facing west, on the heights of Fairview; and the brigade on Stuart's extreme right was soon in touch with the troops directed by General Lee. Then against the three sides of the Federal position the battle raged. From the south and south-east came Anderson and McLaws, the batteries unlimbering on every eminence, and the infantry, hitherto held back, attacking with the vigour which their gallant commanders knew so well how to inspire. And from the west, formed in three lines, Hill's division to the front, came the Second Army Corps. The men knew by this time that the leader whom they trusted beyond all others had been struck down, that he was lying wounded, helpless, far away in rear. Yet his spirit was still with them. Stuart, galloping along the ranks, recalled him with ringing words to their memories, and as the bugles sounded the onset, it was with a cry of "Remember Jackson!" that his soldiers rushed fiercely upon the Federal breastworks.

The advanced line, within the forest, was taken at the first rush; the second, at the foot of the Fairview heights, protected by a swampy stream, a broad belt of abattis, and with thirty guns on the hill behind, proved far more formidable, and Hill's division was forced back. But Rodes and Colston were in close support. The fight was speedily renewed; and then came charge and counter-charge; the storm of the parapets; the rally of the defenders; the rush with the bayonet; and, mowing down men like grass, the fearful sweep of case and canister. Twice the Confederates were repulsed. Twice they reformed, brigade mingled with brigade, regiment with regiment, and charged again in the teeth of the thirty guns.

On both sides ammunition began to fail; the brushwood took fire, the ground became hot beneath the foot, and many wounded perished miserably in the flames. Yet still, with the tangled abattis dividing the opposing lines, the fight went on; both sides struggling fiercely, the Federals with the advantage of position, the Confederates of numbers, for Hooker refused to reinforce his gallant troops. At length the guns which Stuart had established on Hazel Grove, crossing their fire with those of McLaws and Anderson, gained the upper hand over the Union batteries. The storm of shell, sweeping the Fairview plateau, took the breastworks in reverse; the Northern infantry, after five hours of such hot battle as few fields have witnessed, began sullenly to yield, and as Stuart, leading the last charge, leapt his horse over the parapet, the works were evacuated, and the tattered colours of the Confederates waved in triumph on the hill.

"The scene," says a staff-officer, "can never be effaced from the minds of those that witnessed it. The troops were pressing forward with all the ardour and enthusiasm of combat. The white smoke of musketry fringed the front of battle, while the artillery on the hills in rear shook the earth with its thunder and filled the air with the wild shrieking of the shells that plunged into the masses of the retreating foe. To add greater horror and sublimity to the scene, the Chancellorsville House and the woods surrounding it were wrapped in flames. It was then that General Lee rode to the front of his advancing battalions. His presence was the signal for one of those uncontrollable outbursts of enthusiasm which none can appreciate who have not witnessed them.

"The fierce soldiers, with their faces blackened with the smoke of battle, the wounded, crawling with feeble limbs from the fury of the devouring flames, all seemed possessed of a common impulse. One long, unbroken cheer, in which the feeble cry of those who lay help-less on the earth blended with the strong voices of those who still fought, hailed the presence of the victorious chief.

"His first care was for the wounded of both armies, and he was among the foremost at the burning mansion, where some of them lay. But at that moment, when the transports of his troops were drowning the roar of battle with acclamations, a note was brought to him from General Jackson. It was handed to him as he sat on his horse near the Chancellorsville House, and unable to open it with his gauntleted hands, he passed it to me with directions to read it to him. I shall never forget the look of pain and anguish that passed over his face as he listened. In a voice broken with emotion he bade me say to General Jackson that the victory was his. I do not know how others may regard this incident, but for myself, as I gave expression to the thoughts of his exalted mind, I forgot the genius that won the day in my reverence for the generosity that refused its glory."

Lee's reply ran:—

"General,—I have just received your note, informing me that you were wounded. I cannot express my regret at the occurrence. Could I have directed events, I should have chosen for the good of the country to be disabled in your stead.

"I congratulate you upon the victory, which is due to your skill and energy.

"Very respectfully, your obedient servant, R. E. LEE, *General*."

Such was the tribute, not the less valued that it was couched in no exaggerated terms, which was brought to the bedside in the quiet hospital. Jackson was almost alone. As the sound of cannon and mus-ketry, borne across the forest, grew gradually louder, he had ordered all those who had remained with him, except Mr. Smith, to return to the battle-field and attend to their different duties.

His side, injured by his fall from the litter, gave him much pain, but his thoughts were still clear, and his speech coherent. "General Lee," he said, when his aide-de-camp read to him the Commander-in-Chief's brief words, "is very kind, but he should give the praise to God."

During the day the pain gradually ceased; the general grew brighter, and from those who visited the hospital he inquired minutely about the battle and the troops engaged. When conspicuous instances of courage were related his face lit up with enthusiasm, and he uttered his usual "Good, good," with unwonted energy when the gallant behaviour of his old command was alluded to. "Some day," he said, "the men of that brigade will be proud to say to their children, 'I was one of the Stonewall Brigade.'" He disclaimed all right of his own to the name Stonewall: "It belongs to the brigade and not to me." That night he slept well, and was free from pain.

Meanwhile the Confederate army, resting on the heights of Chancellorsville, preparatory to an attack upon Hooker's second stronghold, had received untoward news. Sedgwick, at eleven o'clock in the morning, had carried Marye's Hill, and, driving Early before him, was moving up the plank road. Wilcox' brigade of Anderson's division, then at Banks' Ford, was ordered to retard the advance of the hostile column. McLaws was detached to Salem Church. The Second Army Corps and the rest of Anderson's division remained to hold Hooker in check, and for the moment operations at Chancellorsville were suspended.

McLaws, deploying his troops in the forest, two hundred and fifty yards from a wide expanse of cleared ground, pushed his skirmishers forward to the edge, and awaited the attack of a superior force. Reserving his fire to close quarters, its effect was fearful. But the Federals pushed forward; a school-house occupied as an advanced post was captured, and at this point Sedgwick was within an ace of breaking through. His second line, however, had not yet deployed, and a vigorous counterstroke, delivered by two brigades, drove back the whole of his leading division in great disorder. As night fell the Confederates, careful not to expose themselves to the Union reserves, retired to the forest, and Sedgwick, like Hooker, abandoned all further idea of offensive action.

May 4 The next morning Lee himself, with the three remaining brigades of Anderson, arrived upon the scene. Sedgwick, who had lost 5,000 men the preceding day, May had fortified a position covering Banks' Ford, and occupied it with over 20,000 muskets. Lee, with the divisions of McLaws, Anderson, and Early, was slightly stronger. The attack was delayed, for the Federals held strong ground, difficult to reconnoitre; but once begun the issue was soon decided. Assailed in front and flanks, with no help coming from Hooker, and only a single bridge at Banks' Ford in rear, the Federals rapidly gave ground.

Darkness, however, intensified by a thick fog, made pursuit difficult, and Sedgwick re-crossed the river with many casualties but in good order. During these operations, that is, from four o'clock on Sunday afternoon until after midnight on Monday, Hooker had not moved a single man to his subordinate's assistance. So extraordinary a situation has seldom been seen in war: an army of 60,000 men, strongly fortified, was held in check for six-and-thirty hours by 20,000; while not seven miles away raged a battle on which the whole fate of the campaign depended.

Lee and Jackson had made no false estimate of Hooker's incapacity. Sedgwick's army corps had suffered so severely in men and in *moral* that it was not available for immediate service, even had it been transferred to Chancellorsville; and Lee was now free to concentrate his whole force against the main body of the Federal army. His men, notwithstanding their extraordinary exertions, were confident of victory.

May 5 "As I sheltered myself," says an eye-witness, "in a little farm-house on the plank road the brigades of Anderson's division came splashing through the mud, in wild tumultuous spirits, singing, shouting, jesting, heedless of soaking rags, drenched to the skin, and burning again to mingle in the mad revelry of battle." But it was impossible to push forward, for a violent rain-storm burst upon the Wilderness, and the spongy soil, saturated with the deluge, absolutely precluded all movement across country. Hooker, who had already made preparations for retreat, took advantage of the weather, and as soon as darkness set in put his army in motion for the bridges.

May 6 By eight o'clock on the morning of the 6th the whole force had crossed; and when the Confederate patrols pushed forward, Lee found that his victim had escaped.

The Army of the Potomac returned to its old camp on the hills above Fredericksburg, and Lee reoccupied his position on the opposite ridge. Stoneman, who had scoured the whole country to within a few miles of Richmond, returned to Kelly's Ford on May 8. The raid had effected nothing. The damage done to the railroads and canals was repaired by the time the raiders had regained the Rappahannock. Lee's operations at Chancellorsville had not been affected in the very slightest degree by their presence in his rear, while Stoneman's absence had proved the ruin of the Federal army. Jackson, who had been removed by the Commander-in-Chief's order to Mr. Chandler's house, near Gurney's Station, on the morning of May 5, was asked what he thought of Hooker's plan of campaign. His reply was: "It was in the main a good conception, an excellent plan. But he should not have sent away his cavalry; that was his great blunder. It was that which enabled me to turn him without his being aware of it, and to take him in the rear. Had he kept his cavalry with him, his plan would have been a very good one." This was not his only comment on the great battle. Among other things, he said that he intended to cut the Federals off from the United States Ford, and, taking a position between them and the river, oblige them to attack him, adding, with a smile, "My men sometimes fail to drive the enemy from a position, but they always fail to drive us away." He spoke of General Rodes, and alluded in high terms to his splendid behaviour in the attack on Howard. He hoped he would be promoted, and he said that promotion should be made at once, upon the field, so as to act as an incentive to gallantry in others. He spoke of Colonel Willis, who had commanded the skirmishers, and praised him very highly, and referred most feelingly to the death of Paxton, the commander of the Stonewall Brigade, and of Captain Boswell, his chief engineer. In speaking of his own share in the victory he said: "Our movement was a great success; I think the most successful military movement of my life. But I expect to receive far more credit for it than I deserve. Most men will think I planned it all from the first; but it was not so. I simply took advantage of circumstances as they were presented to me in the providence of God. I feel that His hand led me—let us give Him the glory."

It must always be an interesting matter of speculation what the result would have been had Jackson accomplished his design, on the night he fell, of moving a large part of his command up the White House road, and barring the only line of retreat left open to the Federals.

Hooker, it is argued, had two corps in position which had been hardly engaged, the Second and the Fifth; and another, the First, under Reynolds, was coming up. Of these, 25,000 men might possibly, could they have been manœuvred in the forest, have been sent to drive Jackson back. And, undoubtedly, to those who think more of numbers than of human nature, of the momentum of the mass rather than the mental equilibrium of the general, the fact that a superior force of comparatively fresh troops was at Hooker's disposal will be sufficient to put the success of the Confederates out of court. Yet the question will always suggest itself, would not the report that a victorious enemy, of unknown strength, was pressing forward, in the darkness of the night, towards the only line of retreat, have so demoralised the Federal commander and the Federal soldiers, already shaken by the overthrow of the Eleventh Army Corps, that they would have thought only of securing their own safety? Would Hooker, whose tactics the next day, after he had had the night given him in which to recover his senses, were so inadequate, have done better if he had received no respite? "Would the soldiers of the three army corps not yet engaged, who had been witnesses of the rout of Howard's divisions, have fared better, when they heard the triumphant yells of the advancing Confederates, than the hapless Germans? "The wounding of Jackson," says a most careful historian of the battle, himself a participator in the Union disaster, "was a most fortunate circumstance for the Army of the Potomac. At nine o'clock the capture or destruction of a large part of the army seemed inevitable. There was, at the time, great uncertainty and a feeling akin to panic prevailing among the Union forces round Chancellorsville; and when we consider the position of the troops at this moment, and how many important battles have been won by trivial flank attacks—how Richepanse (attacking through the forest) with a single brigade ruined the Austrians at Hohenlinden—we must admit that the Northern army was in great peril when Jackson arrived within one thousand yards of its vital point (the White House) with 20,000 men and 50 cannon." He must be a great leader indeed who, when his flank is suddenly rolled up and his line of retreat threatened, preserves sufficient coolness to devise a general counterstroke. Jackson had proved himself equal to such a situation at Cedar Run, but it is seldom in these circumstances that Providence sides with the "big battalions."

The Federal losses in the six days' battles were heavy: over 12,000 at Chancellorsville, and 4,700 at Fredericksburg, Salem Church, and Banks' Ford; a total of 17,287. The army lost 13 guns, and nearly 6,000 officers and men were reported either captured or missing.

But a mere statement of the casualties by no means represents the comparative loss of the opposing forces. Victory does not consist in merely killing and maiming a few thousand men. This is the visible result; it is the invisible that tells. The Army of the Potomac, when it retreated across the Rappahannock, was far stronger in mere numbers than the Army of Northern Virginia; but in reality it was far weaker, for the moral of the survivors, and of the general who led them, was terribly affected. That of the Confederates, on the other hand, had been sensibly elevated, and it is moral, not numbers, which is the strength of armies. What, after all, was the loss of 12,200 soldiers to the Confederacy? In that first week of May there were probably 20,000 conscripts in different camps of instruction, more than enough to recruit the depleted regiments to full strength. Nor did the slaughter of Chancellorsville diminish to any appreciable degree the vast hosts of the Union.

And yet the Army of the Potomac had lost more than all the efforts of the Government could replace. The Army of Virginia, on the other hand, had acquired a superiority of spirit which was ample compensation for the sacrifice which had been made. It is hardly too much to say that Lee's force had gained from the victory an increase of strength equivalent to a whole army corps of 80,000 men, while that of his opponent had been proportionately diminished. Why, then, was there no pursuit?

It has been asserted that Lee was so crippled by his losses at Chancellorsville that he was unable to resume operations against Hooker for a whole month. This explanation of his inactivity can hardly be accepted.

On June 16 and 18, 1815, at Quatre-Bras and Waterloo, the Anglo-Dutch army, little larger than that of Northern Virginia, lost 17,000 men; and yet on the 19th Wellington was marching in pursuit of the French; nor did he halt until he arrived within sight of Paris. And on August 28, 29, and 30, 1862, at Groveton and the Second Manassas, Stonewall Jackson lost 4,000 officers and men, one-fifth of his force, but he was not left in rear when Lee invaded Maryland. Moreover, after he had defeated Sedgwick, on the same night that Hooker was recrossing the Rappahannock, Lee was planning a final attack on the Federal intrenchments, and his disappointment was bitter when he learned that his enemy had escaped.

If his men were capable of further efforts on the night of May 5, they were capable of them the next day; and it was neither the ravages of battle nor the disorganisation of the army that held the Confederates fast, but the deficiency of supplies, the damage done to the railways by Stoneman's horsemen, the weakness of the cavalry, and, principally, the hesitation of the Government. After the victory of Chancellorsville, strong hopes of peace were entertained in the South Before Hooker advanced, a large section of the Northern Democrats, despairing of ultimate success, had once more raised the cry that immediate separation was better, than a hopeless contest, involving such awful sacrifices, and it needed all Lincoln's strength to stem the tide of disaffection. The existence of this despondent feeling was well known to the Southern statesmen; and to such an extent did they count upon its growth and increase that they had overlooked altogether the importance of improving a victory, should the army be successful; so now, when the chance had come, they were neither ready to forward such an enterprise, nor could they make up their minds to depart from their passive attitude. But to postpone all idea of counterstroke until some indefinite period is as fatal in strategy as in tactics. By no means an uncommon policy, it has been responsible for the loss of a thousand opportunities.

Had not politics intervened, a vigorous pursuit—not necessarily involving an immediate attack, but drawing Hooker, as Pope had been drawn in the preceding August, into an unfavourable situation, before his army had had time to recover—would have probably been initiated. It may be questioned, however, whether General Lee, even when Longstreet and his divisions joined him, would have been so strong as he had been at the end of April. None felt more deeply than the Commander-in-Chief that the absence of Jackson was an irreparable misfortune. "Give him my affectionate regards," he said to an aide-de-camp who was riding to the hospital; "tell him to make haste and get well, and come back to me as soon as he can. He has lost his left arm, but I have lost my right." "Any victory," he wrote privately, "would be dear at such a price. I know not how to replace him."

His words were prophetic. Exactly two months after Chancellorsville the armies met once more in the clash of battle. During the first two days, on the rolling plain round Gettysburg, a village of Pennsylvania, four Federal army corps were beaten in succession, but ere the sun set on the third Lee had to admit defeat.

And yet his soldiers had displayed the same fiery courage and stubborn persistence which had carried them victorious through the Wilderness. But his "right arm" had not yet been replaced. "If," he said after the war, with unaccustomed emphasis, "I had had Jackson at Gettysburg I should have won the battle, and a complete victory there would have resulted in the establishment of Southern independence."

It was not to be. Chancellorsville, where 130,000 men were defeated by 60,000, is up to a certain point as much the tactical masterpiece of the nineteenth century as was Leuthen of the eighteenth. But, splendid triumph as it was, the battle bore no abiding fruits, and the reason seems very clear. The voice that would have urged pursuit was silent. Jackson's fall left Lee alone, bereft of his alter ego; with none, save Stuart, to whom he could entrust the execution of those daring and delicate manœuvres his inferior numbers rendered necessary; with none on whose resource and energy he could implicitly rely. Who shall say how far his own resolution had been animated and confirmed at other crises by the prompting and presence of the kindred spirit? "They supplemented each other," said Davis, "and together, with any fair opportunity, they were absolutely invincible."

Many a fierce battle still lay before the Army of Northern Virginia; marvellous was the skill and audacity with which Lee manœuvred his ragged regiments in the face of overwhelming odds; fierce and unyielding were the soldiers, but with Stonewall Jackson's death the impulse of victory died away.

May 7 It is needless to linger over the closing scene at Gurney's Station. For some days there was hope that the patient would recover; pneumonia, attributed to his fall from the litter as he was borne from the field, supervened, and he gradually began to sink. On the Thursday his wife and child arrived from Richmond; but he was then almost too weak for conversation, and on Sunday morning it was evident that the end was near.

May 10 As yet he had scarcely realised his condition. If, he said, it was God's will, he was ready to go, but he believed that there was still work for him to do, and that his life would be preserved to do it. At eleven o'clock Mrs. Jackson knelt by his side, and told him that he could not live beyond the evening. "You are frightened, my child," he replied, "death is not so near; I may yet get well." She fell upon the bed, weeping bitterly, and told him again that there was no hope. After a moment's pause, he asked her to call Dr. McGuire. "Doctor," he said, "Anna tells me I am to die to-day; is it so?" When he was answered, he remained silent for a moment or two, as if in intense thought, and then quietly replied, "Very good, very good; it is all right."

About noon, when Major Pendleton came into the room, he asked, "Who is preaching at headquarters to-day?" He was told that Mr. Lacy was, and that the whole army was praying for him. "Thank God," he said; "they are very kind to me." Already his strength was fast ebbing, and although his face brightened when his baby was brought to him, his mind had begun to wander. Now he was on the battle-field, giving orders to his men; now at home in Lexington; now at prayers in the camp. Occasionally his senses came back to him, and about half-past one he was told that he had but two hours to live. Again he answered, feebly but firmly, "Very good; it is all right." These were almost his last coherent words. For some time he lay unconscious, and then suddenly he cried out: "Order A.P. Hill to prepare for action! Pass the infantry to the front! Tell Major Hawks" . . . then stopped, leaving the sentence unfinished. Once more he was silent; but a little while after he said very quietly and clearly, "Let us cross over the river, and rest under the shade of the trees," and the soul of the great captain passed into the peace of God.

[Editor's note: It is interesting that Robert E. Lee's final words were so close to Jackson's. After lingering from a stroke for two weeks, on October 12, 1870, at Washington College, Lexington, Virginia, Lee is said to have uttered, "Tell Hill he must come up!" Calling for A. P. Hill from somewhere in his thoughts. Then he said, "Strike the tent!" and died. This quote is mistrusted by some historians who claim it was never written down by Lee's relatives.]

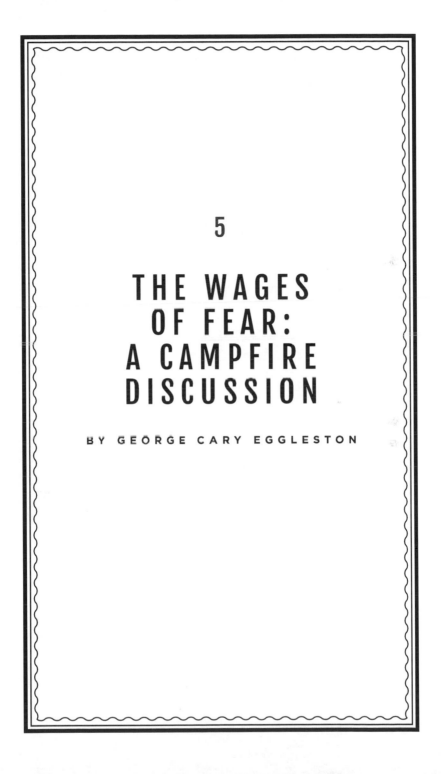

5

THE WAGES OF FEAR: A CAMPFIRE DISCUSSION

BY GEORGE CARY EGGLESTON

One thing that has probably never changed over the centuries is the holding power of soldiers' campfire conversations. This strong example from a Confederate soldier shows the troops taking on a subject often in their minds, and sometimes getting into real discussions.

It was a kind of off-night, the 23d of October, 1862, twenty-four hours after the battle of Pocotaligo, on the South Carolina coast.

We had to stop over there until morning, because the creek was out of its banks, and we couldn't get across without daylight. There were only about a dozen of us, and we had to build a camp-fire under the trees.

After supper we fell to talking, and naturally we talked of war things. There wasn't anything else to talk about then.

There was the long-legged mountaineer, with the deep voice, and the drawl in his speech which aided the suggestion that he kept his voice in his boots and had to pump it up when anything was to be said. Opposite him was the alert, rapid-speaking fellow, who had come in as a conscript and had made a superb volunteer,—a fellow who had an opinion ready made on every subject that could be mentioned, and who was accustomed to wind up most conversations with a remark so philosophical as to seem strangely out of keeping with the rest of the inconsequent things that he had said. Then there were the two mountaineers who never said anything because they never had anything to say. They had reached that point of intellectual development where the theory is accepted that there ought to be thought behind every utterance; and under this misapprehension they abstained from utterance.

Joe was there, but Joe wasn't talking that night. Joe was surly and sullen. He had had to kill his horse at Pocotaligo the day before, and all the honors he had harvested from that action had not reconciled him to the loss. The new horse he had drawn was, in his opinion, "a beast." Of course all horses are beasts, but that isn't precisely what Joe meant. Besides, he had received a letter from his sweetheart just before we left camp,—she's his wife now, and the mother of his dozen or more children,—in which that young woman had expressed doubts as to whether, after all, he was precisely the kind of man to whom she ought to "give her life." Joe was only seventeen years of age at that time, and he minded little things like that. Still again, Joe had the toothache. Besides that, we were hungry after our exceedingly scant meal of roasted sweet potatoes. Besides that, it was raining.

All the circumstances contributed to make us introspective and psychological in our conversation.

The long-legged mountaineer with the deep voice was telling some entirely inconsequent story about somebody who wasn't known to any of us, and none of us was listening. After a while he said: "He was that sort of a feller that never felt fear in his life."

From Joe: "There never was any such fellow."

The long mountaineer: "Well, that's what he *said*, anyhow."

From Joe: "He lied, then."

"Well," continued the long-legged mountaineer, "that's what he said, and he sort o' lived up to it. If he had any fear, he didn't show it till that time I was tellin' you about, when he went all to pieces and showed the white feather."

"There," growled Joe, "what did I tell you? He was lying all the time."

The postscript philosopher on the other side of the fire broke in, saying: "Well, maybe his breakfast went bad on him that morning. An overdone egg would make a coward out of the Duke of Wellington."

Joe made the general reflection that "some people locate their courage in their transverse colons."

"What's a transverse colon?" asked one of the mountaineers. Joe got up, stretched himself, and made no answer. Perhaps none was expected.

"Well," asked the long-legged mountaineer, "ain't they people that don't feel no fear?"

The glib little fellow quickly responded: "Let's find out. Let's hold an experience meeting. I suppose we're a pretty fairly representative body, and I move that each fellow tells honestly how he feels when he is going into battle; for instance, when the skirmishers are at work in front, and we know that the next two minutes will bring on the business."

"Infernally bad," growled Joe; "and anybody that pretends to feel otherwise lies."

The postscript philosopher replied: "I never saw *you* show any fear, Joe."

"That's because I'm too big a coward to show it," said Joe.

Even the two reticent mountaineers understood that.

One of them was moved to break the silence. At last he had, if not a thought, yet an emotion to stand sponsor for utterance.

"*I* always feel," said he, "as though the squegees had took hold of my knees. There ain't anything of me for about a minute—exceptin' a spot in the small of my back. I always wish I was a woman or a baby, or dead or something like that. After a while I git holt of myself and I says to myself, 'Bill, you've got to stand up to the rack, fodder or no fodder.' After that it all comes sort of easy like, you know, because the firin' begins, and after the firin' begins you're doin' somethin', you see, and when you're fightin' like, things don't seem so bad. I s'pose you've all *noticed* that."

From Joe: "In all the works on psychology it has been recognized as a universal principle, that the mind when occupied with a superior consideration is able to free itself from considerations of a lesser sort."

The mountaineer looked at him helplessly and said nothing.

The postscript philosopher began: "I shall never forget my first battle. It wasn't much of a battle either, but it was lively while it lasted. Unfortunately for me it was one of those fights where you have to wait for the enemy to begin. I was tender then. I had just left home, and every time I looked at the little knickknacks mother and the girls had given me to make camp life comfortable,—for bless my soul they thought we *lived* in camp,—every time I looked at these things I grew teary. There oughtn't to be any bric-à-brac of that kind given to a fellow when he goes into the army. It isn't fit. It worries him."

He was silent for a minute. So were the rest of us. We all had bric-à-brac to remember. He resumed:

"We were lying there in the edge of a piece of woods with a sloping meadow in front, crossed by a stone wall heavily overgrown with vines. At the other edge of the meadow was another strip of woods. The enemy were somewhere in there. We knew they were coming, because the pickets had been driven in, and we stood there waiting for them. The waiting was the worst of it, and as we waited I got to feeling in my pockets and—pulled out a little, old three-cornered pincushion. Conscience knows I wouldn't have pulled out that pincushion at that particular minute to have won a battle. I've got it now. I never had any use for a pincushion because I never could pin any two things together the way a woman can, but a man can't make his womenkind believe that: I've kept it all through the war, and when I go back home—if it suits the Yankees that I ever go back at all—I'm going to give it as a souvenir to the little sister that made it for me. And I'm going to tell her that it was that pincushion, little three-cornered thing that it is, that made a man out of me that day.

"My first thought as I pulled it out was that I wanted to go home and give the war up; but then came another kind of a thought. I said, 'The little girl wouldn't have given that pincushion to me if she hadn't understood that I was going off to fight for the country.' So I said to myself, 'Old boy, you've got to stand your hand pat.' And now whenever we go into battle I always brace myself up a little by feeling in my breeches pocket and sort of shaping out that pincushion."

From Joe: "It's a good story, but the rest of us haven't any pincushions. Besides that, it's raining." I couldn't help observing that Joe drew that afternoon's letter out of his pocket and fumbled it a little, while the long-legged mountaineer was straightening out his limbs and his thoughts for his share in the conversation. He said in basso profundo: "The fact is I'm always so skeered just before a fight that I can't remember afterwards how I did feel. I know only this much, that that last three minutes before the bullets begin to whistle and the shells to howl, takes more out of me than six hours straightaway fightin' afterwards does."

From Joe: "There must be a lot in you at the start, then."

There were still two men unheard from in the experience meeting. Some one of us called upon them for an expression of opinion.

"I donno. I never thought," said one.

"Nuther did I," said the other.

"Of course you didn't," said Joe.

Then the postscript philosopher, rising and stretching himself, remarked: "I reckon that if any man goes into a fight without being scared, that man is drunk or crazy."

Then we all lay down and went to sleep.

6

IN THE RANKS

BY REVEREND R. E. M'BRIDE

R. E. M'Bride recalls his experiences as a private soldier in the Army of the Potomac in this excerpt from his book In the Ranks: From the Wilderness to Appomattox CourtHouse, *published in 1881. From a quiet Pennsylvania town to the battlefields and hospitals of this savage war, "Robbie" M'Bride, as he was known as a soldier, not yet a reverend, survived the war and returned home to tell the story of the fighting as seen "in the ranks."*

"War!"

It is a little word. A child may pronounce it; but what word that ever fell from human lips has a meaning full of such intensity of horror as this little word? At its sound there rises up a grim vision of "confused noise and garments rolled in blood."

April 12, 1861, cannon fired by traitor hands, boomed out over Charleston harbor. The dire sound that shook the air that Spring morning did not die away in reverberating echoes from sea to shore, from island to headland. It rolled on through all the land, over mountain and valley, moaning in every home, at every fire-side, "War! War! War!"

Are we a civilized people? What is civilization? Is it possible to elim-inate the tiger from human nature? Who would have dreamed that the men of the North, busy with plowing and sowing, planning, con-triving, inventing, could prove themselves on a hundred battle-fields a fiercely warlike people? The world looked on with wonder as they rushed eagerly into the conflict, pouring out their blood like water and their wealth without measure, for a sentiment, a principle, that may be summed up in the one word—"nationality." "The great uprising" was not the movement of a blind, unreasoning impulse. A fire had been smoldering in the North for years. The first cannon shot that hurtled around the old flag as it floated over the walls of Fort Sumter shook down the barriers that confined it, and the free winds of liberty fanned it to a devouring flame.

The Yankee—let the name be proudly spoken—as he turned the furrow, stood by his work bench, or listened to the jarring clank of his machinery, had mused with heavy heart and shame-flushed cheek how a haughty, brutal, un-American spirit had drawn a line across the land, and said, "Beyond this is not your country. Here your free speech, free labor, and free thought shall never come." While this line was imaginary, he had waited for better days and larger thought to change the current of the times; but when it was transformed into bristling bayonets and frowning cannon, the tiger rose up within him, and with unquestioning faith he took up the gauge of battle. Men talked of the "cold blood of the North." That blood had surged impetuously through the veins of warrior freemen for a hundred generations. Here in the New World it had lost none of its vigor. The sturdy spirit that in other years ruled the hand that wielded the battle-ax, still ruled, when the hand was employed in subduing mountain and prairie.

The North was averse to war, because it was rising to that higher civilization that abhors violence, discards brute methods, and relies on the intellectual and moral. Such a people, driven to desperation, move right forward to the accomplishment of their object with a scorn of cost or consequences unknown to a lower type. Hence it is that the people of the North, without hesitation, grappled with a rebellion the most formidable ever successfully encountered by any government.

Turning away from a half million graves, wherein they had buried their slain, their bravest and best beloved, they forgot all bitterness for joy that peace had come. No people in the world had greater reason for severity than the victors in this strife. War, willful, unprovoked, without the shadow of justification, had been thrust upon them. This had been preceded by a series of usurpations the most unblushing ever endured by a free people. These were a part of the plan of a band of traitors, who had plotted for years to overthrow the existing order of things, and establish an empire with human slavery for its chief corner-stone.

The "Golden Circle," with its center at Havana, Cuba, its radii extending to Pennsylvania on the North, the isthmus on the south, and sweeping from shore to shore, was the bold dream of the men who plotted the destruction of the American republic. Their object was pursued with a cold-blooded disregard of all right, human and divine, worthy of the pagan brutality of the Roman Triumvirate. Prating about the "Constitution" with hypocritical cant, they trampled upon every safeguard of popular liberty, and at last, in defiance of even the forms of law, plunged the people of the Southern States into a war with the government, which, even if successful in securing a separation, could only have been the beginning of woes, as their plans would develop.

But notwithstanding the heinousness of the accomplished crime, not a man was punished. It is doubtful whether popular opinion would have approved the punishment of even the arch-traitor, Jeff Davis. The common sentiment was expressed by the oft-repeated verdict: "Enough of blood has been shed." Whether this was wise or not it is vain to inquire. Perhaps the future will vindicate the wisdom of the generous course of the government. Thus far it has seemed like folly. The South has shown a persistent vindictiveness unequaled in the history of any people, a cruelty toward the helpless victims of their hate that is shameful to the last degree. The cowardly assassination of political opponents, the brutal murder of black men, women, and children, has been defended openly or covertly by pulpit, press, and platform. If any disapprove, their voice is not heard in condemnation of the wrong. This may have resulted partly from the fact that many of the people of the North, notably many so-called statesmen, ignored common sense and gave way to gush and sentiment. There is nothing gained in this prosy world by calling black white. The leaders of the rebellion were guilty of the horrible crime of treason, and we baptized it something else. The result is manifest to all who are not willfully and wickedly blind to the facts.

Yet it is the part of duty to hope for the speedy coming of an era of calmer judgment, of real and healthy patriotism, when every American citizen will claim our whole land as his country. When the civil war began, my home was with the family of Mr. John Dunn, in Butler County, Pennsylvania. The old gentleman was a Democrat, and at first had little to say about the war. One evening he returned from the village in a state of intense excitement. He had heard of the disastrous battle at Bull Run. It is no exaggeration to say that he "pranced" around the room, chewing his tobacco with great vigor, telling how many of our "poor boys" had been slaughtered by the rebels. His apathy was at an end. He could see where the line lay between treason and patriotism, when once that line was traced in blood.

At this time two Butler County companies, C and D, of the Eleventh Pennsylvania Reserve Volunteer Corps, were in camp near Pittsburg. The corps was sent forward to Washington at once, and from that time till the close of their term of service, they gallantly represented the Keystone State in every battle fought by the Army of the Potomac. My brother, Wm. A., was a private in Company C. He enlisted June 10, 1861, and fell, with many other brave men, at the battle of Gaines' Mill, June 27, 1862.

★   ★   ★

In this quiet village [Prospect, Butler County] one chilly morning in December, 1863, the writer mounted the stage-coach and went rattling over the frozen ground toward Pittsburg, to enlist in the volunteer service. Just seventeen years ago that very morning I had begun the business of life on rather limited capital; and although it had been improved with considerable success, yet the kindly prophecies, particularly of my copperhead friends, did not portend a very lengthy nor brilliant military career. The next day I made my way to the provost-marshal's office, and, after due examination, was pronounced all right, and sworn into the service. If I lied about my age, obliging memory has written it over with something else, and it is gone from me.

I selected Company D, of the Eleventh Pennsylvania Regular Volunteer Corps, and was assigned accordingly. The recruits were retained for some time at Camp Copeland, then about the dreariest, most uncomfortable place I ever saw; shelter and provisions insufficient, bad whisky and blacklegs abundant. Joe Stewart, John Alexander, and myself tented together here. They had enlisted for the One Hundredth Pennsylvania, the "Roundheads." Joe was an old acquaintance. He served gallantly till the close of the war. John was a noble boy and found a soldier's death at Cold Harbor. After one of the fruitless charges made there, when the Roundheads came back foiled of their purpose, John was not with them. In the darkness of night which quickly closed around, Joe went out to search for him. As he was picking his way stealthily among the dead and dying, he heard a well known voice calling softly near by, "Joe, Joe, is that you?" It was John, lying there, shot through the breast. He warned his rescuer to be very cautious, as the rebel videttes were near. With much difficulty he got him back to our lines. This was the night of June 2d, and he died on the 4th.

I left the latter part of January to join the regiment, then camped at Bristoe Station, on the Orange and Alexandria Railroad. With me were two recruits for Company E, Abe Eshelman and Mike Coleman. The former was killed at Petersburg; the latter, a live Irishman, was mustered out at the close of the war, after a year and a half of valiant service for his adopted country. We went by Harrisburg, Baltimore, and Washington, thence by the Orange and Alexandria road, every mile historic ground, past Bull Run, where, the soldiers say, the dead would not stay buried, and finally we alight at Bristoe Station. On the right over there are the Bucktails; a little further toward the west the Second is camped. Over the hill toward Brentsville, past the artillery camp, is the Eleventh.

Here I found John Elliot, who had served with the regiment since its organization. He, brother William, and myself had been boy companions before the war, although I was younger than they. I went into the mess with him, S. L. Parker, and Benjamin Mushrush. After being with them but a short time, I was taken with that scourge of the army, measles, and was removed to the surgeon's tent. I was on picket when the disease made itself felt. The day and night on which I was on duty were stormy, rain and snow. As a result, I had a lively time of it. The disease left my voice so impaired that, for a long time, I was unable to speak above a whisper. During my stay at the surgeon's tent, I employed myself studying his books on surgery, and acquired a knowledge on the subject which was utilized at a later period.

John Elliot had enlisted April 25, 1861, although not mustered into the United States service until July 5th of the same year. He felt that he should be mustered out at the former date of 1864. As the time drew near, we conversed frequently on the subject, and he was in some perplexity as to duty in the case. The morning of the 25th found him on picket. I prepared the morning meal for the mess and then relieved him until he should breakfast. Soon he returned in a more than usually cheerful spirit. After chatting pleasantly for a time, he spoke of his term of enlistment. "I have that matter all arranged now," he said, "as far as I am concerned. I am not certain whether the government has a right to hold me any longer or not; but I will stay till it sees fit to discharge me. The country needs soldiers this Spring. I would like to visit home. It's been three years since I saw mother and the boys; but it's all right. God has kept me safely through all these battles, and I can trust him for time to come."

This was the substance of his language, his exact words, as near as I can remember. They are noble words; as grand as ever fell from the lips of Christian hero. Many a time afterward they were an inspiration to me. His face was bright that beautiful Spring morning with a joy that was not of earth. The night watches had been spent communing with God,—yes, face to face. Had he known that the midsummer sun would look down upon his grave, would his decision have been different? I think not. He knew too much of war and battles not to count the cost. From a Southern prison-pen his brave spirit went up to God.

★　★　★

April 29th we broke camp and proceeded to near Culpepper Court-house. Before leaving camp we sent our extra baggage, clothing, etc., to Washington, and, of course, never saw them again. During the night of May 3d we marched for the Rapidan, crossing at Germania Ford. The next evening we camped in order of battle near the Wilderness Tavern. The following morning the division moved out on a country road toward Robertson's Tavern. Passing through woods, we came to an open field, where line of battle was formed. The Bucktails were in front, skirmishing. We could see them on the ridge, and their occasional shouts and rapid firing showed that the battle had begun. For the first time I heard the whistle of the rifle ball, as a stray one now and then whistled over the line of battle.

After waiting thus for some time, we moved back some distance, in the direction from which we had come. Here I spoke a few words with John Elliot, the last we ever exchanged. In the confusion which followed he was made prisoner, and died at Andersonville.

Soon the noise of battle began to deepen in our front and at the right. Hurried orders were received; the line moved by the right flank, double-quick. The Seventh Regiment deployed and vanished into the woods, forward, and the Eleventh followed in line of battle. Moving on through the thick underbrush, the enemy was quickly encountered. Their first volley was deadly. A ball struck Boss M'Cullough in the forehead. He fell dead, a portion of his shattered brain lodging on the arm of John Stanley, a boy of seventeen, who had come to us during the Spring.

John shuddered, shook it from the sleeve of his blouse, raised his gun and began firing. Captain Jones, of Company A, White, of Company C, and many others, fell dead before this first volley. Soon it was discovered that the division was flanked. Our line was at right angles with the position in which the subsequent fighting took place. To crown all, the woods took fire, and soon the only problem that remained was to withdraw as quickly and safely as possible.

While this turmoil was progressing, to me so strange and bewildering, the surgeon, Dr. Lyon, came across me, and directed me to go to a certain point at the edge of the woods, east of the Wilderness Tavern, to help care for the wounded. Thither I made my way. As I passed on through the woods, I was soon out of reach of the bullets, which had been flying thick and fast. When I came to the open ground, I saw more clearly than ever the results of the battle, still going on in the woods beyond. The multitude of wounded and dying men crowded the road. Some were limping painfully along; others were being carried on stretchers, or helped along by comrades.

Reaching the designated place, I found the field tents erected, and all full of suffering men. I took charge of one in which were twenty-seven wounded, several amputations, and other bad cases. They lay with their heads toward the canvas, a narrow path being left between their feet. All that could be done for them was to give them food and water, bathe their wounds, and render any little service by which their sufferings might be mitigated. Their heroic patience astonished me. Men, torn and mangled, would utter no groan, nor give any vocal expression to the agonies which racked them, except sometimes when sleep or delirium found the overmastering will off guard.

Toward evening I learned that the regiment was just beyond the Wilderness tavern; and, getting relieved for a short time, I started to go to them, as I had the extra coffee of the mess. As I came in sight, they moved hurriedly away toward the right, where the battle was raging fiercely. It was useless to follow, and I began to retrace my steps. Pausing a moment on an elevated knoll, I gazed on the strange scene that spread out before me.

From the right on the turnpike, a line, somewhat curved, extended a distance of three or four miles to the left. On the right the line was enveloped in woods, in which a terrific conflict was going on. Sedgwick's corps was standing between the army and disaster. In the center, on elevated ground, beyond some low woods, I could see a rebel line of battle, while the sharp fire of skirmishers in front showed that here the lines of blue and gray would soon smite together. Further toward the left, a line of blue extended along the edge of a narrow field, facing the woods just beyond, into which it poured incessant volleys, while the smoke that rose up from the woods showed that an active foe was there. Behind our line, flat on the ground, lay a second one. A tragedy, grandly, awfully sublime, was enacting before me.

A hundred thousand men were grappling in deadly conflict. While I gazed the line of battle slackened its fire; the second one rose from the ground; then both swept forward across the field and into the woods beyond, bearing the enemy before them. For a few moments there was silence, and then the struggle was renewed as fiercely as ever. I returned to the field-tents to go on with my work of mercy among the suffering.

As night drew on, the battle ceased, and the men lay down to sleep where they had fought, ready to renew the strife at the return of light. In the tents there, while the army beyond was resting, part of our nation's heroes continued the contest through the solemn hours of night. They fought with the giant Pain, and some of them went down into the dark valley, and close by the chill waters they faced the King of Terrors.

I slept none that night. As morning approached, I went to the edge of the little opening which had been cleared in the woods for the tents. While I stood here looking off toward the scene of yesterday's battle, the sound of a single rifle shot rang out on the air, then another and another, and then a deafening roar of musketry burst forth and raged along the whole line, continuing almost without interruption all day.

In the afternoon Lieutenant Boggs and David Steen were brought in wounded, the former by a rifle ball in the thigh, the latter severely bruised by a fragment of shell. He had been wounded at Gaines' Mill and Fredericksburg. After his return this time, I heard him say that he had come to have more dread of going into battle since he had been wounded so often. Still he never shrank from duty. He was killed the following August at Welden Railroad.

Here I saw the only instance of impatience on the part of a wounded man of which I have any recollection. A young fellow lay about the middle of the tent, wounded in the knee, a ball having cut the skin on one side without injuring the bone. His long legs were extended almost across the narrow path along which I was compelled to walk in passing from one to another. He was grumbling and complaining, demanding and receiving attentions in a gruff and uncivil manner. He would also mutter threatenings of what he would do should I hurt him in stepping over his crooked legs outstretched in my way. To all of this I paid no attention and signs of ill-nature continued. Finally, a bright young man opposite, whose leg was amputated at the thigh, raised himself on his elbow and proceeded to express his opinion of such conduct in language much more forcible than pious.

From this place we moved some distance to the left, where the tents were erected in an open field. Here an incident occurred which illustrates the false estimate placed upon the civilization of the North by the masses of the South. A wounded rebel, an intelligent-looking young man, was brought in from the field in an ambulance. We came with a stretcher to carry him into the tent. He looked at us with a frightened, helpless look, and asked:

"You won't hurt me, will you?"

I assured him we would be just as careful as possible. He seemed surprised to be treated with kindness, having been taught, evidently, that the Yankee invader was a barbarian. Removed to the tent, I examined his wound. A bullet had passed through the ankle joint, and the only remedy was amputation. He inquired how it was. It seemed hard to tell him that he must go through life maimed.

"That is a bad foot; but the surgeons will do the best they can for it. You may lose it." Some time after he was removed, I suppose to have his foot amputated, and I saw him no more.

The next move was to Spotsylvania. Grant had grappled with his enemy, intending to hold on "all Summer." The same spirit seemed to animate his army, from General Meade down to the latest recruit in the ranks. The lines of blue came out from the smoking under-brush of the Wilderness, their ranks torn and decimated, and closed in around the bristling batteries and rifle-pits of Spotsylvania with a relentless courage that was sublime.

Here the tents were pitched in a little, open lot, a house to the right as you faced the position where the fighting was in progress. The tents were not sufficient to contain the wounded, and they lay on the ground on the outside by thousands. Those long rows of suffering forms, gashed and mangled in every conceivable manner, told a dreadful tale of human wrath. That gallant division, the Reserves, had preserved their well-earned reputation for stubborn valor at a terrible cost. Their greatest loss was sustained in a single onset against the rebel position. The enemy was posted in strong rifle-pits, beyond a narrow strip of swamp. Orders were given to charge these works. The division moved forward. They had never failed in such an undertaking. Their charge had always pierced the enemy's line. This had been their record during three years of warfare. But men can not accomplish impossibilities. Baffled by the swamp, cut by the merciless fire that blazed out from the pits, they are driven back, rally, re-form and charge the second and third time, and then retire to the position from which they had come out.

The field-tents here were nearer the front than before. Bullets and an occasional shell whistled over us. My work was still the same, caring for the wounded, assisting the surgeon, or occasionally binding up a wound myself.

During the second day, while engaged at the farther end of the tent, I heard at the front a familiar voice. As soon as I was disengaged I went to the front end of the tent, eager to learn from whom the well-known voice proceeded. There lay a large, noble-looking young man, severely wounded in the thigh. He was conversing quietly with a wounded comrade by his side. Voice and face were as familiar as if heard and seen but yesterday. Puzzled and deeply interested, I did not speak, but proceeded to bathe his wound. While thus engaged, his eyes fell upon my face. Looking at me intently a moment, his face brightened, and he exclaimed:

"You are Rob M'Bride, aren't you?"

"Yes; and you are Billy Craig," was the immediate reply.

As soon as he pronounced my name, it all came to me in a moment. We had been school-mates at Courtney's School-house. He was then one of the "big boys," and I a lad of nine or ten. I had not seen him since. He was one of those large-hearted, royal souls that could find pleasure in little acts of kindness, that bound me to him very closely. He bore his sufferings with heroic fortitude. When the time came to remove the wounded, and they were being hurried away in ambulances and rough army wagons, I went to Dr. Lyon and told him of the case. He went with me to an ambulance and ordered room reserved in it for him. I then had him carried to it, made him as comfortable as possible, bade him good-bye and God speed, and saw him no more on earth. He died from his wound some time in June.

★   ★   ★

May 11th, Lewis Grossman, of Company C, was brought in, terribly wounded by a shell. One arm and leg were crushed, and he was otherwise bruised. I did not see him until after the arm and leg were amputated. He was a young man of great physical endurance, or he would never have rallied from the shock. He was as pale as a corpse when first brought into the tent, but rallied in a little while, and was able to take some refreshment. When left to himself his mind wandered, and he would talk as if he were engaged in the quiet pursuits of peace. Unless prevented, he would remove the bandages from the stumps of his amputated limbs. When spoken to, however, he would refrain from this, and talk rationally of the present circumstances. Dr. Lyon finally told me to give my attention entirely to him. This I did until he was sent away. He told me how his wound was received. He was in front, skirmishing. He was in the road in front of a rebel battery, and in the act of loading his gun. Perceiving they were about to fire, he still delayed a moment, thinking to get in another shot before leaping to the shelter of a large tree that stood near. It was a costly delay.

The shell came screaming toward him, burst, and dashed him stunned and mangled to the ground. As he concluded this narrative, he added, with the utmost seriousness: "But they haven't made much off me, after all. I've peppered them in almost every battle the Potomac army has fought since the war began."

He got along finely, and there seemed every prospect of recovery. When some of the boys called on him at Washington, on their way home in June, he requested them to say nothing to his friends about the extent of his wounds. But from some cause—perhaps gangrene—he died August 3d, and is buried in the National Cemetery at Arlington.

Nearly opposite Lewis lay a young man of very fine face and attractive appearance. He was mortally wounded. Most of the time his sufferings were very great, but no earthly skill could bring any relief. As death drew on, his mind wandered. He was fighting his battles over again. He was not the poor, crushed mortality that lay here. His spirit was over yonder, where the cannon's sullen roar and the awful din of musketry, the cheers of the struggling combatants, told of a deadly strife.

Sometimes he was distressed and troubled, sometimes exultant. Anon his face would light up with the strange fire of battle, and he would raise his arm and cheer. Once he said quite distinctly: "Here is a chance for a brave man." Later he became calm, and quietly fell asleep, to wake no more on earth till the great day of God.

One of the Bucktail Regiment lay on the ground in front of the tent, shot through the chest. He was, perhaps, twenty-five years of age, large and well-formed, his face stamped with the marks of intelligence. While engaged near him, I saw another of that band of heroes coming toward him with great strides, an expression of anguish on his face which I can not forget. He threw himself on his knees by the wounded man, kissed him, then covered his face with his hands, and his great manly form shook with convulsive sobbings. Tears trickled down the cheeks of the other. Not a word was spoken until, after a while, the storm of emotion had passed. Then they conversed calmly for a while, and parted with the quiet dignity of brave men who say farewell while the shadow of death lies dark around them.

A man was brought in shot through both thighs. I did not know his name, but had heard his voice among the worshipers in the church-tent at Bristoe Station, and knew that he was a man of God. After a brief examination, the surgeon announced that amputation would be necessary.

"Very well, doctor; get around to it as quick as you can. I suffer terribly."

Another was shot in the thigh, the bone shattered to the hip. When told that the limb must be amputated he objected.

"But you will die if it is not done."

"I can't help that; it shall not be amputated with my consent."

Within twenty-four hours he was dead. Whether wise in his decision or not, he met the result without flinching or complaint.

A boy with his arm torn off by a shell expressed his only complaint in the words, "I never can fight any more."

One evening, worn out by constant labor and watching, I lay down in a vacant place in the tent, from which a dead soldier had been removed, to find rest for mind and body in sleep. As I lay there thinking of the dreadful scenes around me, of the wounded and dying here, the dead just over yonder, I began to wonder what would be the sensations of a man shot in the brain. Suddenly there came a shock, as if the whole machinery of life had stopped at once. How long a time elapsed before consciousness was resumed I do not know; the interval may have been momentary; but as a dim sense of being stole over me again, I was quite convinced that a stray shot had struck me in the head. Rousing myself, I deliberately felt my head, to learn the exact state of things. To my surprise and gratification, I found every thing in due order. I leave it to those who are skilled in the mysteries of the nervous system to explain the phenomenon; but you must allow me to believe that I know something of what it is to be shot in the head.

The time arrived, at length, when the field hospitals must be moved because of the changed position of the army. A heavy rain began on the 11th, and continued for some days, making the roads almost impassable. The wounded that remained were removed as speedily and as mercifully as possible. Some had to be left behind. Nurses were detailed to remain with them. As night came on, every thing was in readiness, and the rest of us were directed to take our departure without delay. Two of us started together after dark. We made our way through the mud and intense darkness about twenty rods, to the edge of a wood. We resolved to go no further, come what might. Doubling myself up at the root of an old stump, I was soon oblivious to both rain and danger. Just as day was breaking, I awoke, and arousing my companion, we hastened away.

This closed my experience in the hospital.

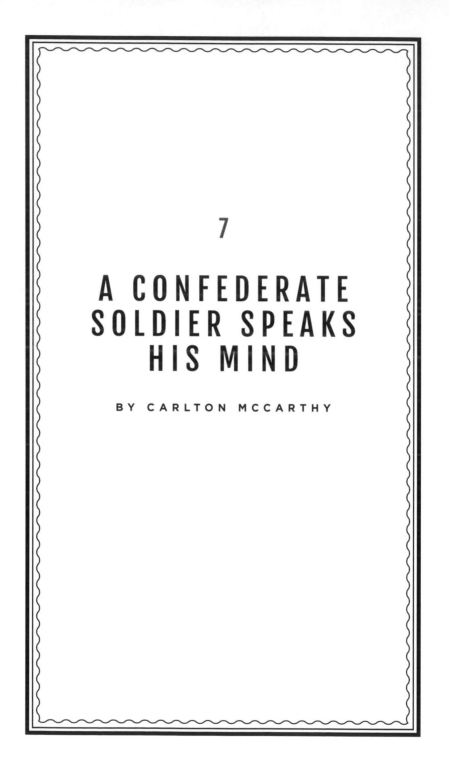

7

A CONFEDERATE SOLDIER SPEAKS HIS MIND

BY CARLTON MCCARTHY

The fortitude and bravery of Confederate soldiers—from officers to privates—has been well documented in many accounts. Less often seen in print are stories that reveal the mindset of the men in gray. What were they thinking? What motivated them and sustained them through years of desperate struggles? Some of the answers to those questions are provided by the book Detailed Minutiae of Soldier Life in the Army of Northern Virginia, 1861–1865, *by Carlton McCarthy. This excerpt, and others in some chapters that follow, provides a rare insight into the thinking of the rebel soldiers who defied a nation.*

We are familiar with the names and deeds of the "generals," from the commander-in-chief down to the almost innumerable brigadiers, and we are all more or less ignorant of the habits and characteristics of the individuals who composed the rank and file of the "grand armies" of 1861–65.

As time rolls on, the historian, condensing matters, mentions "the men" by brigades, divisions, and corps. But here let us look at the individual soldier separated from the huge masses of men composing the armies, and doing his own work and duty.

The fame of Lee and Jackson, world-wide, and as the years increase ever brighter, is but condensed and personified admiration of the Confederate soldier, wrung from an unwilling world by his matchless courage, endurance, and devotion. Their fame is an everlasting monument to the mighty deeds of the nameless host who followed them through so much toil and blood to glorious victories.

The weak, as a rule, are borne down by the strong; but that does not prove that the strong are also the right. The weak suffer wrong, learn the bitterness of it, and finally, by resisting it, become the defenders of right and justice. When the mighty nations of the earth oppress the feeble, they nerve the arms and fire the hearts of God's instruments for the restoration of justice; and when one section of a country oppresses and insults another, the result is the pervasive malady—war! which will work out the health of the nation, or leave it a bloody corpse.

The principles for which the Confederate soldier fought, and in defense of which he died, are to-day the harmony of this country. So long as they were held in abeyance, the country was in turmoil and on the verge of ruin.

It is not fair to demand a reason for actions above reason. The heart is greater than the mind. No man can exactly define the cause for which the Confederate soldier fought. He was above human reason and above human law, secure in his own rectitude of purpose, accountable to God only, having assumed for himself a "nationality," which he was minded to defend with his life and his property, and thereto pledged his sacred honor.

In the honesty and simplicity of his heart, the Confederate soldier had neglected his own interests and rights, until his accumulated wrongs and indignities forced him to one grand, prolonged effort to free himself from the pain of them. He dared not refuse to hear the call to arms, so plain was the duty and so urgent the call. His brethren and friends were answering the bugle-call and the roll of the drum. To stay was dishonor and shame!

He would not obey the dictates of tyranny. To disobey was death. He disobeyed and fought for his life. The romance of war charmed him, and he hurried from the embrace of his mother to the embrace of death. His playmates, his friends, and his associates were gone; he was lonesome, and he sought a reunion "in camp." He would not receive as gospel the dogmas of fanatics, and so he became a "rebel." Being a rebel, he must be punished. Being punished, he resisted. Resisting, he died.

The Confederate soldier opposed immense odds. If the Confederate soldier had then had only this disparity of numbers to contend with, he would have driven every invader from the soil of Virginia.

But the Confederate soldier fought, in addition to these odds, the facilities for the transportation and concentration of troops and supplies afforded by the network of railways in the country north of him, all of which were subject to the control of the government, and backed by a treasury which was turning out money by the ton, one dollar of which was equal to sixty Confederate dollars.

It should be remembered also that, while the South was restricted to its own territory for supplies, and its own people for men, the North drew on the world for material, and on every nation of the earth for men.

The arms and ammunition of the Federal soldiers were abundant and good—so abundant and so good that they supplied both armies, and were greatly preferred by Confederate officers. The equipment of the Federal armies was well nigh perfect. The facilities for manufacture were simply unlimited, and the nation thought no expenditure of treasure too great, if only the country, the Union! could be saved. The factory and the foundry chimneys made a pillar of smoke by day and of fire by night. The latest improvements were hurried to the front, and adopted by both armies almost simultaneously; for hardly had the Federal bought, when the Confederate captured, and used, the very latest.

Commissary stores were piled up all over Virginia, for the use of the invading armies. They had more than they could protect, and their loss was gain to the hungry defenders of the soil.

The Confederate soldier fought a host of ills occasioned by the deprivation of chloroform and morphia, which were excluded from the Confederacy, by the blockade, as contraband of war. The man who has submitted to amputation without chloroform, or tossed on a couch of agony for a night and a day without sleep for the want of a dose of morphia, may possibly be able to estimate the advantages which resulted from the possession by the Federal surgeons of an unlimited supply of these.

The Confederate soldier fought bounties and regular monthly pay; the "Stars and Stripes," the "Star Spangled Banner," "Hail Columbia," "Tramp, Tramp, Tramp," "John Brown's Body," "Rally 'round the Flag," and all the fury and fanaticism which skilled minds could create—opposing this grand array with the modest and homely refrain of "Dixie," supported by a mild solution of "Maryland, My Maryland." He fought good wagons, fat horses, and tons of quartermaster's stores; pontoon trains, of splendid material and construction, by the mile; gunboats, wooden and iron, and men-of-war; illustrated papers, to cheer the "Boys in Blue" with sketches of the glorious deeds they did not do; Bibles by the car load, and tracts by the million—the first to prepare them for death, and the second to urge upon them the duty of dying.

The Confederate soldier fought the "Sanitary Commission," whose members, armed with every facility and convenience, quickly carried the sick and wounded of the Federal army to comfortable quarters, removed the bloody garments, laid the sufferer on a clean and dry couch, clothed him in clean things, and fed him on the best the world could afford and money buy.

He fought the well-built, thoroughly equipped ambulances, the countless surgeons, nurses, and hospital stewards, and the best surgical appliances known to the medical world. He fought the commerce of the United States and all the facilities for war which Europe could supply, while his own ports were closed to all the world. He fought the trained army officers and the regular troops of the United States Army, assisted by splendid native volunteer soldiers, besides swarms of men, the refuse of the earth—Portuguese, Spanish, Italian, German, Irish, Scotch, English, French, Chinese, Japanese—white, black, olive, and brown. He laid down life for life with this hireling host, who died for pay, mourned by no one, missed by no one, loved by no one; who were better fed and clothed, fatter, happier, and more contented in the army than ever they were at home, and whose graves strew the earth in lonesome places, where none go to weep. When one of these fell, two could be bought to fill the gap. The Confederate soldier killed these without compunction, and their comrades buried them without a tear.

The Confederate soldier fought the cries of distress which came from his home—tales of woe, want, insult, and robbery. He fought men who knew that *their* homes (when they had any) were safe, their wives and children, their parents and sisters, sheltered, and their business affairs more than usually prosperous; who could draw sight drafts, have them honored, and make the camp table as bountiful and luxurious as that of a New York hotel. He fought a government founded by the genius of his fathers, which derived its strength from principles they formulated, and which persuaded its soldiers that they were the champions of the constitutional liberty which they were marching to invade, and eventually to destroy.

The relative strength of armies becomes a matter of secondary importance when these facts are considered. The disparity of numbers only would never have produced the result which the combination of these various forces did—the surrender of the Army of Northern Virginia.

The Confederate soldier was purely patriotic. He foresaw clearly, and deliberately chose, the trials which he endured. He was an individual who could not become the indefinite portion of a mass, but fought for himself, on his own account. He was a self-sacrificing hero, but did not claim that distinction or any merit, feeling only that he was in the line of duty to self, country, and God. He fought for a principle, and needed neither driving nor urging, but was eager and determined to fight. He was not a politic man, but a man under fervent feeling, forgetful of the possibilities and calamities of war, pressing his claims to the rights of humanity.

The Confederate soldier was a monomaniac for four years. His mania was the independence of the Confederates States of America, secured by force of arms.

The Confederate soldier was a venerable old man, a youth, a child, a preacher, a farmer, merchant, student, statesman, orator, father, brother, husband, son—the wonder of the world, the terror of his foes!

If the peace of this country can only be preserved by forgetting the Confederate soldier's deeds and his claims upon the South, the blessing is too dearly bought. We have sworn to be grateful to him. Dying, his head pillowed on the bosom of his mother, Virginia, he heard that his name would be honored.

When we fill up, hurriedly, the bloody chasm opened by war, we should be careful that we do not bury therein many noble deeds, some tender memories, some grand examples, and some hearty promises washed with tears.

8

AMERICA'S DEADLIEST DAY: ONE OFFICER'S STORY

BY FREDERICK L. HITCHCOCK

"The air was full of whizzing, singing, buzzing bullets. Once down on the ground under cover of the hill, it required very strong resolution to get up where these missiles of death were flying so thickly, yet that was the duty of us officers, especially us of the field and staff." That vivid description from Frederick L. Hitchcock's book War from the Inside *is but a glimpse of the horrors of battle that took place in the single bloodiest day in American history. Unlike Gettysburg, which lasted three days, Antietam—or "Sharpsburg" as the Confederates called it—took place in a single day. On September 16, 1862, Union forces under General George McClellan had the opportunity to surround and destroy the army of Robert E. Lee at this small Maryland town and nearby Antietam Creek. Although fighting hard, with a horrific loss of life, the Union forces on the field held too much strength in reserve, with the result that Lee's Army of Northern Virginia escaped. As with the Union Army, Lee's forces sustained massive dead and wounded but escaped to fight again. Later, General McClellan was relieved of command by President Abraham Lincoln.*

I was appointed adjutant of the One Hundred and Thirty-second Regiment, Pennsylvania Volunteers, by our great war Governor, Andrew G. Curtin, at the solicitation of Colonel Richard A. Oakford, commanding the regiment, my commission dating the 22d day of August, 1862. I reported for duty to Colonel Oakford at Camp Whipple, where the regiment was then encamped, on the 3d day of September, 1862. This was immediately following the disasters of "Chantilly" and "Second Bull Run," and as I passed through Washington to Camp Whipple, I found the greatest excitement prevailing because of these reverses, and a general apprehension for the safety of the capital in consequence. The wildest rumors were abroad concerning the approach of the victorious rebel troops, and an alarm amounting almost to a panic existed. Being without a horse or other means of transportation, I was obliged to make my way, valise in hand, on foot from Washington over the "long bridge" across the Potomac, to Camp Whipple, some two miles up the river nearly opposite Georgetown. From the wild rumors floating about Washington, I did not know but I should be captured bag and baggage before reaching camp. Undertaking this trip under those circumstances, I think, required almost as much nerve as "real work" did later on.

Getting beyond the long bridge there were abundant evidences of the reported disasters. Straggling troops, army wagons, etc., were pouring in from the "front" in great disorder.

I was assigned quarters, and a copy of the daily routine orders of camp was placed in my hands, and my attention specially called to the fact that the next "order of business" was "dress parade" at six o'clock. I inquired the cause of this special notice to me, and was informed that I was expected to officiate as adjutant of the regiment at that ceremony. I pleaded with the colonel to be allowed a day or so in camp to see how things were done before undertaking such difficult and important duties; that I knew absolutely nothing about any part of military service; had never served a day in any kind of military work, except in a country fire company; had never seen a dress parade of a full regiment in my life, and knew nothing whatever about the duties of an adjutant.

My pleadings were all in vain. The only reply I received was a copy of the "Army Regulations," with the remark that I had two hours in which to study up and master the details of dress parade, and that I could not learn my duties any easier nor better than by actual practice; that my condition was no different from that of my fellow officers; that we were all there in a camp of instruction learning our duties, and there was not a moment to lose. I then began to realize something of the magnitude of the task which lay before me. To do difficult things, without knowing how; that is, to learn how in the doing, was the universal task of the Union volunteer officer.

I took up my "Army Regulations" and attacked the ceremony of dress parade as a life and death matter. Before my two hours were ended, I could repeat every sentence of the ceremony verbatim, and felt that I had mastered the thing, and was not going to my execution in undertaking my duties as adjutant. Alas for the frailty of memory; it failed me at the crucial moment, and I made a miserable spectacle of myself before a thousand officers and men, many of them old friends and acquaintances, all of whom, it seemed to me, were specially assembled on that occasion to witness my début, and see me get "balled up." They were not disappointed. Things tactically impossible were freely done during that ceremony.

Looking back now upon that scene, from the long distance of forty years, I see a green country boy undertaking to handle one thousand men in the always difficult ceremony of a dress parade. (I once heard Governor Hartranft, who attained the rank of a major-general during the war, remark, as he witnessed this ceremony, that he had seen thousands of such parades, and among them all, only one that he considered absolutely faultless.) I wonder now that we got through it at all. Think of standing to give your first command at the right of a line of men five hundred abreast, that is, nearly one thousand feet in length, and trying to make the men farthest away hear your small, unused, and untrained voice. I now can fully forgive my failure. The officers and men were considerate of me, however, and, knowing what was to be done, went through with it after a fashion in spite of my blunders.

Another feature is the utter change in one's individual liberty. To be no longer the arbiter of your own time and movements, but to have it rubbed into you at every turn that you are a very small part of an immense machine, whose business is to march and fight; that your every movement is under the control of your superior officers; that, in fact, you have no will of your own that can be exercised; that your individuality is for the time sunk, is a trial to an American freeman which patriotism alone can overcome. Not the least feature of this transition is the practical obliteration of the Lord's day. This is a great shock to a Christian who has learned to love the Lord's day and its hallowed associations. Routine duty, the march, the fighting, all go right on, nothing stops for Sunday.

On Saturday, September 6, we received orders to join the Army of the Potomac—again under the command of "Little Mac"—at Rockville, Md., distant about eighteen miles. [Reference to General George McCellan] This was our first march. The day was excessively hot, and Colonel Oakford received permission to march in the evening. We broke camp about six o'clock P.M. It was a lovely moonlight night, the road was excellent, and for the first six miles the march was a delight. We marched quite leisurely, not making over two miles an hour, including rests, nevertheless the last half of the distance was very tiresome, owing to the raw and unseasoned condition of our men, and the heavy load they were carrying. We reached the bivouac of the grand Army of the Potomac, of which we were henceforth to be a part, at about three o'clock the next morning. Three miles out from the main camp we encountered the outpost of the picket line and were duly halted. The picket officer had been informed of our coming, and so detained us only long enough to satisfy himself that we were all right.

Here we encountered actual conditions of war with all its paraphernalia for the first time. Up to this time we had been playing at war, so to speak, in a camp of instruction. Now we were entering upon the thing itself, with all its gruesome accessories. Everything here was business, and awful business, too. Here were parks of artillery quiet enough just now, but their throats will speak soon enough, and when they do it will not be the harmless booming of Fourth of July celebrations. Here we pass a bivouac of cavalry, and yonder on either side the road, in long lines of masses, spread out like wide swaths of grain, lie the infantry behind long rows of stacked guns. Here were upward of seventy-five thousand men, all, except the cordon of pickets, sound asleep. In the midst of this mighty host the stillness was that of a graveyard; it seemed almost oppressive.

Halting the regiment, Colonel Oakford and I made our way to the head-quarters of Major-General Sumner, commanding the Second Army Corps, to whom the colonel was ordered to report. We finally found him asleep in his head-quarters wagon. A tap on the canvas top of the wagon quickly brought the response, "Hello! Who's there? What's wanted?"

Colonel Oakford replied, giving his name and rank, and that his regiment was here to report to him, according to orders.

"Oh, yes, colonel, that is right," replied the general. "How many men have you?"

Receiving the colonel's answer, General Sumner said: "I wish you had ten times as many, for we need you badly. Glad you are here, colonel. Make yourselves as comfortable as you can for the rest of the night, and I will assign you to your brigade in the morning." Here was a cordial reception and hospitality galore. "Make yourselves comfortable"—in Hotel "Dame Nature!" Well, we were all weary enough to accept the hospitality. We turned into the adjacent field, "stacked arms," and in a jiffy were rolled up in our blankets and sound asleep. The mattresses supplied by Madame Nature were rather hard, but her rooms were fresh and airy, and the ceilings studded with the stars of glory. My last waking vision that night was a knowing wink from Jupiter and Mars, as much as to say, "sleep sweetly, we are here."

★　★　★

An interesting feature of the issue of rations was the method of supplying the fresh beef. Live cattle were driven to the army and issued alive to the several corps, from which details were made of men who had been butchers, who killed and dressed the beef. The animals were driven into an enclosure and expert marksmen shot them down as wanted. This seemed cruel work, but it was well done; the animal being hit usually at the base of its horns, death was instantaneous. This fresh meat, which we got but seldom after the march began, was cooked and eaten the day it was issued. Enough for one day was all that was issued at a time, and this, after the non-eatable portions had been eliminated, did not overburden the men.

The hard bread was a square cracker about the size of an ordinary soda cracker, only thicker, and very hard and dry. It was supposed to be of the same quality as sea biscuit or pilot bread, but I never saw any equal to that article. The salt pork was usually good for pork, but it was a great trial to us all to come down to camp fare, "hardtack and pork." Sometimes the "hardtack" was very old and poor. I have seen many a one placed in the palm of the hand, a smart blow, a puff of breath . . . a handful of "squirmers"—the boys' illustration of a "full hand." It came to be the rule to eat in daylight for protection against the unknown quantity in the hardtack. If we had to eat in the dark, after a prolonged march, our protection then lay in breaking our cracker into a cup of boiling coffee, stir it well and then flow enough of the coffee over to carry off most of the strangers and take the balance on faith.

On the march each man carried his own rations in haversacks. These were made of canvas and contained pockets for salt, sugar and coffee, besides room for about two days' rations of hard bread and pork. Sometimes five, six, and seven days' rations were issued, then the balance had to be stowed away in knapsacks and pockets of the clothing. When, as was usual in the latter cases, there was also issued sixty to one hundred rounds of ammunition, the man became a veritable pack-mule.

For the first month many of our men went hungry. Having enormous appetites consequent upon this new and most strenuous mode of life, they would eat their five days' supply in two or three, and then have to "skirmish" or go hungry until the next supply was issued. Most, however, soon learned the necessity as well as the benefit of restricting their appetites to the supply. But there were always some improvident ones, who never had a supply ahead, but were always in straights for grub. They were ready to black boots, clean guns, in fact, do any sort of menial work for their comrades for a snack to eat. Their improvidence made them the drudges of the company.

Whatever may be said about other portions of the rations, the coffee was always good. I never saw any poor coffee, and it was a blessing it was so, for it became the soldiers' solace and stay, in camp, on picket and on the march. Tired, footsore, and dusty from the march, or wet and cold on picket, or homesick and shivering in camp, there were rest and comfort and new life in a cup of hot coffee. We could not always have it on picket nor on the march. To make a cup of coffee two things were necessary besides the coffee, namely, water and fire, both frequently very difficult to obtain. On picket, water was generally plentiful, but in the immediate presence of the enemy, fire was forbidden, for obvious reasons. On the march both were usually scarce, as I shall show later on.

How was our coffee made? Each man was provided with a pint tin cup. As much coffee as could comfortably be lifted from the haversack by the thumb and two fingers—depending somewhat on the supply—was placed in the cup, which was filled about three-fourths full of water, to leave room for boiling. It was then placed upon some live coals and brought to a boil, being well stirred in the meantime to get the strength of the coffee. A little cold water was then added to settle it. Eggs, gelatin, or other notions of civilization, for settling, were studiously omitted. Sometimes sugar was added, but most of the men, especially the old vets, took it straight. It was astonishing how many of the "wrinkles of grim visaged war" were temporarily smoothed out by a cup of coffee. This was the mainstay of our meals on the march, a cup of coffee and a thin slice of raw pork between two hardtacks frequently constituting a meal. Extras fell in the way once in a while. Chickens have been known to stray into camp, the result of a night's foraging.

★   ★   ★

The army mule has been much caricatured, satirized, and abused, but the soldier had no more faithful or indispensable servant than this same patient, plodding, hard-pulling, long-eared fellow of the roomy voice and nimble heels. The "boys" told a story which may illustrate the mule's education. A "tenderfoot" driver had gotten his team stalled in a mud hole, and by no amount of persuasion could he get them to budge an inch. Helpers at the wheels and new hands on the lines were all to no purpose. A typical army bummer had been eying the scene with contemptuous silence. Finally he cut loose:

"Say! You 'uns dunno the mule language. Ye dunno the dilec. Let a perfesser in there."

He was promptly given the job. He doffed cap and blouse, marched up to those mules as if he weighed a ton and commanded the army. Clearing away the crowd, he seized the leader's line, and distending his lungs, he shot out in a voice that could have been heard a mile a series of whoops, oaths, adjectives, and billingsgate that would have silenced the proverbial London fish vender. The mules recognized the "dilec" at once, pricked up their ears and took the load out in a jiffy.

"Ye see, gents, them ar mules is used to workin' with a perfesser."

★   ★   ★

We are bound northward through Maryland, the vets tell us, on a chase after the rebs. The army marches in three and four parallel columns, usually each corps in a column by itself, and distant from the other columns equal to about its length in line of battle, say a half to three-fourths of a mile. Roads were utilized as far as practicable, but generally were left to the artillery and the wagon trains, whilst the infantry made roads for themselves directly through the fields.

The whole army marches surrounded by "advance and rear guards," and "flankers," to prevent surprise. Each column is headed by a corps of pioneers who, in addition to their arms, are provided with axes, picks and shovels, with the latter stone walls and fences are levelled sufficiently to permit the troops to pass, and ditches and other obstructions covered and removed. It is interesting to see how quickly this corps will dispose of an ordinary stone wall or rail fence. They go down so quickly that they hardly seem to pause in their march.

We learn that the Johnnies are only a couple of days ahead of us. That they marched rapidly and were on their good behavior, all marauding being forbidden, and they were singing a new song, entitled "My Maryland," thus trying to woo this loyal border State over to the Confederacy. We were told that Lee hung two soldiers for stealing chickens and fruit just before they entered Frederick City.

Much could be written about the discomforts of these marches, the chief of which was the dust more than the heat and the fatigue. No rain had fallen for some time, and the roads and the fields through which we passed were powdered into fine dust, which arose in almost suffocating clouds, so that mouth, lungs, eyes, and ears were filled with it. Sometimes it became so dense that men could not be seen a dozen yards away. The different regiments took turns in heading the columns. There was comparative comfort at the head, but there were so many regiments that during the whole campaign our regiment enjoyed this privilege but once.

Another feature of the march was the inability to satisfy thirst. The dust and heat no doubt produced an abnormal thirst which water did not seem to satisfy. The water we could get was always warm, and generally muddy and filthy. The latter was caused by the multitude of men using the little streams, springs, or wells. Either of these, ordinarily abundant for many more than ever used them, were hardly a cup full apiece for a great army. Hence many a scrimmage took place for the first dash at a cool well or spring.

On our second or third day's march, such a scrap took place between the advanced columns for a well, and in the melee one man was accidentally pushed down into it, head first, and killed. He belonged to one of the Connecticut regiments, I was told. We passed by the well, and were unable to get water, because a dead soldier lay at the bottom of it. His regiment probably got his body out, but we had to march on without stopping to learn whether they did or not.

The problem of water for our army we found to be a troublesome one. Immediately we halted, much of our rest would be taken up in efforts to get water. We lost no opportunity to fill our canteens. Arriving in bivouac for the night, the first thing was a detail to fill canteens and camp kettles for supper coffee. We always bivouacked near a stream, if possible. But, then, so many men wanting it soon roiled it for miles, so that our details often had to follow the stream up three and four miles before they could get clean water. This may seem a strong statement, but if one will stop a moment and think of the effect upon even a good-sized stream, of a hundred thousand men, besides horses and mules, all wanting it for drinking, cooking, washing, and bathing (both the latter as peremptory needs as the former), he will see that the statement is no exaggeration.

The officers at this time experienced difficulty in getting food to eat. The men were supplied with rations and forced to carry them, but rations were not issued to officers—though they might purchase of the commissary such as the men had, when there was a supply. The latter were supposed to provide their own mess, for which purpose their mess-kits were transported in a wagon supplied to each regiment. The field and staff usually made one mess, and the line or company officers another. Sometimes the latter messed with their own men, carrying their rations along on the march the same as the men. This was discouraged by the government, but it proved the only way to be sure of food when needed, and was later on generally adopted.

We had plenty of food with our mess-kit and cook, but on the march, and especially in the presence of the enemy, our wagons could never get within reach of us. Indeed, when we bivouacked, they were generally from eight to ten miles away. The result was we often went hungry, unless we were able to pick up a meal at a farm-house—which seldom occurred, for the reason that most of these farmers were rebel sympathizers and would not feed us "Yanks," or they would be either sold out, or stolen out, of food. The tale generally told was, "You 'uns has stolen all we 'uns had." This accounts for the entry in my diary that the next morning I marched without breakfast, but got a good bath in the Monocacy—near which we encamped—in place of it. I got a "hardtack" and bit of raw pork about 10 A.M.

An interesting feature of our first two days' march was the clearing out of knapsacks to reduce the load. Naturally each man was loaded with extras of various sorts, knicknacks of all varieties, but mostly supposed necessaries of camp life, put in by loving hands at home, a salve for this, a medicine for that, a keepsake from one and another, some the dearest of earth's treasures, each insignificant in itself, yet all taking room and adding weight to over-burdened shoulders. At the mid-day halt, on the first day knapsacks being off for rest, they came open and the sorting began. It was sad, yet comical withal, to notice the things that went out. The most bulky and least treasured went first.

At the second halting, an hour later, still another sorting was made. The sun was hot and the knapsack was heavy. After the second day's march, those knapsacks contained little but what the soldier was compelled to carry, his rations, extra ammunition, and clothing. Were these home treasures lost? Oh, no! Not one. Our friends, the vets, gathered them all in as a rich harvest. They had been there themselves, and knowing what was coming, were on hand to gather the plums as they fell. The only difference was that another mother's or sweetheart's "boy" got the treasures.

★ ★ ★

On our third day's march we were halted for rest, when an orderly rode through the lines saying to the different colonels, "General McClellan will pass this way in ten minutes." This meant that we were to be ready to cheer "Little Mac" when he came along, which, of course, we all did.

Many of the old vets, who had been with him on the Peninsula, and now greeted him again after his reinstatement, were very enthusiastic. But notwithstanding their demonstrations, they rather negatived their praises by the remark, "No fight to-day; Little Mac has gone to the front."

"Look out for a fight when he goes to the rear." On the other hand, they said when "Old Man Sumner"—our corps commander—"goes to the front, look out for a fight."

★   ★   ★

Never did day open more beautiful. We were astir at the first streak of dawn. We had slept, and soundly too, just where nightfall found us under the shelter of the hill near Keedysville. No reveille call this morning. Too close to the enemy. Nor was this needed to arouse us. A simple call of a sergeant or corporal and every man was instantly awake and alert. All realized that there was ugly business and plenty of it just ahead. This was plainly visible in the faces as well as in the nervous, subdued demeanor of all. The absence of all joking and play and the almost painful sobriety of action, where jollity had been the rule, was particularly noticeable.

Before proceeding with the events of the battle, I should speak of the "night before the battle," of which so much has been said and written. My diary says that Lieutenant-Colonel Wilcox, Captain James Archbald, Co. I, and I slept together, sharing our blankets; that it rained during the night; this fact, with the other, that we were close friends at home, accounts for our sharing blankets. Three of us with our gum blankets could so arrange as to keep fairly dry, notwithstanding the rain.

The camp was ominously still this night. We were not allowed to sing or make any noise, nor have any fires—except just enough to make coffee—for fear of attracting the fire of the enemies' batteries. But there was no need of such an inhibition as to singing or frolicking, for there was no disposition to indulge in either. Unquestionably, the problems of the morrow were occupying all breasts. Letters were written home—many of them "last words"—and quiet talks were had, and promises made between comrades. Promises providing against the dreaded possibilities of the morrow. "If the worst happens, Jack." "Yes, Ned, send word to mother and to, and these; she will prize them," and so directions were interchanged that meant so much.

I can never forget the quiet words of Colonel Oakford, as he inquired very particularly if my roster of the officers and men of the regiment was complete, for, said he, with a smile, "We shall not all be here to-morrow night."

Now to resume the story of the battle. We were on the march about six o'clock and moved, as I thought, rather leisurely for upwards of two miles, crossing Antietam creek, which our men waded nearly waist deep, emerging, of course, soaked through, our first experience of this kind. It was a hot morning and, therefore, the only ill effects of this wading was the discomfort to the men of marching with soaked feet. It was now quite evident that a great battle was in progress. A deafening pandemonium of cannonading, with shrieking and bursting shells, filled the air beyond us, towards which we were marching. An occasional shell whizzed by or over, reminding us that we were rapidly approaching the "debatable ground."

Soon we began to hear a most ominous sound which we had never before heard, except in the far distance at South Mountain, namely, the rattle of musketry. It had none of the deafening bluster of the cannonading so terrifying to new troops, but to those who had once experienced its effect, it was infinitely more to be dreaded. The fatalities by musketry at close quarters, as the two armies fought at Antietam and all through the Civil War, as compared with those by artillery, are at least as 100 to 1, probably much more than that.

These volleys of musketry we were approaching sounded in the distance like the rapid pouring of shot upon a tinpan, or the tearing of heavy canvas, with slight pauses interspersed with single shots, or desultory shooting. All this presaged fearful work in store for us, with what results to each personally the future, measured probably by moments, would reveal.

How does one feel under such conditions? To tell the truth, I realized the situation most keenly and felt very uncomfortable. Lest there might be some undue manifestation of this feeling in my conduct, I said to myself, this is the duty I undertook to perform for my country, and now I'll do it, and leave the results with God. My greater fear was not that I might be killed, but that I might be grievously wounded and left a victim of suffering on the field.

The nervous strain was plainly visible upon all of us. All moved doggedly forward in obedience to orders, in absolute silence so far as talking was concerned. The compressed lip and set teeth showed that nerve and resolution had been summoned to the discharge of duty. A few temporarily fell out, unable to endure the nervous strain, which was simply awful. There were a few others, it must be said, who skulked, took counsel of their cowardly legs, and, despite all efforts of "file closers" and officers, left the ranks. Of these two classes most of the first rejoined us later on, and their dropping out was no reflection on their bravery. The nervous strain produced by the excitement and danger gave them the malady called by the vets, the "cannon quickstep."

On our way into "position" we passed the "Meyer Spring," a magnificent fountain of sweet spring water. It was walled in, and must have been ten or twelve feet square and at least three feet deep, and a stream was flowing from it large enough to make a respectable brook. Many of us succeeded in filling our canteens from this glorious spring, now surrounded by hundreds of wounded soldiers. What a Godsend it was to those poor fellows.

About eight o'clock we were formed into line of battle and moved forward through a grove of trees but before actually coming under musketry fire of the enemy we were moved back again, and swung around nearly a mile to the left to the base of a circular knoll to the left of the Roulette farm-house and the road which leads up to the Sharpsburg pike, near the Dunkard church. The famous "sunken road"—a road which had been cut through the other side of this knoll—extended from the Roulette Lane directly in front of our line towards Sharpsburg. I had ridden by the side of Colonel Oakford, except when on duty, up and down the column, and as the line was formed by the colonel and ordered forward, we dismounted and sent our horses to the rear by a servant. I was immediately sent by the colonel to the left of the line to assist in getting that into position. A rail fence separated us from the top of the knoll. Bullets were whizzing and singing by our ears, but so far hitting none where I was. Over the fence and up the knoll in an excellent line we went. In the center of the knoll, perhaps a third of the way up, was a large tree, and under and around this tree lay a body of troops doing nothing. They were in our way, but our orders were forward, and through and over them we went.

Reaching the top of the knoll we were met by a terrific volley from the rebels in the sunken road down the other side, not more than one hundred yards away, and also from another rebel line in a corn-field just beyond. Some of our men were killed and wounded by this volley. We were ordered to lie down just under the top of the hill and crawl forward and fire over, each man crawling back, reloading his piece in this prone position and again crawling forward and firing. These tactics undoubtedly saved us many lives, for the fire of the two lines in front of us was terrific. The air was full of whizzing, singing, buzzing bullets. Once down on the ground under cover of the hill, it required very strong resolution to get up where these missiles of death were flying so thickly, yet that was the duty of us officers, especially us of the field and staff. My duty kept me constantly moving up and down that whole line.

On my way back to the right of the line, where I had left Colonel Oakford, I met Lieutenant-Colonel Wilcox, who told me the terrible news that Colonel Oakford was killed. Of the details of his death, I had no time then to inquire. We were then in the very maelstrom of the battle. Men were falling every moment. The horrible noise of the battle was incessant and almost deafening. Except that my mind was so absorbed in my duties, I do not know how I could have endured the strain.

Yet out of this pandemonium memory brings several remarkable incidents. They came and went with the rapidity of a quickly revolving kaleidoscope. You caught stupendous incidents on the instant, and in an instant they had passed. One was the brave death of the major of this regiment that was lying idle under the tree. The commanding officer evidently was not doing his duty, and this major was endeavoring to rally his men and get them at work. He was swinging his hat and cheering his men forward, when a solid shot decapitated him. His poor body went down as though some giant had picked it up and furiously slammed it on the ground, and I was so near him that I could almost have touched him with my sword.

The inaction of this regiment lying behind us under that tree was very demoralizing to our men, setting them a bad example. General Kimball, who commanded our brigade, was seated on his horse just under the knoll in the rear of our regiment, evidently watching our work, and he signalled me to come to him, and then gave me orders to present his compliments to the commanding officer of that regiment and direct him to get his men up and at work. I communicated this order as directed. The colonel was hugging the ground, and merely turned his face towards me without replying or attempting to obey the order. General Kimball saw the whole thing, and again called me to him and, with an oath, commanded me to repeat the order to him at the muzzle of my revolver, and shoot him if he did not immediately obey.

Said General Kimball: "Get those cowards out of there or shoot them." My task was a most disagreeable one, but I must deliver my orders, and did so, but was saved the duty of shooting by the other officers of the regiment bravely rallying their men and pushing them forward to the firing-line, where they did good work. What became of that skulking colonel, I do not know.

The air was now thick with smoke from the muskets, which not only obscured our vision of the enemy, but made breathing difficult and most uncomfortable. The day was excessively hot, and no air stirring, we were forced to breathe this powder smoke, impregnated with saltpetre, which burned the coating of nose, throat, and eyes almost like fire.

Captain Abbott, commanding Company G, from Mauch Chunk, a brave and splendid officer, was early carried to the rear, a ball having nearly carried away his under jaw. He afterwards told me that his first sensation of this awful wound was his mouth full of blood, teeth, and splintered bones, which he spat out on the ground, and then found that unless he got immediate help he would bleed to death in a few minutes.

Fortunately he found Assistant Surgeon Hoover, who had been assigned to us just from his college graduation, who, under the shelter of a hay-stack, with no anæsthetic, performed an operation which Dr. Gross, of Philadelphia, afterwards said had been but once before successfully performed in the history of surgery, and saved his life. Lieutenant Anson C. Cranmer, Company C, was killed, and the ground was soon strewn with the dead and wounded. Soon our men began to call for more ammunition, and we officers were kept busy taking from the dead and wounded and distributing to the living. Each man had eighty rounds when we began the fight. One man near me rose a moment, when a missile struck his gun about midway, and actually capsized him. He pulled himself together, and, finding he was only a little bruised, picked up another gun, with which the ground was now strewn, and went at it again.

Directly, a lull in the enemy's firing occurred, and we had an opportunity to look over the hill a little more carefully at their lines. Their first line in the sunken road seemed to be all dead or wounded, and several of our men ran down there, to find that literally true. They brought back the lieutenant-colonel, a fine-looking man, who was mortally wounded. I shook his hand, and he said, "God bless you, boys, you are very kind." He asked to be laid down in some sheltered place, for, said he, "I have but a few moments to live."

I well remember his refined, gentlemanly appearance, and how profoundly sorry I felt for him. He was young, lithely built, of sandy complexion, and wore a comparatively new uniform of Confederate gray, on which was embroidered the insignia of the "5th Ga., C. S. A." He said, "You have killed all my brave boys; they are there in the road." And they were, I saw them next day lying four deep in places as they fell, a most awful picture of battle carnage. This lull was of very short duration, and like the lull of a storm presaged a renewal of the firing with greater fury, for a fresh line of rebel troops had been brought up. This occurred three times before we were relieved.

During the fiercest of the firing, another remarkable incident occurred, which well illustrated the fortunes of war. I heard a man shouting, "Come over here men, you can see 'em better," and there, over the brow of the knoll, absolutely exposed, was Private George

Coursen, of Company K, sitting on a boulder, loading and firing as calmly as though there wasn't a rebel in the country. I yelled to him to come back under the cover of the hill-top, but he said he could see the rebels better there, and refused to leave his vantage-ground. I think he remained there until we were ordered back and did not receive a scratch. His escape was nothing less than a miracle. He seemed to have no idea of fear.

A remarkable fact about our experience during this fight was that we took no note of time. When we were out of ammunition and about to move back I looked at my watch and found it was 12.30 P.M. We had been under fire since eight o'clock. I couldn't believe my eyes; was sure my watch had gone wrong. I would have sworn that we had not been there more than twenty minutes, when we had actually been in that very hell of fire for four and a half hours.

Just as we were moving back, the Irish brigade came up, under command of General Thomas Francis Meagher. They had been ordered to complete our work by a charge, and right gallantly they did it. Many of our men, not understanding the order, joined in that charge. General Meagher rode a beautiful white horse, but made a show of himself by tumbling off just as he reached our line. The boys said he was drunk, and he certainly looked and acted like a drunken man. He regained his feet and floundered about, swearing like a crazy man. The brigade, however, made a magnificent charge and swept everything before it.

Another incident occurred during the time we were under fire. My attention was arrested by a heavily built general officer passing to the rear on foot. He came close by me and as he passed he shouted: "You will have to get back. Don't you see yonder line of rebels is flanking you?" I looked in the direction he pointed, and, sure enough, on our right and now well to our rear was an extended line of rebel infantry with their colors flying, moving forward almost with the precision of a parade. They had thrown forward a beautiful skirmish line and seemed to be practically masters of the situation. My heart was in my mouth for a couple of moments, until suddenly the picture changed, and their beautiful line collapsed and went back as if the d——l was after them. They had run up against an obstruction in a line of the "boys in blue," and many of them never went back. This general officer who spoke to me, I learned, was Major-General Richardson, commanding the First Division, then badly wounded, and who died a few hours after.

Our regiment now moved back and to the right some three-quarters of a mile, where we were supplied with ammunition, and the men were allowed to make themselves a cup of coffee and eat a "hard-tack." I was faint for want of food, for I had only a cup of coffee in the early morning, and was favored with a hardtack by one of the men, who were always ready and willing to share their rations with us. We now learned that our brigade had borne the brunt of a long and per-sistent effort by Lee to break our line at this point, and that we were actually the third line which had been thrown into this breach, the other two having been wiped out before we advanced; that as a matter of fact our brigade, being composed so largely of raw troops—our regiment being really more than half the brigade in actual number—was designed to be held in reserve.

But the onslaught of the enemy had been so terrific, that by eight o'clock A.M. our reserve line was all there was left and we had to be sent in. The other three regiments were veterans, old and tried. They had an established reputation of having never once been forced back or whipped, but the One Hundred and Thirty-second was new and, except as to numbers, an unknown quantity. We had been unmerci-fully guyed during the two preceding weeks, as I have said before, as a lot of "greenhorns," "pretty boys" in "pretty new clothes," "mamma's darlings," etc., etc., to the end of the vets' slang calendar. Now that we had proved our metal under fire, the atmosphere was completely changed. Not the semblance of another jibe against the One Hundred and Thirty-second Pennsylvania Volunteers.

We did not know how well we had done, only that we had tried to do our duty under trying circumstances, until officers and men from other regiments came flocking over to congratulate and praise us. I didn't even know we had passed through the fire of a great battle until the colonel of the Fourteenth Indiana came over to condole with us on the loss of Colonel Oakford, and incidentally told us that this was undoubtedly the greatest battle of the war thus far, and that we probably would never have such another.

After getting into our new position, I at once began to look up our losses. I learned that Colonel Oakford was killed by one of the rebel sharp-shooters just as the regiment scaled the fence in its advance up the knoll, and before we had fired a shot. It must have occurred almost instantly after I left him with orders for the left of the line. I was probably the last to whom he spoke. He was hit by a minie-ball in the left shoulder, just below the collar-bone. The doctor said the ball had severed one of the large arteries, and he died in a very few minutes. He had been in command of the regiment a little more than a month, but during that brief time his work as a disciplinarian and drill-master had made it possible for us to acquit ourselves as creditably as they all said we had done. General Kimball was loud in our praise and greatly lamented Colonel Oakford's death, whom he admired very much. He was a brave, able, and accomplished officer and gentleman, and his loss to the regiment was irreparable.

Had Colonel Oakford lived his record must have been brilliant and his promotion rapid, for very few volunteer officers had so quickly mastered the details of military tactics and routine. He was a thorough disciplinarian, an able tactician, and the interests and welfare of his men were constantly upon his heart.

My diary records the fact that I saw Captain Willard, of the Fourteenth Connecticut, fall as we passed their line on our way to the rear; that he appeared to have been hit by a grape-shot or piece of shell. I did not know him, only heard that he was a brother of E. N. Willard, of Scranton. The Fourteenth Connecticut men said he was a fine man and splendid officer.

Among the wounded—reported mortally—was Sergeant Martin Hower, of Company K, one of our very best non-commissioned officers. I saw him at the hospital, and it was very hard to be able to do nothing for him. It seemed our loss must reach upward of two hundred killed, wounded and missing. Out of seven hundred and ninety-eight who answered to roll-call in the morning, we had with us less than three hundred at the close of the fight.

Of the missing, many of them were of those who joined the Irish brigade in their charge, and who did not find us again for a day or so. It may seem strange that a man should not be able to find his regiment for so long a time, when really it is so close at hand. But when one remembers that our army of about seventy-five thousand men had upward of two hundred regiments massed within say two square miles, and that they were constantly changing position, it will be seen that looking for any one regiment is almost like looking for a needle in a hay-mow.

During the afternoon of this day we were again moved further to the right and placed as supports of a battery. We were posted about two hundred yards directly in front of the guns on low ground. The battery was evidently engaged in another artillery duel. We were in a comparatively safe position, so long as the rebel guns directed their firing at our battery; but after a time they began "feeling for the supports," first dropping their shells beyond our guns, then in front of them, until they finally got a pretty good range on our line and filled the air with bursting shells over our heads. One and another was carried to the rear, wounded, and the line became very restive. We were required to lie perfectly quiet. We found this very much more trying than being at work, and the line began to show symptoms of wavering, when General Kimball, who with his staff had dismounted and was resting near us, immediately mounted his horse and, riding up and down the line, shouted: "Stand firm, trust in God, and do your duty."

It was an exceedingly brave act, and its effect was electric upon the men. There was no more wavering, and the rebel battery, evidently thinking they had not found the "supports," soon ceased firing upon us. It was now near night and the firing very perceptibly slackened in our vicinity, though a mile or more to the left it still continued very heavy. This, we afterwards learned, was the work at what has passed into history as "Burnside's" bridge—the effort of Burnside's corps to capture the stone bridge over Antietam creek, near the village of Sharpsburg, and the heights beyond. These were gallantly carried after a terrific fight quite late in the afternoon.

Our work, so far as this battle was concerned, was done. We rested "on our arms" where we were for the next forty-eight hours, expecting all the next day a renewal of the fighting; but nothing was done in our neighborhood beyond a few shots from the battery we were supporting. On the second day it became known that Lee had hauled off, and there was no immediate prospect of further fighting. Our companies were permitted to gather up their dead, and burying parties were organized.

We were allowed to go over the field freely. It was a gruesome sight. Our own dead had been cared for, but the rebel dead remained as they had fallen. In the hot sun the bodies had swollen and turned black. Nearly all lay with faces up and eyes wide open, presenting a spectacle to make one shudder. . . . Their limbs and bodies were so enlarged that their clothing seemed ready to burst. Some ghouls had been among them, whether from their own lines or from ours, could not be known, but every man's pockets had been ripped out and the contents taken.

In company with Captain Archbald I went over the position occupied by our regiment and brigade, the famous "sunken road," that is, the lane or road extending from near the "Roulette house" towards Sharpsburg. For some distance it had been cut through the opposite side of the knoll upon which we fought, and had the appearance of a sunken road. It was literally filled with rebel dead, which in some places lay three and four bodies deep. We afterwards saw pictures of this road in the illustrated papers, which partially portrayed the horrible scene. Those poor fellows were the Fifth Georgia regiment. This terrible work was mostly that of our regiment, and bore testimony to the effectiveness of the fire of our men.

The position was an alluring one: the road was cut into the hill about waist high, and seemed to offer secure protection to a line of infantry, and so no doubt this line was posted there to hold the knoll and this Sharpsburg road. It proved, however, nothing but a death-trap, for once our line got into position on the top of this crescent-shaped ridge we could reach them by a direct fire on the center and a double flanking fire at the right and left of the line, and only about one hundred yards away. With nothing but an open field behind them there was absolutely no escape, nothing but death or surrender, and they evidently chose the former, for we saw no white flag displayed. We could now understand the remark of their lieutenant-colonel, whom our boys brought in, as already mentioned: "You have killed all my poor boys. They lie there in the road." I learned later that the few survivors of this regiment were sent South to guard rebel prisoners.

The lines of battle of both armies were not only marked by the presence of the dead, but by a vast variety of army equipage, such as blankets, canteens, haversacks, guns, gunslings, bayonets, ramrods, some whole, others broken—verily, a besom of destruction had done its work faithfully here. Dead horses were everywhere, and the stench from them and the human dead was horrible. "Uncle" Billy Sherman has said, "War is hell!" yet this definition, with all that imagination can picture, fails to reveal all its bloody horrors.

The positions of some of the dead were very striking. One poor fellow lay face down on a partially fallen stone wall, with one arm and one foot extended, as if in the act of crawling over. His position attracted our attention, and we found his body literally riddled with bullets—there must have been hundreds—and most of them shot into him after he was dead, for they showed no marks of blood. Probably the poor fellow had been wounded in trying to reach shelter behind that wall, was spotted in the act by our men, and killed right there, and became thereafter a target for every new man that saw him. Another man lay, still clasping his musket, which he was evidently in the act of loading when a bullet pierced his heart, literally flooding his gun with his life's blood, a ghastly testimonial to his heroic sacrifice.

We witnessed the burying details gathering up and burying the dead. The work was rough and heartless, but only comporting with the character of war. The natural reverence for the dead was wholly absent. The poor bodies, all of them heroes in their death, even though in a mistaken cause, were "planted" with as little feeling as though they had been so many logs. A trench was dug, where the digging was easiest, about seven feet wide and long enough to accommodate all the bodies gathered within a certain radius; these were then placed side by side, cross-wise of the trench, and buried without anything to keep the earth from them. In the case of the Union dead, the trenches were usually two or three feet deep, and the bodies were wrapped in blankets before being covered, but with the rebels no blankets were used, and the trenches were sometimes so shallow as to leave the toes exposed after a shower.

No ceremony whatever attended this gruesome service, but it was generally accompanied by ribald jokes, at the expense of the poor "Johnny" they were "planting." This was not the fruit of debased natures or degenerate hearts on the part of the boys, who well knew it might be their turn next, under the fortunes of war, to be buried in like manner, but it was recklessness and thoughtlessness, born of the hardening influences of war.

Having now given some account of the scenes in which I participated during the battle and the day after, let us look at another feature of the battle, and probably the most heart-breaking of all, the field hospital. There was one established for our division some three hundred yards in our rear, under the shelter of a hill. Here were gathered as rapidly as possible the wounded, and a corps of surgeons were busily engaged in amputating limbs and dressing wounds. It should be understood that the accommodations were of the rudest character. A hospital tent had been hurriedly erected and an old house and barn utilized. Of course, I saw nothing of it or its work until the evening after the battle, when I went to see the body of our dead colonel and some of our Scranton boys who were wounded.

Outside the hospital were piles of amputated arms, legs, and feet, thrown out with as little care as so many pieces of wood. There were also many dead soldiers—those who had died after reaching the hospital—lying outside, there being inside scant room only for the living. Here, on bunches of hay and straw, the poor fellows were lying so thickly that there was scarce room for the surgeon and attendants to move about among them. Others were not allowed inside, except officers and an occasional friend who might be helping. Our chaplain spent his time here and did yeoman service helping the wounded. Yet all that could be done with the limited means at hand seemed only to accentuate the appalling need. The pallid, appealing faces were patient with a heroism born only of the truest metal. I was told by the surgeons that such expressions as this were not infrequent as they approached a man in his "turn": "Please, doctor, attend to this poor fellow next; he's worse than I," and this when his own life's blood was fast oozing away.

Most of the wounded had to wait hours before having their wounds dressed, owing to insufficient force and inadequate facilities. I was told that not a surgeon had his eyes closed for three days after this battle. The doctors of neighboring towns within reach came and voluntarily gave their services, yet it is doubtless true that hundreds of the wounded perished for want of prompt and proper care. This is one of the unavoidable incidents of a great battle—a part of the horrors of war. The rebel wounded necessarily were second to our own in receiving care from the surgeons, yet they, too, received all the attention that was possible under the circumstances. Some of their surgeons remained with their wounded, and I am told they and our own surgeons worked together most energetically and heroically in their efforts to relieve the sufferings of all, whether they wore the blue or the gray. Suffering, it has been said, makes all the world akin. So here, in our lines, the wounded rebel was lost sight of in the suffering brother.

We remained on the battle-field until September 21, four days after the fight.

My notes of this day say that I was feeling so miserable as to be scarcely able to crawl about, yet was obliged to remain on duty; that Lieutenant-Colonel Wilcox, now in command, and Major Shreve were in the same condition. This was due to the nervous strain through which we had passed, and to insufficient and unwholesome food. As stated before, we had been obliged to eat whatever we could get, which for the past four days had been mostly green field corn roasted as best we could. The wonder is that we were not utterly prostrated. Nevertheless, I not only performed all my duties, but went a mile down the Antietam creek, took a bath, and washed my underclothing, my first experience in the laundry business.

We had been now for two weeks and more steadily on the march, our baggage in wagons somewhere en route, without the possibility of a change of clothing or of having any washing done. Most of this time marching in a cloud of dust so thick that one could almost cut it, and perspiring freely, one can imagine our condition. Bathing as frequently as opportunity offered, yet our condition was almost unendurable. For with the accumulation of dirt upon our body, there was added the ever-present scourge of the army, body lice. These vermin, called by the boys "graybacks," were nearly the size of a grain of wheat, and derived their name from their bluish-gray color. They seemed to infest the ground wherever there had been a bivouac of the rebels, and following them as we had, during all of this campaign, sleeping frequently on the ground just vacated by them, no one was exempt from this plague. They secreted themselves in the seams of the clothing and in the armpits chiefly. A good bath, with a change of underclothing, would usually rid one of them, but only to acquire a new crop in the first camp. The clothing could be freed of them by boiling in salt water or by going carefully over the seams and picking them off. The latter operation was a frequent occupation with the men on any day which was warm enough to permit them to disrobe for the purpose. One of the most laughable sights I ever beheld was the whole brigade, halted for a couple of hours' rest one hot day, with clothing off, "skirmishing," as the boys called it, for "graybacks." This was one of the many unpoetical features of army life which accentuated the sacrifices one made to serve his country.

How did we ordinarily get our laundrying done? The enlisted men as a rule always did it themselves. Occasionally in camp a number of them would club together and hire some "camp follower" or some other soldier to do it. Officers of sufficient rank to have a servant, of course, readily solved the question. Those of us of lesser rank could generally hire it done, except on the march. Then we had to be our own laundrymen. Having, as in the above instance, no change of clothing at hand, the washing followed a bath, and consisted in standing in the running water and rubbing as much of the dirt out of the underwear as could be done without soap, for that could not be had for love or money; then hanging them on the limb of a tree and sitting in the sun, as comfortable as possible, whilst wind and sun did the drying. A "snap-shot" of such a scene would no doubt be interesting. But "snap-shots" unfortunately were not then in vogue, and so a picture of high art must perish. We could not be over particular about having our clothes dry. The finishing touches were added as we wore them back to camp.

My diary notes that there were nine hundred and ninety-eight rebel dead gathered and buried from in front of the lines of our division. This line was about a quarter of a mile long, and this was mostly our work (our division), although Richardson's division had occupied part of this ground before us, but had been so quickly broken that they had not made much impression upon the enemy. Our division had engaged them continuously and under a terrific fire from eight o'clock A.M. until 12.30 P.M. It may be asked why during that length of time and under such a fire all were not annihilated. The answer is, that inaccuracy and unsteadiness in firing on both sides greatly reduce its effectiveness, and taking all possible advantage of shelter by lying prone upon the ground also prevents losses; but the above number of rebel dead, it should be remembered, represents, probably, not more than twenty to twenty-five per cent of their casualties in that area of their lines; the balance were wounded and were removed. So that with nine hundred and ninety-eight dead it can be safely estimated that their losses exceeded four thousand killed and wounded in that area. This would indicate what was undoubtedly true, that we were in the very heart of that great battle.

Here I wish to say that some chroniclers of battles have undertaken to measure the effectiveness and bravery of the different regiments, batteries, etc., by the numbers they have lost in certain battles; for example, one historian has made a book grading the regiments by the number of men they lost in action, assuming that the more men killed and wounded, the more brilliant and brave had been its work. This assumption is absolutely fallacious. Heavy losses may be the result of great bravery with splendid work. On the other hand, they may be the result of cowardice or inefficiency. Suppose, under trying circumstances, officers lose their heads and fail to properly handle their men, or if the latter prove cowardly and incapable of being moved with promptness to meet the exigency, great loss usually ensues, and this would be chargeable to cowardice or inefficiency. According to the loss way of estimating fighting regiments, the least deserving are liable to be credited with the best work. The rule is, the better drilled, disciplined, and the better officered, the less the losses in any position on the firing-line.

This fixing up of quarters had been done in contemplation of remaining here through the winter, and we had taken our cue from like actions of our brigade officers, who were supposed to know something about the movements of the army. When we got orders on the 29th of October to prepare for the march, I was assured by the adjutant-general of our brigade that it was nothing more than a day's reconnoissance, and that we were certainly not going to move our quarters. He knew as much about it as I did. Within an hour after this order another came directing us to move in heavy marching order, with three days' rations and sixty rounds of ammunition. And so we moved out of Harper's Ferry on the 31st of October, leaving our fixed-up quarters, with my four-dollar stove, to Geary's division, which succeeded to our camp.

We crossed the Shenandoah on a pontoon bridge and skirted the mountain under Loudon Heights over the same route south that we had taken on our way in from the Leesburg raid. We marched very leisurely, making during the first four days only about twenty-five miles, to a village bearing the serious name of Snickersville. Here we had the first evidence of the presence of the enemy. We were hurried through this village and up through the gap in the mountain called "Snicker's Gap" to head off the rebels. We soon came on to their scouts and pickets, who fled precipitately without firing a gun. Part of our division halted on the top of the gap, while a couple of regiments skirmished through the woods both sides of the road down to the foot of the mountain on the other side. The enemy had taken "French leave," and so our men returned and our division bivouacked here for the night.

We now learned that these giant armies were moving south in parallel columns, the mountain separating them. At every gap or pass in the mountain a bristling head or a clinched fist, so to speak, of one would be thrust through and the other would try to hit it. This was our mission, as we double-quicked it through this gap. When we got there the "fist" had been withdrawn, and our work for the time was over. But our bivouac here—how beautiful it was! The fields were clean and green, with plenty of shade, for right in the gap were some good farms. Then the cavalry had not cleaned the country of everything eatable, as was usual, they being always in the advance. There was milk and bread to be had, and somehow—I never dared to inquire too closely about it—some good mutton came into camp that night, so that we had a splendid breakfast next morning. Some fine honey was added to the bill of fare. The man who brought in the latter claimed that a rebel hive of bees attacked him whilst on picket duty, and he confiscated the honey as a measure of retaliation.

But the special feature that makes that camp linger in my memory was the extraordinary beauty of the scene in the valley below us when the evening camp-fires were lighted. We were on a sort of table-land two or three hundred feet above the broad valley, which widened out at this point and made a most charming landscape. As the darkness drew on the camp-fires were lighted, and the scene became one of weird, bewitching beauty. Almost as far as the eye could reach, covering three and possibly four square miles, were spread out the blazing camp-fires of that mighty host of our "Boys in Blue."

No drums were beaten and the usual retreat call was not sounded, but the thousands of camp-fires told of the presence of our men. A martial city was cooking its evening coffee and resting its weary limbs in the genial camp-fire glow, whilst weary hearts were refreshed with the accompanying chat about friends and dearer ones at home. The scouting "Johnny Rebs" (and there were no doubt plenty of them viewing the scene) could have gotten from it no comforting information to impart as to our numbers. Most of the Army of the Potomac, now largely augmented by new regiments, was there, probably not less than one hundred thousand men. It was a picture not of a lifetime, but of the centuries. It made my blood leap as I realized that I was looking down upon the grandest army, all things considered, of any age or time. Its mission was to save to liberty and freedom the life of the best government the world ever saw. In its ranks was the best blood of a free people.

In intelligence it was far superior to any other army that ever existed. Scholars of all professions, tradesmen and farmers, were there, fighting side by side, animated by the same patriotic impulse. I said to myself, it is impossible that that army should be beaten. It is the strong right arm of the Union, and under God it shall assuredly deal the deathblow to the rebellion.

This it certainly did, though at a fearful cost, for it was fighting the same blood.

The inspiration of that scene made me glad from the bottom of my heart that I had the privilege of being just one in that glorious army. After forty years, what would I take for that association with all its dangers and hardships? What for these pictures and memories? They are simply priceless. I only wish I could so paint the pictures and reproduce the scenes that they might be an inspiration to the same patriotism that moved this mighty host.

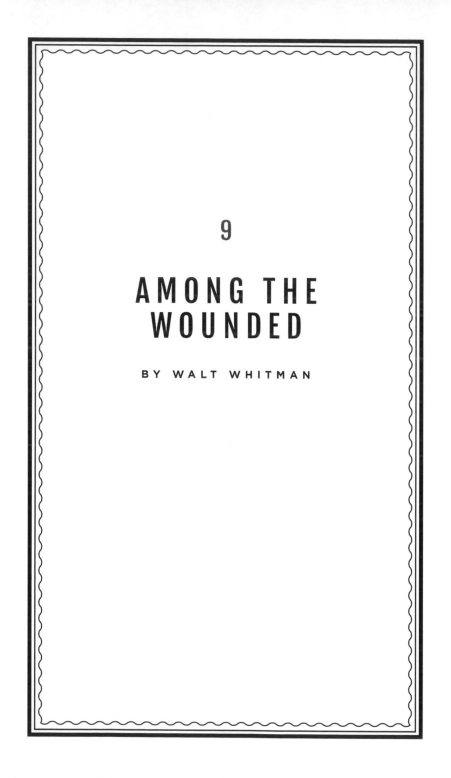

9

AMONG THE WOUNDED

BY WALT WHITMAN

One of America's greatest writers describes what he saw during his frequent visits to hospitals during the Civil War.

As this tremendous war goes on, the public interest becomes more general and gathers more and more closely about the wounded, the sick, and the Government hospitals, the surgeons, and all appertaining to the medical department of the army. Up to the date of this writing (December 9, 1864) there have been, as I estimate, near four hundred thousand cases under treatment, and there are to-day, probably, taking the whole service of the United States, two hundred thousand, or an approximation to that number, on the doctors' list. Half of these are comparatively slight ailments or hurts. Every family has directly or indirectly some representative among this vast army of the wounded and sick.

The following sketch is made to gratify the general interest in this field of the war, and also for a few special persons through whose means alone I have aided the men. It extends over a period of two years, coming down to the present hour, and exhibits the army hospitals at Washington, the camp hospitals in the field, etc. A very few cases are given as specimens of thousands. The account may be relied upon as faithful, though rapidly thrown together. It will put the reader in as direct contact as may be with scenes, sights, and cases of these immense hospitals. As will be seen, it begins back two years since, at a very gloomy period of the contest.

Began my visits (December 21, 1862) among the camp hospitals in the Army of the Potomac, under General Burnside. Spent a good part of the day in a large brick mansion on the banks of the Rappahannock, immediately opposite Fredericksburg. It is used as a hospital since the battle, and seems to have received only the worst cases. Outdoors, at the foot of a tree, within ten yards of the front of the house, I notice a heap of amputated feet, legs, arms, hands, etc.—about a load for a one-horse cart. Several dead bodies lie near, each covered with its brown woollen blanket. In the dooryard, toward the river, are fresh graves, mostly of officers, their names on pieces of barrel staves or broken board, stuck in the dirt. (Most of these bodies were subsequently taken up and transported North to their friends.)

The house is quite crowded, everything impromptu, no system, all bad enough, but I have no doubt the best that can be done; all the wounds pretty bad, some frightful, the men in their old clothes, unclean and bloody. Some of the wounded are rebel officers, prisoners. One, a Mississippian—a captain—hit badly in the leg, I talked with some time; he asked me for papers, which I gave him. (I saw him three months afterward in Washington, with leg amputated, doing well.)

I went through the rooms, down stairs and up. Some of the men were dying. I had nothing to give at that visit, but wrote a few letters to folks home, mothers, etc. Also talked to three or four who seemed most susceptible to it, and needing it.

December 22 to 31.—Am among the regimental brigade and division hospitals somewhat. Few at home realize that these are merely tents, and sometimes very poor ones, the wounded lying on the ground, lucky if their blanket is spread on a layer of pine or hemlock twigs, or some leaves. No cots; seldom even a mattress on the ground. It is pretty cold. I go around from one case to another. I do not see that I can do any good, but I cannot leave them. Once in a while some youngster holds on to me convulsively, and I do what I can for him; at any rate stop with him, and sit near him for hours, if he wishes it. Besides the hospitals, I also go occasionally on long tours through the camps, talking with the men, etc.; sometimes at night among the groups around the fires, in their shebang enclosures of bushes. I soon get acquainted anywhere in camp with officers or men, and am always well used. Sometimes I go down on picket with the regiments I know best. As to rations, the army here at present seems to be tolerably well supplied, and the men have enough, such as it is. Most of the regiments lodge in the flimsy little shelter tents. A few have built themselves huts of logs and mud, with fireplaces.

I might give a long list of special cases, interesting items of the wounded men here, but have not space.

Left Falmouth, January, 1863, by Aquia creek railroad, and so on Government steamer up the Potomac. Many wounded were with us on cars and boat. The cars were just common platform ones. The railroad journey of ten or twelve miles was made mostly before sunrise. The soldiers guarding the road came out from their tents or shebangs of bushes with rumpled hair and half-awake look. Those on duty were walking their posts, some on banks over us, others down far below the level of the track. I saw large cavalry camps off the road. At Aquia Creek Landing were numbers of wounded going North. While I waited some three hours, I went around among them. Several wanted word sent home to parents, brothers, wives, etc., which I did for them (by mail the next day from Washington). On the boat I had my hands full. One poor fellow died going up.

Am now (January, February, etc., 1863) in and around Washington, daily visiting the hospitals. Am much in Campbell, Patent-office, Eighth-street, H-street, Armory-square, and others. Am now able to do a little good, having money (as almoner of others home), and getting experience. I would like to give lists of cases, for there is no end to the interesting ones; but it is impossible without making a large volume, or rather several volumes. I must, therefore, let one or two days' visits at this time suffice as specimens of scores and hundreds of subsequent ones, through the ensuing spring, summer, and fall, and, indeed, down to the present week.

Sunday, January 25.—Afternoon and till 9 in the evening, visited Campbell hospital. Attended specially to one case in Ward I, very sick with pleurisy and typhoid fever, young man, farmer's son— D. F. Russell, Company E, Sixtieth New York—down-hearted and feeble; a long time before he would take any interest; soothed and cheered him gently; wrote a letter home to his mother, in Malone, Franklin county, N.Y., at his request; gave him some fruit and one or two other gifts; enveloped and directed his letter, etc. Then went thoroughly through Ward 6; observed every case in the ward (without, I think, missing one); found some cases I thought needed little sums of money; supplied them (sums of perhaps thirty, twenty-five, twenty, or fifteen cents); distributed a pretty bountiful supply of cheerful reading matter, and gave perhaps some twenty to thirty persons, each one some little gift, such as oranges, apples, sweet crackers, figs, etc., etc., etc.

Thursday, January 29.—Devoted the main part of the day, from 11 to 3.30 o'clock, to Armory-square hospital; went pretty thoroughly through Wards F, G, H, and I—some fifty cases in each ward. In Ward H supplied the men throughout with writing paper and a stamped envelope each, also some cheerful reading matter; distributed in small portions, about half of it in this ward, to proper subjects, a large jar of first-rate preserved berries; also other small gifts. In Wards G, H, and I, found several cases I thought good subjects for small sums of money, which I furnished in each case. The poor wounded men often come up "dead broke," and it helps their spirits to have even the small sum I give them.

My paper and envelopes all gone, but distributed a good lot of amusing reading matter; also, as I thought judicious, tobacco, oranges, apples, etc. Some very interesting cases in Ward I: Charles Miller, Bed No. 19, Company D, Fifty-third Pennsylvania, is only sixteen years of age, very bright, courageous boy, left leg amputated below the knee; next bed below him, young lad very sick—gave the two each appropriate gifts; in the bed above also amputation of the left leg—gave him a part of a jar of raspberries; Bed No. 1, this ward, gave a small sum also; also to a soldier on crutches, sitting on his bed near.

Evening, same day.—Went to see D. F. R., Campbell hospital, before alluded to; found him remarkably changed for the better—up and dressed (quite a triumph; he afterwards got well and went back to his regiment). Distributed in the wards a quantity of note-paper and forty or fifty, mostly paid, envelopes, of which the men were much in need; also a four-pound bag of gingersnaps I bought at a baker's in Seventh street.

Here is a case of a soldier I found among the crowded cots in the Patent hospital—(they have removed most of the men of late and broken up that hospital). He likes to have some one to talk to, and we will listen to him. He got badly wounded in the leg and side at Fredericksburg that eventful Saturday, 13th December. I Ie lay the succeeding two days and nights helpless on the field, between the city and those grim batteries, for his company and his regiment had been compelled to leave him to his fate. To make matters worse, he lay with his head slightly down hill, and could not help himself. At the end of some fifty hours he was brought off, with other wounded, under a flag of truce.

We ask him how the Rebels treated him during those two days and nights within reach of them—whether they came to him—whether they abused him? He answers that several of the Rebels, soldiers and others, came to him, at one time and another. A couple of them, who were together, spoke roughly and sarcastically, but did not act. One middle-aged man, however, who seemed to be moving around the field among the dead and wounded for benevolent purposes, came to him in a way he will never forget. This man treated our soldier kindly, bound up his wounds, cheered him, gave him a couple of biscuits gave him a drink of whiskey and water, asked him if he could eat some beef.

This good Secesh, however, did not change our soldier's position, for it might have caused the blood to burst from the wounds where they were clotted and stagnated. Our soldier is from Pennsylvania; has had a pretty severe time; the wounds proved to be bad ones. But he retains a good heart, and is at present on the gain. It is not uncommon for the men to remain on the field this way, one, two, or even four or five days.

I continue among the hospitals during March, April, etc., without intermission. My custom is to go through a ward, or a collection of wards, endeavoring to give some trifle to each, without missing any. Even a sweet biscuit, a sheet of paper, or a passing word of friendliness, or but a look or nod, if no more. In this way I go through large numbers without delaying, yet do not hurry. I find out the general mood of the ward at the time; sometimes see that there is a heavy weight of listlessness prevailing, and the whole ward wants cheering up. I perhaps read to the men, to break the spell, calling them around me, careful to sit away from the cot of any one who is very bad with sickness or wounds. Also I find out, by going through in this way, the cases that need special attention, and can then devote proper time to them. Of course I am very cautious, among the patients, in giving them food. I always confer with the doctor, or find out from the nurse or ward-master about a new case. But I soon get sufficiently familiar with what is to be avoided, and learn also to judge almost intuitively what is best.

I do a good deal of writing letters by the bedside, of course—writing all kinds, including love letters. Many sick and wounded soldiers have not written home to parents, brothers, sisters, and even wives, for one reason or another, for a long, long time. Some are poor writers; some cannot get paper and envelopes; many have an aversion to writing, because they dread to worry the folks at home—the facts about them are so sad to tell. I always encourage the men to write, and promptly write for them.

As I write this, in May, 1863, the wounded have begun to arrive from Hooker's command, from bloody Chancellorsville. I was down among the first arrivals. The men in charge of them told me the bad cases were yet to come. If that is so, I pity them, for these are bad enough. You ought to see the scene of the wounded arriving at the landing here, foot of Sixth street, at night. Two boat-loads came about half-past seven last night. A little after eight it rained, a long and violent shower. The poor, pale, helpless soldiers had been debarked, and lay around on the wharf and neighborhood, anywhere. The rain was, probably, grateful to them; at any rate they were exposed to it.

The few torches light up the spectacle. All around on the wharf, on the ground, out on side places, etc., the men are lying on blankets, old quilts, etc., with the bloody rags bound around their heads, arms, legs, etc. The attendants are few, and at night few outsiders also—only a few hard-worked transportation men and drivers. (The wounded are getting to be common, and people grow callous.) The men, whatever their condition, lie there and patiently wait till their turn comes to be taken up. Near by the ambulances are now arriving in clusters, and one after another is called to back up and take its load. Extreme cases are sent off on stretchers. The men generally make little or no ado, whatever their sufferings—a few groans that cannot be repressed, and occasionally a scream of pain as they lift a man into the ambulance.

To-day, as I write, hundreds more are expected; and to-morrow and the next day more, and so on for many days.

The soldiers are nearly all young men, and far more Americans than is generally supposed—I should say nine tenths are native born. Among the arrivals from Chancellorsville I find a large proportion of Ohio, Indiana, and Illinois men. As usual there are all sorts of wounds.

Some of the men are fearfully burnt from the explosion of artillery caissons. One ward has a long row of officers, some with ugly hurts. Yesterday was perhaps worse than usual: amputations are going on; the attendants are dressing wounds. As you pass by you must be on your guard where you look. I saw, the other day, a gentleman, a visitor, apparently from curiosity, in one of the wards, stop and turn a moment to look at an awful wound they were probing, etc.; he turned pale, and in a moment more he had fainted away and fallen on the floor.

I buy, during the hot weather, boxes of oranges from time to time, and distribute them among the men; also preserved peaches and other fruits; also lemons and sugar for lemonade. Tobacco is also much in demand. Large numbers of the men come up, as usual, without a cent of money. Through the assistance of friends in Brooklyn and Boston, I am again able to help many of those that fall in my way. It is only a small sum in each case, but it is much to them. As before, I go around daily and talk with the men, to cheer them up.

My note-books are full of memoranda of the cases of this summer, and the wounded from Chancellorsville, but space forbids my transcribing them.

As I sit writing this paragraph (sundown, Thursday, June 25) I see a train of about thirty huge four-horse wagons, used as ambulances, filled with wounded, passing up Fourteenth street, on their way, probably, to Columbian, Carver, and Mount Pleasant hospitals. This is the way the men come in now, seldom in small numbers, but almost always in these long, sad processions. Through the past winter, while our army lay opposite Fredericksburg, the like strings of ambulances were of frequent occurrence along Seventh street, passing slowly up from the steam-boat wharf, from Aquia creek.

This afternoon, July 22, 1863, I spent a long time with a young man I have been with considerable, named Oscar F. Wilber, Company G, One Hundred Fifty-fourth New York, low with chronic diarrhoea and a bad wound also. He asked me to read him a chapter in the New Testament. I complied and asked him what I should read. He said, "Make your own choice." I opened at the close of one of the first books of the Evangelists, and read the chapters describing the latter hours of Christ and the scenes at the crucifixion. The poor wasted young man asked me to read the following chapter also, how Christ rose again. I read very slowly, for Oscar was feeble. It pleased him very much, yet the tears were in his eyes. He asked me if I enjoyed religion. I said, "Perhaps not, my dear, in the way you mean, and yet may-be it is the same thing." He said, "It is my chief reliance." He talked of death, and said he did not fear it. I said, "Why, Oscar, don't you think you will get well?" He said, "I may, but it is not probable." He spoke calmly of his condition. The wound was very bad; it discharged much. Then the diarrhoea had prostrated him, and I felt that he was even then the same as dying. He behaved very manly and affectionate. The kiss I gave him as I was about leaving, he returned fourfold. He gave me his mother's address, Mrs. Sally D. Wilber, Alleghany post-office, Cattaraugus county, N. Y. I had several such interviews with him. He died a few days after the one just described.

August, September, October, etc.—I continue among the hospitals in the same manner, getting still more experience, and daily and nightly meeting with most interesting cases. Through the winter of 1863–4, the same. The work of the army hospital visitor is indeed a trade, an art, requiring both experience and natural gifts, and the greatest judgment. A large number of the visitors to the hospitals do no good at all, while many do harm. The surgeons have great trouble from them. Some visitors go from curiosity—as to a show of animals.

Others give the men improper things. Then there are always some poor fellows, in the crises of sickness or wounds, that imperatively need perfect quiet—not to be talked to by strangers. Few realize that it is not the mere giving of gifts that does good; it is the proper adaption. Nothing is of any avail among the soldiers except conscientious personal investigation of cases, each for itself; with sharp, critical faculties, but in the fullest spirit of human sympathy and boundless love. The men feel such love more than anything else. I have met very few persons who realize the importance of humoring the yearnings for love and friendship of these American young men, prostrated by sickness and wounds.

February, 1864.—I am down at Culpepper and Brandy station, among the camp of First, Second, and Third Corps, and going through the division hospitals. The condition of the camps here this winter is immensely improved from last winter near Falmouth. All the army is now in huts of logs and mud, with fireplaces; and the food is plentiful and tolerably good. In the camp hospitals I find diarrhoea more and more prevalent, and in chronic form. It is at present the great disease of the army. I think the doctors generally give too much medicine, oftener making things worse. Then they hold on to the cases in camp too long. When the disease is almost fixed beyond remedy, they send it up to Washington. Alas! how many such wrecks have I seen landed from boat and railroad and deposited in the Washington hospitals, mostly but to linger awhile and die, after being kept at the front too long.

The hospitals in front, this winter, are also much improved. The men have cots, and often wooden floors, and the tents are well warmed.

March and April, 1864.—Back again in Washington. They are breaking up the camp hospitals in Meade's army, preparing for a move. As I write this, in March, there are all the signs. Yesterday and last night the sick were arriving here in long trains, all day and night. I was among the new-comers most of the night. One train of a thousand came into the depot, and others followed. The ambulances were going all night, distributing them to the various hospitals here. When they come in, some literally in a dying condition, you may well imagine it is a lamentable sight. I hardly know which is worse, to see the wounded after a battle, or these wasted wrecks.

I remain in capital health and strength, and go every day, as before, among the men, in my own way, enjoying my life and occupation more than I can tell.

Of the army hospitals now in and around Washington, there are thirty or forty. I am in the habit of going to all, and to Fairfax seminary, Alexandria, and over Long Bridge to the convalescent camp, etc. As a specimen of almost any one of these hospitals, fancy to yourself a space of three to twenty acres of ground, on which are grouped ten or twelve very large wooden barracks, with, perhaps, a dozen or twenty, and sometimes more than that number, of small buildings, capable all together of accommodating from five hundred to a thousand or fifteen hundred persons. Sometimes these large wooden barracks, or wards, each of them, perhaps, from a hundred to a hundred and fifty feet long, are arranged in a straight row, evenly fronting the street; others are planned so as to form an immense V; and others again arranged around a hollow square. They make all together a huge cluster, with the additional tents, extra wards for contagious diseases, guard-houses, sutler's stores, chaplain's house, etc. In the middle will probably be an edifice devoted to the offices of the surgeon in charge and the ward surgeons, principal attachés, clerks, etc. Then around this center radiate or are gathered the wards for the wounded and sick.

These wards are either lettered alphabetically, Ward G, Ward K, or else numerically, 1, 2, 3, etc. Each has its ward surgeon and corps of nurses. Of course there is, in the aggregate, quite a muster of employees, and over all the surgeon in charge. Any one of these hospitals is a little city in itself. Take, for instance, the Carver hospital, out a couple of miles, on a hill, northern part of Fourteenth street. It has more inmates than an ordinary country town. The same with the Lincoln hospital, east of the Capitol, or the Finley hospital, on high grounds northeast of the city; both large establishments. Armory-square hospital, under Dr. Bliss, in Seventh street (one of the best anywhere), is also temporarily enlarged this summer, with additional tents, sheds, etc. It must have nearly a hundred tents, wards, sheds, and structures of one kind and another. The worst cases are always to be found here.

A wanderer like me about Washington pauses on some high land which commands the sweep of the city (one never tires of the noble and ample views presented here, in the generally fine, soft, peculiar air and light), and has his eyes attracted by these white clusters of barracks in almost every direction. They make a great show in the landscape, and I often use them as landmarks. Some of these clusters are very full of inmates. Counting the whole, with the convalescent camps (whose inmates are often worse off than the sick in the hospitals), they have numbered, in this quarter and just down the Potomac, as high as fifty thousand invalid, disabled, or sick and dying men.

My sketch has already filled up so much room that I shall have to omit any detailed account of the wounded of May and June, 1864, from the battles of the Wilderness, Spottsylvania, etc. That would be a long history in itself. The arrivals, the numbers, and the severity of the wounds, out-viewed anything that we have seen before. For days and weeks a melancholy tide set in upon us. The weather was very hot. The wounded had been delayed in coming, and much neglected. Very many of the wounds had worms in them. An unusual proportion mortified. It was among these that, for the first time in my life, I began to be prostrated with real sickness, and was, before the close of the summer, imperatively ordered North by the physician to recuperate and have an entire change of air.

What I know of first Fredericksburg, Chancellorsville, Wilderness, etc., makes clear to me that there has been, and is yet, a total lack of science in elastic adaptation to the needs of the wounded after a battle. The hospitals are long afterward filled with proofs of this.

I have seen many battles, their results, but never one where there was not, during the first few days, an unaccountable and almost total deficiency of everything for the wounded—appropriate sustenance, nursing, cleaning, medicines, stores, etc. (I do not say surgical attendance, because the surgeons cannot do more than human endurance permits.) Whatever pleasant accounts there may be in the papers of the North, this is the actual fact. No thorough previous preparation, no system, no foresight, no genius. Always plenty of stores, no doubt, but always miles away; never where they are needed, and never the proper application. Of all harrowing experiences, none is greater than that of the days following a heavy battle. Scores, hundreds, of the noblest young men on earth, uncomplaining, lie helpless, mangled, faint, alone, and so bleed to death, or die from exhaustion, either actually untouched at all, or with merely the laying of them down and leaving them, when there ought to be means provided to save them.

The reader has doubtless inferred the fact that my visits among the wounded and sick have been as an independent missionary, in my own style, and not as an agent of any commission. Several noble women and men of Brooklyn, Boston, Salem, and Providence, have voluntarily supplied funds at times. I only wish they could see a tithe of the actual work performed by their generous and benevolent assistance among the suffering men.

He who goes among the soldiers with gifts, etc., must beware how he proceeds. It is much more of an art than one would imagine. They are not charity-patients, but American young men, of pride and independence. The spirit in which you treat them, and bestow your donations, is just as important as the gifts themselves; sometimes more so. Then there is continual discrimination necessary. Each case requires some peculiar adaptation to itself. It is very important to slight nobody—not a single case. Some hospital visitors, especially the women, pick out the handsomest looking soldiers, or have a few for their pets. Of course some will attract you more than others, and some will need more attention than others; but be careful not to ignore any patient. A word, a friendly turn of the eye or touch of the hand in passing, if nothing more.

One hot day toward the middle of June I gave the inmates of Carver hospital a general ice-cream treat, purchasing a large quantity, and going around personally through the wards to see to its distribution.

Here is a characteristic scene in a ward: It is Sunday afternoon (middle of summer, 1864), hot and oppressive, and very silent through the ward. I am taking care of a critical case, now lying in a half lethargy. Near where I sit is a suffering Rebel from the Eighth Louisiana; his name is Irving. He has been here a long time, badly wounded, and lately had his leg amputated. It is not doing very well. Right opposite me is a sick soldier boy laid down with his clothes on, sleeping, looking much wasted, his pallid face on his arm. I see by the yellow trimming on his jacket that he is a cavalry boy. He looks so handsome as he sleeps, one must needs go nearer to him. I step softly over, and find by his card that he is named William Cone, of the First Maine Cavalry, and his folks live in Skowhegan.

Well, poor John Mahay is dead. He died yesterday. His was a painful and lingering case. I have been with him at times for the past fifteen months. He belonged to Company A, One Hundred and First New York, and was shot through the lower region of the abdomen at second Bull Run, August, 1862. One scene at his bedside will suffice for the agonies of nearly two years. The bladder had been perforated by a bullet going entirely through him. Not long since I sat a good part of the morning by his bedside, Ward E, Armory-square; the water ran out of his eyes from the intense pain, and the muscles of his face were distorted, but he utters nothing except a low groan now and then. Hot moist cloths were applied, and relieved him somewhat.

Poor Mahay, a mere boy in age, but old in misfortune, he never knew the love of parents, was placed in his infancy in one of the New York charitable institutions, and subsequently bound out to a tyrannical master in Sullivan county (the scars of whose cowhide and club remained yet on his back). His wound here was a most disagreeable one, for he was a gentle, cleanly, and affectionate boy. He found friends in his hospital life, and, indeed, was a universal favorite. He had quite a funeral ceremony.

Through Fourteenth street to the river, and then over the long bridge and some three miles beyond, is the huge collection called the convalescent camp. It is a respectable sized army in itself, for these hospitals, tents, sheds, etc., at times contain from five to ten thousand men. Of course there are continual changes. Large squads are sent off to their regiments or elsewhere, and new men received. Sometimes I found large numbers of paroled returned prisoners here. During October, November, and December, 1864, I have visited the military hospitals about New York City, but have not room in this article to describe these visits.

I have lately been (November 25) in the Central-park hospital, near One Hundred and Fourth street; it seems to be a well-managed institution. During September, and previously, went many times to the Brooklyn city hospital, in Raymond street, where I found (taken in by contract) a number of wounded and sick from the army. Most of the men were badly off, and without a cent of money, many wanting tobacco. I supplied them, and a few special cases with delicacies; also repeatedly with letter-paper, stamps, envelopes, etc., writing the addresses myself plainly—(a pleased crowd gathering around me as I directed for each one in turn). This Brooklyn hospital is a bad place for soldiers, or anybody else. Cleanliness, proper nursing, watching, etc., are more deficient than in any hospital I know. For dinner on Sundays I invariably found nothing but rice and molasses. The men all speak well of Drs. Yale and Kissam for kindness, patience, etc., and I think, from what I saw, there are also young medical men. In its management otherwise, this is the poorest hospital I have been in, out of many hundreds.

Among places, apart from soldiers', visited lately (December 7) I must specially mention the great Brooklyn general hospital and other public institutions at Flatbush, including the extensive lunatic asylum, under charge of Drs. Chapin and Reynolds. Of the latter (and I presume I might include these county establishments generally) I have deliberately to put on record about the profoundest satisfaction with professional capacity, completeness of house arrangements to ends required, and the right vital spirit animating all, that I have yet found in any public curative institution among civilians.

In Washington, in camp and everywhere, I was in the habit of reading to the men. They were very fond of it, and liked declamatory, poetical pieces. Miles O'Reilly's pieces were also great favorites. I have had many happy evenings with the men. We would gather in a large group by ourselves, after supper, and spend the time in such readings, or in talking, and occasionally by an amusing game called the game of Twenty Questions.

For nurses, middle-aged women and mothers of families are best. I am compelled to say young ladies, however refined, educated, and benevolent, do not succeed as army nurses, though their motives are noble; neither do the Catholic nuns, among these home-born American young men. Mothers full of motherly feeling, and however illiterate, but bringing reminiscences of home, and with the magnetic touch of hands, are the true women nurses. Many of the wounded are between fifteen and twenty years of age.

I should say that the Government, from my observation, is always full of anxiety and liberality toward the sick and wounded. The system in operation in the permanent hospitals is good, and the money flows without stint. But the details have to be left to hundreds and thousands of subordinates and officials. Among these, laziness, heartlessness, gouging, and incompetency are more or less prevalent. Still, I consider the permanent hospitals, generally, well conducted.

A very large proportion of the wounded come up from the front without a cent of money in their pockets. I soon discovered that it was about the best thing I could do to raise their spirits and show them that somebody cared for them, and practically felt a fatherly or brotherly interest in them, to give them small sums, in such cases, using tact and discretion about it.

A large majority of the wounds are in the arms and legs. But there is every kind of wound in every part of the body. I should say of the sick, from my experience in the hospitals, that the prevailing maladies are typhoid fever and the camp fevers generally, diarrhoea, catarrhal affections and bronchitis, rheumatism and pneumonia. These forms of sickness lead, all the rest follow. There are twice as many sick as there are wounded. The deaths range from six to ten per cent of those under treatment.

I must bear my most emphatic testimony to the zeal, manliness, and professional spirit and capacity generally prevailing among the surgeons, many of them young men, in the hospitals and the army. I will not say much about the exceptions, for they are few (but I have met some of those few, and very foolish and airish they were). I never ceased to find the best young men, and the hardest and most disinterested workers, among these surgeons, in the hospitals. They are full of genius, too. I have seen many hundreds of them, and this is my testimony.

During my two years in the hospitals and upon the field, I have made over six hundred visits, and have been, as I estimate, among from eighty thousand to one hundred thousand of the wounded and sick, as sustainer of spirit and body in some slight degree, in their time of need. These visits varied from an hour or two, to all day or night; for with dear or critical cases I watched all night. Sometimes I took up my quarters in the hospital, and slept or watched there several nights in succession. I may add that I am now just resuming my occupation in the hospitals and camps for the winter of 1864–5, and probably to continue the seasons ensuing.

To many of the wounded and sick, especially the youngsters, there is something in personal love, caresses, and the magnetic flood of sympathy and friendship, that does, in its way, more good than all the medicine in the world. I have spoken of my regular gifts of delicacies, money, tobacco, special articles of food, knick-knacks, etc., etc. But I steadily found more and more that I could help, and turn the balance in favor of cure, by the means here alluded to, in a curiously large proportion of cases. The American soldier is full of affection and the yearning for affection. And it comes wonderfully grateful to him to have this yearning gratified when he is laid up with painful wounds or illness, far away from home, among strangers. Many will think this merely sentimentalism, but I know it is the most solid of facts. I believe that even the moving around among the men, or through the ward, of a hearty, healthy, clean, strong, generous-souled person, man or woman, full of humanity and love, sending out invisible, constant currents thereof, does immense good to the sick and wounded.

To those who might be interested in knowing it, I must add, in conclusion, that I have tried to do justice to all the suffering that fell in my way. While I have been with wounded and sick in thousands of cases from the New England States, and from New York, New Jersey, and Pennsylvania, and from Michigan, Wisconsin, Indiana, Illinois, and the Western States, I have been with more or less from all the States North and South, without exception. I have been with many from the border States, especially from Maryland and Virginia, and found far more Union Southerners than is supposed. I have been with many Rebel officers and men among our wounded, and given them always what I had, and tried to cheer them the same as any. I have been among the army teamsters considerably, and indeed always find myself drawn to them. Among the black soldiers, wounded or sick, and in the contraband camps, I also took my way whenever in their neighborhood, and I did what I could for them.

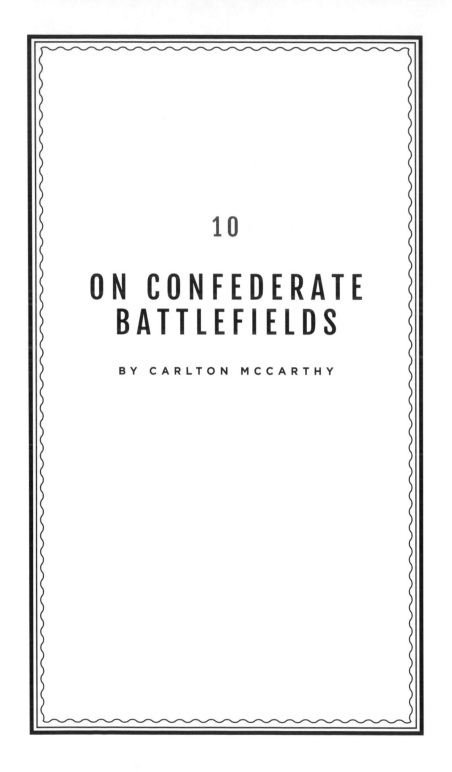

10

ON CONFEDERATE
BATTLEFIELDS

BY CARLTON MCCARTHY

In vivid prose, personal and in great detail, a Confederate soldier describes the marches, the battles, and the agony that followed.

A battle-field, when only a few thousands of men are engaged, is a more extensive area than most persons would suppose. When large bodies of men—twenty to fifty thousand on each side—are engaged, a mounted man, at liberty to gallop from place to place, could scarcely travel the field over during the continuance of the battle; and a private soldier, in the smallest affair, sees very little indeed of the field. What occurs in his own regiment, or probably in his own company, is about all, and is sometimes more than he actually sees or knows. Thus it is that, while the field is extensive, it is to each individual limited to the narrow space of which he is cognizant.

The dense woods of Virginia, often choked with heavy undergrowth, added greatly to the difficulty of observing the movements of large bodies of troops extended in line of battle. The commanders were compelled to rely almost entirely upon the information gained from their staff officers and the couriers of those in immediate command on the lines.

The beasts of burden which travel the Great Desert scent the oasis and the well miles away, and, cheered by the prospect of rest and refreshment, press on with renewed vigor; and in the book of Job it is said of the horse, "He saith among the trumpets, Ha! ha! and he smelleth the battle afar off, the thunder of the captains, and the shoutings." So a soldier, weary and worn, recognizing the signs of approaching battle, did quicken his lagging steps and cry out for joy at the prospect.

The column, hitherto moving forward with the steadiness of a mighty river, hesitates, halts, steps back, then forward, hesitates again, halts. The colonels talk to the brigadier, the brigadiers talk to the major-general, some officers hurry forward and others hurry to the rear. Infantry stands to one side of the road while cavalry trots by to the front. Now some old wagons marked "Ord. Dept." go creaking and rumbling by. One or two light ambulances, with a gay and careless air, seem to trip along with the ease of a dancing-girl. They and the surgeons seem cheerful. Some, not many, ask "What is the matter?" Most of the men there know exactly: they are on the edge of battle.

Presently a very quiet, almost sleepy looking man on horseback, says, "Forward, 19th!" and away goes the leading regiment. A little way ahead the regiment jumps a fence, and—pop! bang! whiz! thud! is all that can be heard, until the rebel yell reverberates through the woods. Battle? No! skirmishers advancing.

Step into the woods now and watch these skirmishers. See how cheerfully they go in. How rapidly they load, fire, and re-load. They stand six and twelve feet apart, calling to each other, laughing, shouting and cheering, but advancing. There: one fellow has dropped his musket like something red hot. His finger is shot away. His friends congratulate him, and he walks sadly away to the rear. Another staggers and falls with a ball through his neck, mortally wounded. Two comrades raise him to his feet and try to lead him away, but one of them receives a ball in his thigh which crushes the bone, and he falls groaning to the ground.

The other advises his poor dying friend to lie down, helps him to do so, and runs to join his advancing comrades. When he overtakes them he finds every man securely posted behind a tree, loading, firing, and conducting himself generally with great deliberation and prudence. They have at last driven the enemy's skirmishers in upon the line of battle, and are waiting. A score of men have fallen here, some killed outright, some slightly, some sorely, and some mortally wounded. The elements now add to the horrors of the hour. Dense clouds hovering near the tree tops add deeper shadows to the woods. Thunder, deep and ominous, rolls in prolonged peals across the sky, and lurid lightning darts among the trees and glistens on the gun barrels. But still they stand.

Now a battery has been hurried into position, the heavy trails have fallen to the ground, and at the command "Commence firing!" the cannoniers have stepped in briskly and loaded. The first gun blazes at the muzzle and away goes a shell. The poor fellows in the woods rejoice as it crashes through the trees over their heads, and cheer when it explodes over the enemy's line. Now, what a chorus! Thunder, gun after gun, shell after shell, musketry, pelting rain, shouts, groans, cheers, and commands!

But help is coming. At the edge of the woods, where the skirmishers entered, the brigade is in line. Somebody has ordered, "Load!"

The ramrods glisten and rattle down the barrels of a thousand muskets. "F-o-o-o or r-r-r-w-a-a-a-r r-r-d!" is the next command, and the brigade disappears in the woods, the canteens rattling, the bushes crackling, and the officers never ceasing to say, "Close up, men; close up! guide c-e-n-t-e-r-r-r-r!"

The men on that skirmish line have at last found it advisable to lie down at full length on the ground, though it is so wet, and place their heads against the trees in front. They cannot advance and they cannot retire without, in either case, exposing themselves to almost certain death. They are waiting for the line of battle to come to their relief.

At last, before they see, they hear the line advancing through the pines. The snapping of the twigs, the neighing of horses, and hoarse commands, inspire a husky cheer, and when the line of the old brigade breaks through the trees in full view, they fairly yell! Every man jumps to his feet, the brigade presses firmly forward, and soon the roll of musketry tells all who are waiting to hear that serious work is progressing away down in the woods. All honor to the devoted infantry. The hour of glory has arrived for couriers, aides-de-camp, and staff officers generally. They dash about from place to place like spirits of unrest. Brigade after brigade and division after division is hurried into line, and pressed forward into action. Battalions of artillery open fire from the crests of many hills, and the battle is begun.

Ammunition trains climb impassable places, cross ditches without bridges, and manage somehow to place themselves in reach of the troops. Ambulances, which an hour before went gayly forward, now slowly and solemnly return loaded. Shells and musket balls which must have lost their way, go flitting about here and there, wounding and killing men who deem themselves far away from danger. The [Black] cooks turn pale as these unexpected visitors enter the camps at the rear, and the rear is "extended" at once.

But our place now is at the front, on the field. We are to watch the details of a small part of the great expanse. As we approach, a ludicrous scene presents itself. A strongarmed artilleryman is energetically thrashing a dejected looking individual with a hickory bush, and urging him to the front. He has managed to keep out of many a fight, but now he *must* go in. The captain has detailed a man to *whip* him in, and the man is doing it. With every blow the poor fellow yells and begs to be spared, but his determined guardian will not cease. They press on, the one screaming and the other lashing, till they reach the battery in position and firing on the retiring enemy. A battery of the enemy is replying, and shells are bursting overhead, or ploughing huge furrows in the ground. Musket balls are "rapping" on the rims of the wheels and sinking with a deep "thud" into the bodies of the poor horses. Smoke obscures the scene, but the cannoniers in faint outline can be seen cheerfully serving the guns.

As the opposing battery ceases firing, and having limbered up, scampers away, and the last of the enemy's infantry slowly sinks into the woods out of sight and out of reach, a wild cheer breaks from the cannoniers, who toss their caps in the air and shout, shake hands and shout again, while the curtain of smoke is raised by the breeze and borne away.

The cavalry is gone. With jingle and clatter they have passed through the lines and down the hill, and are already demanding surrender from many a belated man. There will be no rest for that retreating column. Stuart, with a twinkle in his eye, his lips puckered as if to whistle a merry lay, is on their flanks, in their rear, and in their front. The enemy will send their cavalry after him, of course, but he will stay with them, nevertheless.

Add now the stream of wounded men slowly making their way to the rear; the groups of dejected prisoners plodding along under guard, and you have about as much of a battle as one private soldier ever sees.

But after the battle, man will tell to man what each has seen and felt, until every man will feel that he has seen the whole. Hear, then, the stories of battle.

An artilleryman—he must have been a driver—says: when the firing had ceased an old battery horse, his lower jaw carried away by a shot, with blood streaming from his wound, staggered up to him, gazed beseechingly at him, and, groaning piteously, laid his bloody jaws on his shoulder, and so made his appeal for sympathy. He was beyond help.

The pathetic nature of this story reminds a comrade that a new man in the battery, desiring to save the labor incident to running up the gun after the rebound, determined to hold on to the handspike, press the trail into the ground, and hold her fast. He did try, but the rebound proceeded as usual, and the labor-saving man was "shocked" at the failure of his effort. Nothing daunted, the same individual soon after applied his lips to the vent of the gun, which was choked, and endeavored to clear it by an energetic blast from his lungs. The vent was not cleared but the lips of the recruit were nicely browned, and the detachment greatly amused.

At another gun it has happened that No. 1 and No. 3 have had a difficulty. No. 3 having failed to serve the vent, there was a premature explosion, and No. 1, being about to withdraw the rammer, fell heavily to the ground, apparently dead. No. 3, seeing what a calamity he had caused, hung over the dead man and begged him to speak and exonerate him from blame. After No. 3 had exhausted all his eloquence and pathos, No. 1 suddenly rose to his feet and informed him that the premature explosion was a fact, but the death of No. 1 was a joke intended to warn him that if he ever failed again to serve that vent, he would have his head broken by a blow from a rammer-head. This joke having been completed in all its details, the firing was continued.

Another man tells how Eggleston had his arm torn away by a solid shot, and, as he walked away, held up the bleeding, quivering stump, exclaiming, "Never mind, boys; I'll come back soon and try 'em with this other one." Alas! poor fellow, he had fought his last fight.

Poor Tom, he who was always, as he said, "willing to give 'em half a leg, or so," was struck about the waist by a shot which almost cut him in two. He fell heavily to the ground, and, though in awful agony, managed to say: "Tell mother I died doing my duty." While the fight lasted, several of the best and bravest received wounds apparently mortal, and were laid aside covered by an old army blanket. They refused to die, however, and remain to this day to tell their own stories of the war and of their marvelous recovery.

At the battle of the Wilderness, May, 1864, a man from North Carolina precipitated a severe fight by asking a very simple and reasonable question. The line of battle had been pressed forward and was in close proximity to the enemy. The thick and tangled undergrowth prevented a sight of the enemy, but every man felt he was near. Everything was hushed and still. No one dared to speak above a whisper. It was evening, and growing dark. As the men lay on the ground, keenly sensible to every sound, and anxiously waiting, they heard the firm tread of a man walking along the line. As he walked they heard also the jingle-jangle of a pile of canteens hung around his neck. He advanced with deliberate mien to within a few yards of the line and opened a terrific fight by quietly saying, "Can any you fellows tell a man whar he can git some water?" Instantly the thicket was illumined by the flash of a thousand muskets, the men leaped to their feet, the officers shouted, and the battle was begun. Neither side would yield, and there they fought till many died.

Soon, however, the reserve brigade began to make its way through the thicket. The first man to appear was the brigadier, thirty yards ahead of his brigade, his sword between his teeth, and parting the bushes with both hands as he spurred his horse through the tangled growth. Eager for the fight, his eyes glaring and his countenance lit up with fury, his first word was "Forward!" and forward went the line.

On the march from Petersburg to Appomattox, after a sharp engagement, some men of Cutshaw's artillery battalion, acting as infantry, made a stand for a while on a piece of high ground. They noticed, hanging around in a lonely, distracted way, a tall, lean, shaggy fellow holding, or rather leaning on, a long staff, around which hung a faded battle-flag. Thinking him out of his place and skulking, they suggested to him that it would be well for him to join his regiment. He replied that his regiment had all run away, and he was merely waiting a chance to be useful. Just then the enemy's advancing skirmishers poured a hot fire into the group, and the artillerymen began to discuss the propriety of leaving. The color-bearer, remembering their insinuations, saw an opportunity for retaliation. Standing, as he was, in the midst of a shower of musket balls, he seemed almost ready to fall asleep. But suddenly his face was illumined with a singularly pleased and childish smile. Quietly walking up close to the group, he said, "Any you boys want to *charge*?" The boys answered, "Yes." "Well," said the imperturbable, "I'm the man to carry this here old flag for you. Just follow me." So saying he led the squad full into the face of the advancing enemy, and never once seemed to think of stopping until he was urged to retire with the squad. He came back smiling from head to foot, and suffered no more insinuations.

At Gettysburg, when the artillery fire was at its height, a brawny fellow, who seemed happy at the prospect for a hot time, broke out singing:

> *Backward, roll backward,*
> *O Time in thy flight:*
> *Make me a child again,*
> *just for this fight!*

Another fellow near him replied, "Yes; and a *gal* child at that."

At Fredericksburg a good soldier, now a farmer in Chesterfield County, Virginia, was desperately wounded and lay on the field all night. In the morning a surgeon approached him and inquired the nature of his wound. Finding a wound which is always considered fatal, he advised the man to remain quietly where he was and die. The man insisted on being removed to a hospital, saying in the most emphatic manner, that though every man ever wounded as he was (his bowels were punctured by the ball) had died, he was determined not to die. The surgeon, struck by the man's courage and nerve, consented to remove him, advising him, however, not to cherish the hope of recovery. After a hard struggle he did recover, and is to-day a living example of the power of a determined will.

At the Wilderness, when the fight was raging in the tangled woods and a man could scarcely trust himself to move in any direction for fear of going astray or running into the hands of the enemy, a mere boy was wounded. Rushing out of the woods, his eyes staring and his face pale with fright, he shouted, "Where's the rear. Mister! I say, Mister! where's the rear?" Of course he was laughed at. The very grim fact that there was no "rear," in the sense of safety, made the question irresistibly ludicrous. The conduct of this boy was not exceptional. It was no uncommon thing to see the best men badly demoralized and eager to go to the rear because of a wound scarcely worthy of the name. On the other hand, it sometimes happened that men seriously wounded could not be convinced of their danger, and remained on the field.

The day General Stuart fell, mortally wounded, there was a severe fight in the woods not far from the old Brook Church, a few miles from Richmond; the enemy was making a determined stand, in order to gain time to repair a bridge which they were compelled to use, and the Confederate infantry skirmishers were pushing them hard. The fighting was stubborn and the casualties on the Confederate side very numerous. In the midst of the fight a voice was heard shouting, "Where's my boy? I'm looking for my boy!" Soon the owner of the voice appeared, tall, slim, aged, with silver gray hair, dressed in a full suit of broadcloth. A tall silk hat and a clerical collar and cravat completed his attire. His voice, familiar to the people of Virginia, was deep and powerful. As he continued to shout, the men replied, "Go back, old gentleman; you'll get hurt here. Go back; go back!"

"No, no," said he. "I can go anywhere my boy has to go, and the Lord is here. I want to see my boy, and I will see him!" Then the order, "Forward!" was given and the men made once more for the enemy. The old gentleman, his beaver in one hand, a big stick in the other, his long hair flying, shouting, "Come on, boys!" disappeared in the depths of the woods, well in front. He was a Methodist minister, an old member of the Virginia Conference, but his carriage that day was soldierly and grand. One thought—that his boy was there—made the old man feel that he might brave the danger, too. No man who saw him there will ever forget the parson who led the charge at Brook Church.

At the battle of Spottsylvania Court House, a gun in position somewhat in advance of the line was so much exposed to the enemy's fire that it was abandoned. Later in the day the battery being ordered to move, the captain directed the sergeant to take his detachment and bring in the gun. The sergeant and his gunner, with a number of men, went out to bring in the gun by hand. Two men lifted the trail and the sergeant ordered, "All together!" The gun moved, but moved *in a circle*. The fire was hot, and *all hands were on the same side*—the side farthest from the enemy! After some persuasion the corporal and the sergeant managed to induce a man or two to get on the other side, with them, and they were moving along very comfortably when a shrapnel whacked the sergeant on his breast, breaking his ribs and tearing away the muscle of one arm. He fell into the arms of the corporal. Seeing that their only hope of escaping from this fire was work, the cannoniers bent to the wheels, and the gun rolled slowly to shelter.

It was at Spottsylvania Court House that the Federal infantry rushed over the works, and, engaging in a hand-to-hand fight, drove out the Confederate infantry. On one part of the line the artillerymen stood to their posts, and when the Federal troops passing the works had massed themselves inside, fired to the right and left, up and down the lines, cutting roadways through the compact masses of men, and holding their positions until the Confederate infantry reformed, drove out the enemy and re-occupied the line. Several batteries were completely overrun, and the cannoniers sought and found safety in front of the works, whence the enemy had made their charge.

At another point on the lines, where there was no infantry support, the enemy charged repeatedly and made every effort to carry the works, but were handsomely repulsed by artillery alone. An examination of the ground in front of the works after the fight, disclosed the fact that all the dead and wounded were victims of artillery fire. The dead were literally torn to pieces, and the wounded dreadfully mangled. Scarcely a man was hurt on the Confederate side.

At Fort Harrison, a few miles below Richmond, in 1864, a ludicrous scene resulted from the firing of a salute with shotted guns. Federal artillery occupied the fort, and the lines immediately in front of it were held by the "Department Battalion," composed of the clerks in the various government offices in Richmond, who had been ordered out to meet an emergency. Just before sundown the detail for picket duty was formed, and about to march out to the picket line, the clerks presenting quite a soldierly appearance. Suddenly bang! went a gun in the fort, and a shell came tearing over. Bang! again, and bang! bang! and more shells exploding. Pow! pow! what consternation! In an instant the beautiful line melted away as by magic. Every man took to shelter, and the place was desolate. The firing was rapid, regular, and apparently aimed to strike the Confederate lines, but ceased as suddenly as it had begun.

General Custis Lee, whose tent was near by, observing the panic, stepped quietly up to the parapet of the works, folded his arms, and walked back and forth without uttering a word or looking to the right or to the left. His cool behavior, coupled with the silence of the guns, soon reassured the trembling clerks, and one by one they dropped into line again. General Butler had heard some news that pleased him, and ordered a salute with shotted guns. That was all.

Two boys who had volunteered for service with the militia in the same neighborhood, were detailed for picket duty. It was the custom to put three men on each post, two militia boys and one veteran. The boys and an old soldier of Johnston's division were marched to their post, where they found, ready dug, a pit about five feet deep and three feet wide. It was quite dark, and the boys, realizing fully their exposed position, at once occupied the pit. The old soldier saw he had an opportunity to have a good time, knowing that those boys would keep wide awake. Giving them a short lecture about the importance of great watchfulness, he warned them to be ready to leave there very rapidly at any moment, and, above all, to keep very quiet. His words were wasted, as the boys would not have closed their eyes or uttered a word for the world. These little details arranged, the cunning old soldier prepared to make himself comfortable. First he gathered a few small twigs and made a *very small* fire. On the fire he put a battered old tin cup. Into this he poured some coffee from his canteen. From some mysterious place in his clothes he drew forth sugar and dropped it into the cup. Next, from an old worn haversack, he took a "chunk" of raw bacon and a "pone" of corn bread. Then, drawing a large pocket knife, in a dexterous manner he sliced and ate his bread and meat, occasionally sipping his coffee. His evening meal leisurely completed, he filled his pipe, smoked, and stirred up the imaginations of the boys by telling how dangerous a duty they were performing; told them how easy it would be for the Yankees to creep up and shoot them or capture and carry them off. Having finished his smoke, he knocked out the ashes and dropped the pipe in his pocket. Then he actually unrolled his blanket and oil-cloth. It made the perspiration start on the brows of the boys to see the man's folly. Then taking off his shoes, he laid down on one edge, took hold of the blanket and oil-cloth, rolled himself over to the other side, and with a kind "good night" to the boys, began to snore. The poor boys stood like statues in the pit till broad day. In the morning the old soldier thanked them for not disturbing him, and quietly proceeded to prepare his breakfast.

After the fight at Fisher's Hill, in 1864, Early's army, in full retreat and greatly demoralized, was strung out along the valley pike. The Federal cavalry was darting around picking up prisoners, shooting drivers, and making themselves generally disagreeable. It happened that an artilleryman, who was separated from his gun, was making pretty good time on foot, getting to the rear, and had the appearance of a demoralized infantryman who had thrown away his musket. So one of these lively cavalrymen trotted up, and, waving his sabre, told the artilleryman to "surrender!" But he didn't stop. He merely glanced over his shoulder, and kept on. Then the cavalryman became indignant and shouted, "Halt, d—n you; halt!" And still he would not. "Halt," said the cavalryman, "halt, you d—n s— of a ——; halt!" Then the artilleryman halted, and remarking that he didn't allow any man to speak to him that way, seized a huge stick, turned on the cavalryman, knocked him out of his saddle, and proceeded on his journey to the rear.

This artilleryman fought with a musket at Sailor's Creek. He found himself surrounded by the enemy, who demanded surrender. He refused; said they must take him; and laid about him with the butt of his musket till he had damaged some of the party considerably. He was, however, overpowered and made a prisoner.

Experienced men, in battle, always availed themselves of any shelter within reach. A tree, a fence, a mound of earth, a ditch, anything. Sometimes their efforts to find shelter were very amusing and even silly. Men lying on the ground have been seen to put an old canteen before their heads as a shelter from musket balls; and during a heavy fire of artillery, seemed to feel safer under a tent. Only recruits and fools neglected the smallest shelter. The more experienced troops knew better when to give up than green ones, and never fought well after they were satisfied that they could not accomplish their purpose. Consequently it often happened that the best troops failed where the raw ones did well. The old Confederate soldier would decide some questions for himself. To the last he maintained the right of private judgment, and especially on the field of battle.

11

LOVE, LOSS, AND ARMY LIFE OF THE COMMON SOLDIER

BY LEANDER STILLWELL

In the ranks of the Union Army, pain and drama sometimes went beyond the battlefields.

Soon after our occupation of Corinth a change in the position of our forces took place, and all the command at Owl creek was transferred to Bethel, a small station on the Mobile and Ohio railroad, some twenty or twenty-five miles to the northwest. We left Owl creek on the morning of June 6th, and arrived at Bethel about dark the same evening. Thanks to my repeated long walks in the woods outside of our lines, I was in pretty fair health at this time, but still somewhat weak and shaky.

On the morning we took up the line of march, while waiting for the "fall in" call, I was seated at the foot of a big tree in camp, with my knapsack, packed, at my side. Enoch Wallace came to me and said: "Stillwell, are you going to try to carry your knapsack?" I answered that I reckoned I had to, that I had asked Hen. King (our company teamster) to let me put it in his wagon, and he wouldn't—said he already had too big a load. Enoch said nothing more, but stood silently looking down at me a few seconds, then picked up my knapsack and threw it into our wagon, which was close by, saying to King, as he did so, "Haul that knapsack"—and it was hauled.

I shall never forget this act of kindness on the part of Enoch. It would have been impossible for me to have made the march carrying the knapsack. The day was hot, and much of the road was over sandy land, and through long stretches of black-jack barrens, that excluded every breath of a breeze. The men suffered much on the march, and fell out by scores. When we stacked arms at Bethel that evening, there were only four men of Co. D in line, just enough to make one stack of guns, but my gun was in the stack.

There was no earthly necessity for making this march in one day. We were simply "changing stations;" the Confederate army of that region was down in Mississippi, a hundred miles or so away, and there were no armed foes in our vicinity excepting some skulking bands of guerrillas. Prior to this our regiment had made no marches, except little short movements during the siege of Corinth, none of which exceeded two or three miles. And nearly all the men were weak and debilitated by reason of the prevailing type of illness, and in no condition whatever to be cracked through twenty miles or more on a hot day.

We should have marched only about ten miles the first day, with a halt of about ten minutes every hour, to let the men rest a little, and get their wind. Had that course been pursued, we would have reached our destination in good shape, with the ranks full, and the men would have been benefited by the march. As it was, it probably caused the death of some, and the permanent disabling of more. The trouble at that time was the total want of experience on the part of the most of our officers of all grades, combined with an amazing lack of common sense by some of high authority. I am not blaming any of our regimental officers for this foolish "forced march"—for it amounted to that—the responsibility rested higher up.

Our stay at Bethel was brief and uneventful. However, I shall always remember the place on account of a piece of news that came to me while we were there, and which for a time nearly broke me all up. It will be necessary to go back some years in order to explain it. I began attending the old Stone school house at Otter creek when I was about eight years old. One of my schoolmates was a remarkably pretty little girl, with blue eyes and auburn hair, nearly my own age. We kept about the same place in our studies, and were generally in the same classes. I always liked her, and by the time I was about fifteen years old was head over heels in love. She was far above me in the social scale of the neighborhood.

Her folks lived in a frame house on "the other side of the creek," and were well-to-do, for that time and locality. My people lived in a log cabin, on a little farm in the broken country that extended from the south bank of Otter creek to the Mississippi and Illinois rivers. But notwithstanding the difference in our respective social and financial positions, I knew that she had a liking for me, and our mutual relations became quite "tender" and interesting. Then the war came along, I enlisted and went South.

We had no correspondence after I left home; I was just too deplorably bashful to attempt it, and, on general principles, didn't have sense enough to properly carry on a proceeding of that nature. It may be that here was where I fell down. But I thought about her every day, and had many boyish day dreams of the future, in which she was the prominent figure. Soon after our arrival at Bethel I received a letter from home. I hurriedly opened it, anxious, as usual, to hear from the folks, and sitting down at the foot of a tree, began reading it. All went well to nearly the close, when I read these fatal words:

"Billy Crane and Lucy Archer got married last week."

The above names are fictitious, but the bride was my girl.

I can't explain my feelings—if you ever have had such an experience, you will understand. I stole a hurried glance around to see if anybody was observing my demeanor, then thrust the letter into my jacket pocket, and walked away. Not far from our camp was a stretch of swampy land, thickly set with big cypress trees, and I bent my steps in that direction. Entering the forest, I sought a secluded spot, sat down on an old log, and read and re-read that heart-breaking piece of intelligence. There was no mistaking the words; they were plain, laconic, and nothing ambiguous about them. And, to intensify the bitterness of the draught, it may be set down here that the groom was a dudish young squirt, a clerk in a country store, who lacked the pluck to go for a soldier, but had stayed at home to count eggs and measure calico. In my opinion, he was not worthy of the girl, and I was amazed that she had taken him for a husband.

I remember well some of my thoughts as I sat with bitterness in my heart, alone among those gloomy cypresses. I wanted a great big battle to come off at once, with the 61st Illinois right in front, that we might run out of cartridges, and the order would be given to fix bayonets and charge! Like Major Simon Suggs, in depicting the horrors of an apprehended Indian war, I wanted to see blood flow in a "great gulgin' torrent, like the Tallapoosa river." Well, it was simply a case of pure, intensely ardent boy-love, and I was hit, hard, but survived. And I now heartily congratulate myself on the fact that this youthful shipwreck ultimately resulted in my obtaining for a wife the very best woman (excepting only my mother) that I ever knew in my life.

I never again met my youthful flame, to speak to her, and saw her only once, and then at a distance, some years after the close of the war when I was back in Illinois on a visit to my parents. Several years ago her husband died, and in course of time she married again, this time a man I never knew, and the last I heard of or concerning her, she and her second husband were living somewhere in one of the Rocky Mountain States.

★   ★   ★

On this march I was a participant in an incident which was somewhat amusing, and also a little bit irritating. Shortly before noon of the first day, Jack Medford, of my company, and myself, concluded we would "straggle," and try to get a country dinner. Availing ourselves of the first favorable opportunity, we slipped from the ranks, and struck out. We followed an old country road that ran substantially parallel to the main road on which the column was marching, and soon came to a nice looking old log house standing in a grove of big native trees. The only people at the house were two middle-aged women and some children. We asked the women if we could have some dinner, saying that we would pay for it. They gave an affirmative answer, but their tone was not cordial and they looked "daggers." Dinner was just about prepared, and when all was ready, we were invited, with evident coolness, to take seats at the table. We had a splendid meal, consisting of corn bread, new Irish potatoes, boiled bacon and greens, butter and buttermilk. Compared with sow-belly and hardtack, it was a feast. Dinner over, we essayed to pay therefor. Their charge was something less than a dollar for both of us, but we had not the exact change. The smallest denomination of money either of us had was a dollar greenback, and the women said that they had no money at all to make change. Thereupon we proffered them the entire dollar. They looked at it askance, and asked if we had any "Southern" or Confederate money.

We said we had not, that this was the only kind of money we had. They continued to look exceedingly sour, and finally remarked that they were unwilling to accept any kind of money except "Southern." We urged them to accept the bill, told them it was United States money, and that it would pass readily in any place in the South occupied by our soldiers; but no, they were obdurate, and declined the greenback with unmistakable scorn. Of course we kept our temper; it never would have done to be saucy or rude after getting such a good dinner, but, for my part, I felt considerably vexed. But there was nothing left to do except thank them heartily for their kindness and depart.

From their standpoint their course in the matter was actuated by the highest and most unselfish patriotism, but naturally we couldn't look at it in that light. I will say here, "with malice towards none, and with charity for all," that in my entire sojourn in the South during the war, the women were found to be more intensely bitter and malignant against the old government of the United States, and the national cause in general, than were the men. Their attitude is probably another illustration of the truth of Kipling's saying, "The female of the species is more deadly than the male."

This probably is a fitting place for something to be said about our method of traveling by rail during the Civil war, as compared with the conditions of the present day in that regard. At the time I am now writing, about fifteen thousand United States soldiers have recently been transported on the cars from different places in the interior of the country, to various points adjacent to the Mexican border, for the purpose of protecting American interests. And it seems that in some cases the soldiers were carried in ordinary passenger coaches. Thereupon bitter complaints were made on behalf of such soldiers because Pullman sleepers were not used! And these complaints were effective, too, for, according to the press reports of the time, the use of passenger coaches for such purposes was summarily stopped and Pullmans were hurriedly concentrated at the places needed, and the soldiers went to war in them. Well, in our time, the old regiment was hauled over the country many times on trains, the extent of our travels in that manner aggregating hundreds and hundreds of miles. And such a thing as even ordinary passenger coaches for the use of the enlisted men was never heard of. And I have no recollection now that (during the war) any were provided for the use of the commissioned officers, either, unless they were of pretty high rank.

The cars that we rode in were the box or freight cars in use in those days. Among them were cattle cars, flat or platform cars, and in general every other kind of freight car that could be procured. We would fill the box cars, and in addition clamber upon the roofs thereof and avail ourselves of every foot of space. And usually there was a bunch on the cow-catchers. The engines used wood for fuel; the screens of the smoke-stacks must have been very coarse, or maybe they had none at all, and the big cinders would patter down on us like hail. So, when we came to the journey's end, by reason of the cinders and soot we were about as dirty and black as any regiment of sure-enough colored troops that fought under the Union flag in the last years of the war.

When the regiment was sent home in September, 1865, some months after the war was over, the enlisted men made even that trip in our old friends, the box cars. It is true that on this occasion there was a passenger coach for the use of the commissioned officers, and that is the only time that I ever saw such a coach attached to a train on which the regiment was taken anywhere. Now, don't misunderstand me. I am not kicking because, more than half a century after the close of the Civil War, Uncle Sam sent his soldier boys to the front in Pullmans. The force so sent was small and the government could well afford to do it, and it was right. I just want you to know that in my time, when we rode, it was in any kind of an old freight car, and we were awful glad to get that. And now on this matter, "The words of Job are ended."

On the afternoon of December 18th, suddenly, without any pre-vious warning or notification, the bugle sounded "Fall in!" and all the regiment fit for duty and not on guard at once formed on the regimental parade ground. From there we marched to the depot, and with the 43rd Illinois of our brigade got on the cars, and were soon being whirled over the road in a northerly direction. It was a warm, sunshiny day, and we common soldiers supposed we were going on just some little temporary scout, so we encumbered ourselves with nothing but our arms, and haversacks, and canteens. Neglecting to take our blankets was a grievous mistake, as later we found out to our sorrow. We arrived at Jackson a little before sundown, there left the cars, and, with the 43rd, forthwith marched out about two miles east of town.

A little after dark we halted in an old field on the left of the road, in front of a little old country graveyard called Salem Cemetery, and there bivouacked for the night. Along in the evening the weather turned intensely cold. It was a clear, star-lit night, and the stars glittered in the heavens like little icicles. We were strictly forbidden to build any fires, for the reason, as our officers truly said, the Confederates were not more than half a mile away, right in our front. As before stated, we had no blankets, and how we suffered with the cold! I shall never forget that night of December 18th, 1862. We would form little columns of twenty or thirty men, in two ranks, and would just trot round and round in the tall weeds and broom sedge to keep from chilling to death. Sometimes we would pile down on the ground in great bunches, and curl up close together like hogs, in our efforts to keep warm. But some part of our bodies would be exposed, which soon would be stinging with cold, then up we would get and renew the trotting process.

At one time in the night some of the boys, rendered almost desperate by their suffering started to build a fire with some fence rails. The red flames began to curl around the wood, and I started for the fire, intending to absorb some of that glowing heat, if, as Uncle Remus says, "it wuz de las' ack." But right then a mounted officer dashed up to the spot, and sprang from his horse. He was wearing big cavalry boots, and jumped on that fire with both feet and stamped it out in less time than I am taking to tell about it. I heard afterwards that he was Col. Engelmann, of the 43rd Illinois, then the commander of our brigade.

Having put out the fire, he turned on the men standing around, and swore at them furiously. He said that the rebels were right out in our front, and in less than five minutes after we had betrayed our presence by fires, they would open on us with artillery, and "shell hell out of us"—and more to the same effect. The boys listened in silence, meek as lambs, and no more fires were started by us that night. But the hours seemed interminably long, and it looked like the night would never come to an end.

At last some little woods birds were heard, faintly chirping in the weeds and underbrush near by, then some owls set up a hooting in the woods behind us, and I knew that dawn was approaching. When it became light enough to distinguish one another, we saw that we presented a doleful appearance—all hollow-eyed, with blue noses, pinched faces, and shivering as if we would shake to pieces. Permission was then given to build small fires to cook our breakfast, and we didn't wait for the order to be repeated. I made a quart canful of strong, hot coffee, toasted some bacon on a stick, and then, with some hardtack, had a good breakfast and felt better.

Christmas Day in the year eighteen hundred and sixty-two was a gloomy one, in every respect, for the soldiers of the Union army in West Tennessee. Five days before, the Confederate General Van Dorn had captured Grant's depot of supplies at Holly Springs, and government stores of the value of a million and a half of dollars had gone up in smoke and flame. About the same time Forrest had struck the Mobile and Ohio railroad, on which we depended to bring us from the north our supplies of hardtack and bacon, and had made a wreck of the road from about Jackson, Tennessee, nearly to Columbus, Kentucky.

For some months previous to these disasters the regiment to which I belonged, the 61st Illinois Infantry, had been stationed at Bolivar, Tennessee, engaged in guarding the railroad from that place to Toone's Station, a few miles north of Bolivar. On December 18, with another regiment of our brigade, we were sent by rail to Jackson to assist in repelling Forrest, who was threatening that place. On the following day the two regiments, numbering in the aggregate about 500 men, in connection with a small detachment of our cavalry, had a lively and spirited little brush with the Confederate forces about two miles east of Jackson, near a country burying ground called Salem Cemetery, which resulted in our having the good fortune to give them a salutary check.

Reinforcements were sent out from Jackson, and Forrest disappeared. The next day our entire command marched about fifteen miles eastwardly in the direction of the Tennessee river. It was doubtless supposed by our commanding general that the Confederates had retreated in that direction, but he was mistaken. Forrest had simply whipped around Jackson, struck the railroad a few miles north thereof, and then had continued north up the road, capturing and destroying as he went. On the succeeding day, December 21st, we all marched back to Jackson, and my regiment went into camp on a bleak, muddy hillside in the suburbs of the town, and there we remained until December 29th, when we were sent to Carroll Station, about eight miles north of Jackson.

I well remember how gloomy I felt on the morning of that Christmas Day at Jackson, Tennessee. I was then only a little over nineteen years of age. I had been in the army nearly a year, lacking just a few days, and every day of that time, except a furlough of two days granted at our camp of instruction before we left Illinois for the front, had been passed with the regiment in camp and field.

Christmas morning my thoughts naturally turned to the little old log cabin in the backwoods of western Illinois, and I couldn't help thinking about the nice Christmas dinner that I knew the folks at home would sit down to on that day.

There would be a great chicken pot pie, with its savory crust and a superabundance of light, puffy dumplings; delicious light, hot biscuits; a big ball of our own home-made butter, yellow as gold;

broad slices of juicy ham, the product of hogs of our own fattening, and home cured with hickory-wood smoke; fresh eggs from the barn in reckless profusion, fried in the ham gravy; mealy Irish potatoes, baked in their jackets; coffee with cream about half an inch thick; apple butter and crab apple preserves; a big plate of wild honey in the comb; and winding up with a thick wedge of mince pie that mother knew so well how to make—such mince pie, in fact, as was made only in those days, and is now as extinct as the dodo.

And when I turned from these musings upon the bill of fare they would have at home to contemplate the dreary realities of my own possible dinner for the day—my oyster can full of coffee and a quarter ration of hardtack and sow-belly comprised the menu. If the eyes of some old soldier should light upon these lines, and he should thereupon feel disposed to curl his lip with unutterable scorn and say: "This fellow was a milksop and ought to have been fed on Christian Commission and Sanitary goods, and put to sleep at night with a warm rock at his feet"—I can only say in extenuation that the soldier whose feelings I have been trying to describe was only a boy—and, boys, you probably know how it was yourselves during the first year of your army life. But, after all, the soldier had a Christmas dinner that day, and it is of that I have started out to speak.

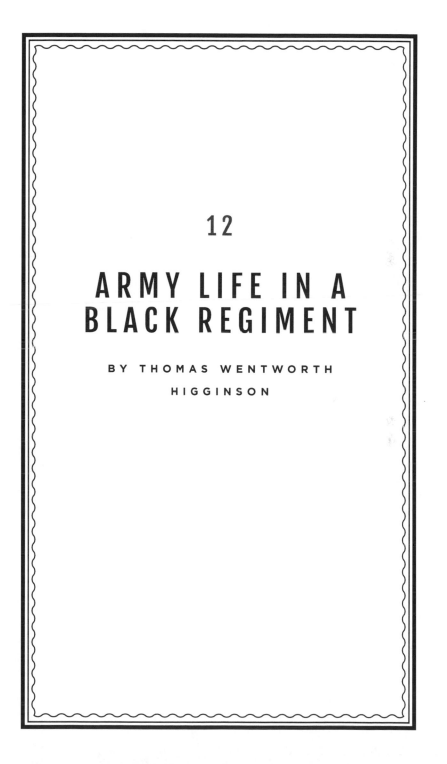

12

ARMY LIFE IN A BLACK REGIMENT

BY THOMAS WENTWORTH HIGGINSON

Once they were slaves; now they are soldiers—armed and ready to fight.

The Edisto expedition cost me the health and strength of several years. I could say, long after, in the words of one of the men, "I'se been a sickly person, eber since de expeditious." Justice to a strong constitution and good habits compels me, however, to say that, up to the time of my injury, I was almost the only officer in the regiment who had not once been off duty from illness. But at last I had to yield, and went North for a month. We heard much said, during the war, of wounded officers who stayed unreasonably long at home. I think there were more instances of those who went back too soon. Such at least was my case. On returning to the regiment I found a great accumulation of unfinished business; every member of the field and staff was prostrated by illness or absent on detailed service; two companies had been sent to Hilton Head on fatigue duty, and kept there unexpectedly long: and there was a visible demoralization among the rest, especially from the fact that their pay had just been cut down, in violation of the express pledges of the government. A few weeks of steady sway made all right again; and during those weeks I felt a perfect exhilaration of health, followed by a month or two of complete prostration, when the work was done. This passing, I returned to duty, buoyed up by the fallacious hope that the winter months would set me right again.

We had a new camp on Port Royal Island, very pleasantly situated, just out of Beaufort. It stretched nearly to the edge of a shelving bluff, fringed with pines and overlooking the river; below the bluff was a hard, narrow beach, where one might gallop a mile and bathe at the farther end. We could look up and down the curving stream, and watch the few vessels that came and went. Our first encampment had been lower down that same river, and we felt at home.

The new camp was named Camp Shaw, in honor of the noble young officer who had lately fallen at Fort Wagner, under circumstances which had endeared him to all the men. As it happened, they had never seen him, nor was my regiment ever placed within immediate reach of the Fifty-Fourth Massachusetts. This I always regretted, feeling very desirous to compare the military qualities of the Northern and Southern blacks. As it was, the Southern regiments with which the Massachusetts troops were brigaded were hardly a fair specimen of their kind, having been raised chiefly by drafting, and, for this and other causes, being afflicted with perpetual discontent and desertion.

We had, of course, looked forward with great interest to the arrival of these new colored regiments, and I had ridden in from the picket-station to see the Fifty-Fourth. Apart from the peculiarity of its material, it was fresh from my own State, and I had relatives and acquaintances among its officers. Governor Andrew, who had formed it, was an old friend, and had begged me, on departure from Massachusetts, to keep him informed as to our experiment. I had good reason to believe that my reports had helped to prepare the way for this new battalion, and I had sent him, at his request, some hints as to its formation. In the streets of Beaufort I had met Colonel Shaw, riding with his lieutenant-colonel and successor, Edward Hallowell, and had gone back with them to share their first meal in camp. I should have known Shaw anywhere by his resemblance to his kindred, nor did it take long to perceive that he shared their habitual truthfulness and courage. Moreover, he and Hallowell had already got beyond the commonplaces of inexperience, in regard to colored troops, and, for a wonder, asked only sensible questions. For instance, he admitted the mere matter of courage to be settled, as regarded the colored troops, and his whole solicitude bore on this point, Would they do as well in line-of-battle as they had already done in more irregular service, and on picket and guard duty? Of this I had, of course, no doubt, nor, I think, had he; though I remember his saying something about the possibility of putting them between two fires in case of need, and so cutting off their retreat. I should never have thought of such a project, but I could not have expected him to trust them as I did, until he had been actually under fire with them. That, doubtless, removed all his anxieties, if he really had any.

This interview had occurred on the 4th of June. Shaw and his regiment had very soon been ordered to Georgia, then to Morris Island; Fort Wagner had been assaulted, and he had been killed. Most of the men knew about the circumstances of his death, and many of them had subscribed towards a monument for him—a project which originated with General Saxton, and which was finally embodied in the "Shaw School-house" at Charleston. So it gave us all pleasure to name this camp for him, as its predecessor had been named for General Saxton.

The new camp was soon brought into good order. The men had great ingenuity in building screens and shelters of light poles, filled in with the gray moss from the live-oaks. The officers had vestibules built in this way, before all their tents; the cooking-places were walled round in the same fashion; and some of the wide company-streets had sheltered sidewalks down the whole line of tents. The sergeant on duty at the entrance of the camp had a similar bower, and the architecture culminated in a "Praise-House" for school and prayer-meetings, some thirty feet in diameter. As for chimneys and flooring, they were provided with that magic and invisible facility which marks the second year of a regiment's life.

★　★　★

Then the duties of inspection and drill, suspended during active service, resume their importance with a month or two of quiet. It really costs unceasing labor to keep a regiment in perfect condition and ready for service. The work is made up of minute and endless details, like a bird's pruning her feathers or a cat's licking her kittens into their proper toilet. Here are eight hundred men, every one of whom, every Sunday morning at farthest, must be perfectly *soigné* in all personal proprieties; he must exhibit himself provided with every article of clothing, buttons, shoe-strings, hooks and eyes, company letter, regimental number, rifle, bayonet, bayonet-scabbard, cap-pouch, cartridge-box, cartridge-box belt, cartridge-box belt-plate, gun-sling, canteen, haversack, knapsack, packed according to rule, forty cartridges, forty percussion caps; and every one of these articles polished to the highest brightness or blackness as the case may be, and moreover hung or slung or tied or carried in precisely the correct manner.

The men had that year a Christmas present which they enjoyed to the utmost—furnishing the detail, every other day, for provost-guard duty in Beaufort. It was the only military service which they had ever shared within the town, and it moreover gave a sense of self-respect to be keeping the peace of their own streets. I enjoyed seeing them put on duty those mornings; there was such a twinkle of delight in their eyes, though their features were immovable. As the "reliefs" went round, posting the guard, under charge of a corporal, one could watch the black sentinels successively dropped and the whites picked up—gradually changing the complexion, like Lord Somebody's black stockings which became white stockings—till at last there was only a squad of white soldiers obeying the "Support Arms! Forward, March!" of a black corporal.

Then, when once posted, they glorified their office, you may be sure. Discipline had grown rather free-and-easy in the town about that time, and it is said that the guardhouse never was so full within human memory as after their first tour of duty. I remember hearing that one young reprobate, son of a leading Northern philanthropist in those parts, was much aggrieved at being taken to the lock-up merely because he was found drunk in the streets. "Why," said he, "the white corporals always showed me the way home." And I can testify that, after an evening party, some weeks later, I heard with pleasure the officers asking eagerly for the countersign.

One of the sergeants of the guard, on one of these occasions, made to one who questioned his authority an answer that could hardly have been improved. The questioner had just been arrested for some offence.

"Know what dat mean?" said the indignant sergeant, pointing to the chevrons on his own sleeve. "Dat mean *Guv'ment.*" Volumes could not have said more, and the victim collapsed. The thing soon settled itself, and nobody remembered to notice whether the face beside the musket of a sentinel were white or black. It meant Government, all the same.

The men were also indulged with several raids on the mainland, under the direction of Captain J. E. Bryant, of the Eighth Maine, the most experienced scout in that region, who was endeavoring to raise by enlistment a regiment of colored troops. On one occasion Captains Whitney and Heasley, with their companies, penetrated nearly to Pocataligo, capturing some pickets and bringing away all the slaves of a plantation, the latter operation being entirely under the charge of Sergeant Harry Williams (Co. K), without the presence of any white man.

The whole command was attacked on the return by a rebel force, which turned out to be what was called in those regions a "dog-company," consisting of mounted riflemen with half a dozen trained bloodhounds. The men met these dogs with their bayonets, killed four or five of their old tormentors with great relish, and brought away the carcass of one. I had the creature skinned, and sent the skin to New York to be stuffed and mounted, meaning to exhibit it at the Sanitary Commission Fair hi Boston; but it spoiled on the passage. These quadruped allies were not originally intended as "dogs of war," but simply to detect fugitive slaves, and the men were delighted at this confirmation of their tales of dog-companies, which some of the officers had always disbelieved.

Captain Bryant, during his scouting adventures, had learned to outwit these bloodhounds, and used his skill in eluding escape, during another expedition of the same kind. He was sent with Captain Metcalf's company far up the Combahee River to cut the telegraphic wires and intercept despatches. Our adventurous chaplain and a telegraphic operator went with the party. They ascended the river, cut the wires, and read the despatches for an hour or two. Unfortunately, the attached wire was too conspicuously hung, and was seen by a passenger on the railway train in passing.

The train was stopped and a swift stampede followed; a squad of cavalry was sent in pursuit, and our chaplain, with Lieutenant Osborn, of Bryant's projected regiment, were captured; also one private, the first of our men who had ever been taken prisoners. In spite of an agreement at Washington to the contrary, our chaplain was held as prisoner of war, the only spiritual adviser in uniform, so far as I know, who had that honor. I do not know but his reverence would have agreed with Scott's pirate-lieutenant, that it was better to live as plain Jack Bunce than die as Frederick Altamont; but I am very sure that he would rather have been kept prisoner to the close of the war, as a combatant, than have been released on parole as a non-resistant.

After his return, I remember, he gave the most animated accounts of the whole adventure, of which he had enjoyed every instant, from the first entrance on the enemy's soil to the final capture. I suppose we should all like to tap the telegraphic wires anywhere and read our neighbor's messages, if we could only throw round this process the dignity of a Sacred Cause. This was what our good chaplain had done, with the same conscientious zest with which he had conducted his Sunday foraging in Florida. But he told me that nothing so impressed him on the whole trip as the sudden transformation in the black soldier who was taken prisoner with him. The chaplain at once adopted the policy, natural to him, of talking boldly and even defiantly to his captors, and commanding instead of beseeching. He pursued the same policy always and gained by it, he thought. But the [Black man] adopted the diametrically opposite policy, also congenial to his crushed race, all the force seemed to go out of him, and he surrendered himself like a tortoise to be kicked and trodden upon at their will. This manly, well-trained soldier at once became a slave again, asked no questions, and, if any were asked, made meek and conciliatory answers. He did not know, nor did any of us know, whether he would be treated as a prisoner of war, or shot, or sent to a rice-plantation. He simply acted according to the traditions of his race, as did the chaplain on his side. In the end the soldier's cunning was vindicated by the result; he escaped, and rejoined us in six months, while the chaplain was imprisoned for a year.

The men came back very much exhausted from this expedition, and those who were in the chaplain's squad narrowly escaped with their lives. One brave fellow had actually not a morsel to eat for four days, and then could keep nothing on his stomach for two days more, so that his life was despaired of; and yet he brought all his equipments safe into camp. Some of these men had led such wandering lives, in woods and swamps, that to hunt them was like hunting an otter; shyness and concealment had grown to be their second nature.

After these little episodes came two months of peace. We were clean, comfortable, quiet, and consequently discontented. It was therefore with eagerness that we listened to a rumor of a new Florida expedition, in which we might possibly take a hand. . . .

General Saxton, examining with some impatience a long list of questions from some philanthropic Commission at the North, respecting the traits and habits of the freedmen, bade some staff-officer answer them all in two words, "Intensely human." We all admitted that it was a striking and comprehensive description.

For instance, as to courage. So far as I have seen, the mass of men are naturally courageous up to a certain point. A man seldom runs away from danger which he ought to face, unless others run; each is apt to keep with the mass, and colored soldiers have more than usual of this gregariousness. In almost every regiment, black or white, there are a score or two of men who are naturally daring, who really hunger after dangerous adventures, and are happiest when allowed to seek them. Every commander gradually finds out who these men are, and habitually uses them; certainly I had such, and I remember with delight their bearing, their coolness, and their dash. Some of them were [Black], some [mixed race]. One of them would have passed for white, with brown hair and blue eyes, while others were so black you could hardly see their features. These picked men varied in other respects too; some were neat and well-drilled soldiers, while others were slovenly, heedless fellows, the despair of their officers at inspection, their pride on a raid. They were the natural scouts and rangers of the regiment; they had the two-o'clock-in-the-morning courage, which Napoleon thought so rare. The mass of the regiment rose to the same level under excitement, and were more excitable, I think, than whites, but neither more nor less courageous. Perhaps the best proof of a good average of courage among them was in the readiness they always showed for any special enterprise. I do not remember ever to have had the slightest difficulty in obtaining volunteers, but rather in keeping down the number. The previous pages include many illustrations of this, as well as of then: endurance of pain and discomfort. For instance, one of my lieutenants, a very daring Irishman, who had served for eight years as a sergeant of regular artillery in Texas, Utah, and South Carolina, said he had never been engaged in anything so risky as our raid up the St. Mary's. But in truth it seems to me a mere absurdity to deliberately argue the question of courage, as applied to men among whom I waked and slept, day and night, for so many months together. As well might he who has been wandering for years upon the desert, with a Bedouin escort, discuss the courage of the men whose tents have been his shelter and whose spears his guard. We, their officers, did not go there to teach lessons, but to receive them. There were more than a hundred men in the ranks who had voluntarily met more dangers in their escape from slavery than any of my young captains had incurred in all their lives. . . .

I used to think that I should not care to read "Uncle Tom's Cabin" in our camp; it would have seemed tame. Any group of men in a tent would have had more exciting tales to tell. I needed no fiction when I had Fanny Wright, for instance, daily passing to and fro before my tent, with her shy little girl clinging to her skirts. Fanny was a modest little [mixed race] woman, a soldier's wife, and a company laundress. She had escaped from the main-land in a boat, with that child and another. Her baby was shot dead in her arms, and she reached our lines with one child safe on earth and the other in heaven. I never found it needful to give any elementary instructions in courage to Fanny's husband, you may be sure.

I often asked myself why it was that, with this capacity of daring and endurance, they had not kept the land in a perpetual flame of insurrection; why, especially since the opening of the war, they had kept so still. The answer was to be found in the peculiar temperament of the races, in their religious faith, and in the habit of patience that centuries had fortified. The shrewder men all said substantially the same thing. What was the use of insurrection, where everything was against them? They had no knowledge, no money, no arms, no drill, no organization, above all, no mutual confidence. It was the tradition among them that all insurrections were always betrayed by somebody.

They had no mountain passes to defend like the Maroons [escaped slaves] of Jamaica—no unpenetrable swamps, like the Maroons of Surinam. Where they had these, even on a small scale, they had used them—as in certain swamps round Savannah and in the everglades of Florida, where they united with the Indians, and would stand fire—so I was told by General Saxton, who had fought them there—when the Indians would retreat.

It always seemed to me that, had I been a slave, my life would have been one long scheme of insurrection. But I learned to respect the patient self-control of those who had waited till the course of events should open a better way. When it came they accepted it. Insurrection on their part would at once have divided the Northern sentiment; and a large part of our army would have joined with the Southern army to hunt them down. By their waiting till we needed them, their freedom was secured.

Two things chiefly surprised me in their feeling toward their former masters—the absence of affection and the absence of revenge.

Certainly this indifference did not proceed from any want of personal affection, for they were the most affectionate people among whom I had ever lived. They attached themselves to every officer who deserved love, and to some who did not; and if they failed to show it to their masters, it proved the wrongfulness of the mastery.

But side by side with this faculty of patience, there was a certain tropical element in the men, a sort of fiery ecstasy when aroused, which seemed to link them by blood with the French Turcos, and made them really resemble their natural enemies, the Celts, far more than the Anglo-Saxon temperament. To balance this there were great individual resources when alone, a sort of Indian wiliness and subtlety of resource. Their gregariousness and love of drill made them more easy to keep in hand than white American troops, who rather like to straggle or go in little squads, looking out for themselves, without being bothered with officers. The blacks prefer organization.

The point of inferiority that I always feared, though I never had occasion to prove it, was that they might show less fibre, less tough and dogged resistance, than whites, during a prolonged trial—a long, disastrous march, for instance, or the hopeless defence of a besieged town. I should not be afraid of their mutinying or running away, but of their drooping and dying. It might not turn out so; but I mention it for the sake of fairness, and to avoid overstating the merits of these troops. As to the simple general fact of courage and reliability I think no officer in our camp ever thought of there being any difference between black and white. And certainly the opinions of these officers, who for years risked their lives every moment on the fidelity of their men, were worth more than those of all the world beside.

No doubt there were reasons why this particular war was an especially favorable test of the colored soldiers. They had more to fight for than the whites. Besides the flag and the Union, they had home and wife and child. They fought with ropes round their necks, and when orders were issued that the officers of colored troops should be put to death on capture, they took a grim satisfaction. It helped their esprit de corps immensely. With us, at least, there was to be no play-soldier. Though they had begun with a slight feeling of inferiority to the white troops, this compliment substituted a peculiar sense of self-respect. And even when the new colored regiments began to arrive from the North my men still pointed out this difference—that in case of ultimate defeat, the Northern troops, black or white, would go home, while the First South Carolina must fight it out or be re-enslaved. This was one thing that made the St. John's River so attractive to them and even to me—it was so much nearer the everglades. I used seriously to ponder, during the darker periods of the war, whether I might not end my days as an outlaw, a leader of Maroons.

It used to seem to me that never, since Cromwell's time, had there been soldiers in whom the religious element held such a place. "A religious army," "a gospel army," were their frequent phrases. In their prayer-meetings there was always a mingling, often quaint enough, of the warlike and the pious. "If each one of us was a praying man," said Corporal Thomas Long in a sermon, "it appears to me that we could fight as well with prayers as with bullets—for the Lord has said that if you have faith even as a grain of mustard-seed cut into four parts, you can say to the sycamore-tree, 'Arise, and it will come up.'" And though Corporal Long may have got a little perplexed in his botany, his faith proved itself by works, for he volunteered and went many miles on a solitary scouting expedition into the enemy's country in Florida, and got back safe, after I had given him up for lost.

The extremes of religious enthusiasm I did not venture to encourage, for I could not do it honestly; neither did I discourage them, but simply treated them with respect, and let them have their way, so long as they did not interfere with discipline. In general they promoted it. The mischievous little drummer-boys, whose scrapes and quarrels were the torment of my existence, might be seen kneeling together in their tents to say their prayers at night, and I could hope that their slumbers were blessed by some spirit of peace, such as certainly did not rule over their waking. The most reckless and daring fellows in the regiment were perfect fatalists in their confidence that God would watch over them, and that if they died, it would be because their time had come. This almost excessive faith, and the love of freedom and of their families, all co-operated with their pride as soldiers to make them do their duty. I could not have spared any of these incentives. Those of our officers who were personally the least influenced by such considerations, still saw the need of encouraging them among the men.

The question was often asked, whether the Southern slaves or the Northern free blacks made the best soldiers. It was a compliment to both classes that each officer usually preferred those whom he had personally commanded. I preferred those who had been slaves, for their greater docility and affectionateness, for the powerful stimulus which their new freedom gave, and for the fact that they were fighting, in a manner, for their own homes and firesides. Every one of these considerations afforded a special aid to discipline, and cemented a peculiar tie of sympathy between them and their officers. They seemed like clansmen, and had a more confiding and filial relation to us than seemed to me to exist in the Northern colored regiments.

So far as the mere habits of slavery went, they were a poor preparation for military duty. Inexperienced officers often assumed that, because these men had been slaves before enlistment, they would bear to be treated as such afterwards. Experience proved the contrary. The more strongly we marked the difference between the slave and the soldier, the better for the regiment. One half of military duty lies in obedience, the other half in self-respect. A soldier without self-respect is worthless.

Consequently there were no regiments in which it was so important to observe the courtesies and proprieties of military life as in these. I had to caution the officers to be more than usually particular in returning the salutations of the men; to be very careful in their dealings with those on picket or guard-duty; and on no account to omit the titles of the non-commissioned officers. So, in dealing out punishments, we had carefully to avoid all that was brutal and arbitrary, all that savored of the overseer.

In all ways we had to educate their self-respect. For instance, at first they disliked to obey their own non-commissioned officers. "I don't want him to play de white man ober me," was a sincere objection. They had been so impressed with a sense of inferiority that the distinction extended to the very principles of honor. "I ain't got colored-man principles," said Corporal London Simmons, indignantly defending himself from some charge before me. "I'se got white-gemman principles. I'se do my best. If Cap'n tell me to take a man, s'pose de man be as big as a house, I'll clam hold on him till I die, inception [excepting] I'm sick."

But it was plain that this feeling was a bequest of slavery, which military life would wear off. We impressed it upon them that they did not obey their officers because they were white, but because they were their officers, just as the Captain must obey me, and I the General; that we were all subject to military law, and protected by it in turn. Then we taught them to take pride in having good material for noncommissioned officers among themselves, and in obeying them. On my arrival there was one white first sergeant, and it was a question whether to appoint others. This I prevented, but left that one, hoping the men themselves would at last petition for his removal, which at length they did. He was at once detailed on other duty. The picturesqueness of the regiment suffered, for he was very tall and fair, and I liked to see him step forward in the center when the line of first sergeants came together at dress-parade. But it was a help to discipline to eliminate the Saxon, for it recognized a principle.

Afterwards I had excellent battalion-drills without a single white officer, by way of experiment; putting each company under a sergeant, and going through the most difficult movements, such as division-columns and oblique-squares. And as to actual discipline, it is doing no injustice to the line-officers of the regiment to say that none of them received from the men more implicit obedience than Color-Sergeant Rivers. I should have tried to obtain commissions for him and several others before I left the regiment, had their literary education been sufficient; and such an attempt was finally made by Lieutenant-Colonel Trowbridge, my successor in immediate command, but it proved unsuccessful. It always seemed to me an insult to those brave men to have novices put over their heads, on the ground of color alone; and the men felt it the more keenly as they remained longer in service. There were more than seven hundred enlisted men in the regiment, when mustered out after more than three years' service. The ranks had been kept full by enlistment, but there were only fourteen line-officers instead of the full thirty. The men who should have filled those vacancies were doing duty as sergeants in the ranks.

In what respect were the colored troops a source of disappointment? To me in one respect only—that of health. Their health improved, indeed, as they grew more familiar with military life; but I think that neither their physical nor moral temperament gave them that toughness, that obstinate purpose of living, which sustains the more materialistic Anglo-Saxon. They had not, to be sure, the same predominant diseases, suffering in the pulmonary, not in the digestive organs; but they suffered a good deal. They felt malaria less, but they were more easily choked by dust and made ill by dampness. On the other hand, they submitted more readily to sanitary measures than whites, and, with efficient officers, were more easily kept clean. They were injured throughout the army by an undue share of fatigue duty, which is not only exhausting but demoralizing to a soldier; by the un-suitableness of the rations, which gave them salt meat instead of rice and hominy; and by the lack of good medical attendance. Their childlike constitutions peculiarly needed prompt and efficient surgical care; but almost all the colored troops were enlisted late in the war, when it was hard to get good surgeons for any regiments, and especially for these. In this respect I had nothing to complain of, since there were no surgeons in the army for whom I would have exchanged my own.

And this late arrival on the scene affected not only the medical supervision of the colored troops, but their opportunity for a career. It is not my province to write their history, nor to vindicate them, nor to follow them upon those larger fields compared with which the adventures of my regiment appear but a partisan warfare. Yet this, at least, may be said. The operations on the South Atlantic coast, which long seemed a merely subordinate and incidental part of the great contest, proved to be one of the final pivots on which it turned.

All now admit that the fate of the Confederacy was decided by Sherman's march to the sea. Port Royal was the objective point to which he marched, and he found the Department of the South, when he reached it, held almost exclusively by colored troops. Next to the merit of those who made the march was that of those who held open the door. That service will always remain among the laurels of the black regiments.

13

DRUMMER BOY
FROM MAINE

BY GEORGE T. ULMER

He was so small that he often went unnoticed—even by the enemy.

THE BOMBARDMENT OF FORT SUMTER

This was the beginning and the first sound of actual war which inspired me, and kindled the fire of patriotism in my youthful breast. The little spark lay smoldering for two long years, 'till at last it burst forth into a full blaze. When Fort Sumter was bombarded, I was a midget of a boy; a barefooted, ragged newsboy in the city of New York. The bombardment was threatened for several weeks before it actually occurred; and many nights I would have been bankrupted, but that everyone was on the "qui vive" for the event, and I got myself into lots of trouble by shouting occasionally, "Fort Sumter Bombarded!" I needed money; it sold my papers, and I forgave myself. When the authentic news did come, I think it stirred up within me as big a piece of fighting desire as it did in larger and older people. I mourned the fact that I was then too small to fight, but lived in hopes that the war would last until I should grow. If I could have gone south, I felt that I could have conquered the rebellious faction alone, so confident was I of my fighting abilities.

In the fall of '61 my dear mother died, and my father who had a great desire to make possibilities out of improbabilities, and believing a farm the proper place to bring up a family of boys, bought one away in the interior of Maine. The farm was very hilly, covered with huge pines and liberally planted with granite ledges. I used to think God wanted to be generous to this state and gave it so much land it had to be stood up edgeways. Picture to yourself, dear reader, four boys taken from the busy life of a great city, place them in the wilderness of Maine, where they had to make a winrow of the forest to secure a garden spot for the house, pry out the stumps and blast the ledges to sow the seed, then ask yourself what should the harvest be?

Father's business required all of his time in New York City, and we were left with two hired men to develop the farm, our brains and muscles, but mine didn't seem to develop worth a cent. I didn't care for the farmer's life. The plow and scythe had no charms for me. My horny, hardened little hand itched and longed to beat the drums that would marshall men to arms.

After eight months of hard work we had cleared up quite a respectable little farm, an oasis in that forest of pines. A new house and barn had been built, also new fences and stone walls, but not much credit for this belonged to me. Soon after, we received a letter from father stating that he would be with us in a short time and bring us a new mother and a little step-sister. This was joyous news, the anticipation of a new mother, and above all a step-sister, inspired us with new ambition. The fences and barn received a coat of whitewash, the stones were picked out of the road in front of the house, the wood-pile was repiled and everything put into apple-pie order. We did not know what day they would arrive. So each day about the time the stage coach from Belfast should pass the corners, we would perch ourselves on the fence in front of the house to watch for it, and when it did come in sight, wonder if the folks were in it; if they were, it would turn at the corners and come toward our house. Day after day passed, and they did not come, and we had kind of forgotten about it. Finally one day while we were all busy burning brush, brother Charlie came rushing towards us shouting, "The stage coach is coming! The stage is coming!" Well, such a scampering for the house! We didn't have time to wash or fix up, and our appearance would certainly not inspire our city visitors with much paternal pride or affection; we looked like charcoal burners. Our faces, hands and clothes were black and begrimed from the burning brush, but we couldn't help it; we were obliged to receive and welcome them as we were. I pulled up a handful of grass and tried to wipe my face, but the grass being wet, it left streaks all over it, and I looked more like a bogie man than anything else. We all struggled to brush up and smooth our hair, but it was no use, the stage coach was upon us, the door opened, father jumped out, and as we crowded around him, he looked at us in perfect amazement and with a kind of humiliated expression behind a pleasant fatherly smile he exclaimed, "Well, well, you are a nice dirty looking lot of boys. Lizzie," addressing his wife and helping her to alight, "This is our family, a little smoky; I can't tell which is which, so we'll have to wait till they get their faces washed to introduce them by their names." But our new mother was equal to the occasion for coming to each of us, and taking our dirty faces in her hands, kissed us, saying at the same time, "Philip, don't you mind, they are all nice, honest, hard-working boys, and I know I shall like them, even if this country air has turned their skins black." At this moment a tiny voice called, "Please help me out." All the boys started with a rush, each eager to embrace the little step-sister. I was there first, and in an instant, in spite of my dirty appearance, she sprang from the coach right into my arms; my brothers struggled to take her from me, but she tightened her little arms about my neck and clung to me as if I was her only protector. I started and ran with her, my brothers in full chase, down the road, over the stone walls, across the field, around the stumps with my prize, the brothers keeping up the chase till we were all completely tired out, and father compelled us to stop and bring the child to the house.

Afterward we took our turns at caressing and admiring her; finally we apologized for our behavior and dirty faces, listened to father's and mother's congratulations, concluded father's choice for a wife was a good one, and that our little step-sister was just exactly as we wanted her to be, and the prospect of a bright, new and happy home seemed to be already realized.

* * *

The war grew more and more serious. Newspapers were eagerly sought; and every word about the struggle was read over and over again. A new call for troops was made, another and still another, and I was all the time fretting and chafing in the corn or potato field, because I was so young and small. I could not work; the fire of patriotism was burning me up. My eldest brother had arrived at the age and required size to fit him for the service; he enlisted and went to the front. This added new fuel to the flame already within me, and one day I threw down the hoe and declared that I would go to the war! I would join my brother at all hazards. My folks laughed at me and tried to dissuade me from so unwise a step, but my mind was made up, and I was bound to enlist. Enlist I did, when I was only fourteen years of age and extremely small for my years, but I thought I would answer for a drummer boy if nothing else. I found that up hill work, however, but I was bound to "get there," and—I did.

It was easy enough to enlist, but to get mustered into the service was a different thing. I tried for eight long weeks. I enlisted in my own town, but was rejected. I enlisted in an adjoining town—rejected, and so on for weeks and weeks. But I did not give up. . . .

The Yankee yearning for fight had possession of me, and I could neither eat, sleep nor work. I was bound to be a soldier. I prayed for it, and I sometimes thought, my prayers were answered; that the war should last 'till I was big enough to be one—for it did.

I had enlisted four times in different towns, and each time I went before a mustering officer, I was rejected. "Too small" I was every time pronounced, but I was not discouraged or dismayed—the indomitable pluck and energy of those downeast boys pervaded my system. I was bound to get there, for what I didn't know, I did not care or didn't stop to think. I only thought of the glory of being a soldier, little realizing what an absurd-looking one I would make; but the ambition was there, the pluck was there, and the patriotism of a man entered the breast of the wild dreamy boy. I wanted to go to the front—and I went. After several unsuccessful attempts to be mustered into the service at Augusta, which was twenty-five miles from our little farm, I thought I would enlist from the town of Freedom and thereby get before a different mustering officer who was located in Belfast. I had grown, I thought, in the past six weeks, and before a new officer, I thought my chances of being accepted would improve; so on a bright morning in September I mounted my "gig," behind my little old gray horse, who seemed to say, as he turned his head to look at me when I jumped on to the seat, "What a fool you are, making me haul you all that distance, when you know they won't have you!" but kissing my little step-sister good bye, with a wave of my hand to father and brothers who stood in the yard and door of the dear old home, I drove away, and as I did so I could see the expressions of ridicule and doubt on their faces, while underneath it all there was a tinge of sadness and fear. They did not think for a moment I would be mustered into the army, yet fear took possession of them when I drove off, for they knew my determined disposition.

Well, I arrived in Belfast. Instead of driving direct to the stable and hotel, and putting my horse up, I drove direct to the office of the mustering officer. I did not need to fasten my trusty horse, for he knew it would only be a few moments, and as I went to the office door, he turned his head and whinnied as if he were laughing at me. I entered that office like a young Napoleon. I had made up my mind to walk in before the officer very erect and dignified, even to raising myself on tiptoe. On telling the clerk my errand, he ushered me into an inner office, and imagine my surprise—my consternation—when, swinging around in his chair, I found myself in the presence of the very officer who had rejected me in Augusta so many times.

"Damn it," said he, "will you never let up? Go home to your mother, boy, don't pester me any more. I will not accept you, and let that end it."

I tremblingly told him I had grown since he saw me last, and that by the time I was mustered in I would grow some more, and that I would drum and fight, if it should prove actually necessary.

Thus I pleaded with him for fully one hour. Finally he said, "Well, damned if I don't muster you in, just to get rid of you. Sergeant, make out this young devil's papers and let him go and get killed." My heart leaped into my mouth. I tried to thank him, but he would not have it. He hurried me through, and at 5:30 P. M., September 15, 1863, I was a United States soldier. And when I donned that uniform, what a looking soldier! The smallest clothes they issued looked on me as if it would make a suit for my entire family, but in spite of the misfit, I took them and put them on, with the pants legs rolled up to the knees, and the overcoat dragging on the ground.

I went out of that office as proud as a peacock, but a laughing-stock for the boys, and all who gazed at me. I think even the old horse smiled and looked askance; he acted as if I was fooling him, and hungry as he was, when he turned towards the stable, he dragged along as if he either were sorry or ashamed to draw me among people; but I cared not for their jeers and laughs. I was now a soldier and anxious to get home. I pictured the feeling and joyous greetings of my brothers and sister as they would see me ride up in my uniform; how the boys would envy me, and how the sister would throw her arms about me and kiss me, and how her bosom would heave with pride as she gazed upon the uniform that covered her hero brother.

Oh! I pictured it all in my boyish fancy, and hastened all my arrangements, so full of joy that I could scarcely eat. I would not wait till morning, but started home about midnight, arriving there just at sunrise.

It was on the 17th of September, 1863, one of those bright, balmy days that we have in good old New England, seated in a "gig," might be seen the writer of this little sketch, dressed in soldiers' clothes, covered by one of those familiar cape overcoats that nearly covered the "gig" and poor old horse. I felt as proud as if I was the general in command of all the army.

Instead of giving the family a surprise, they had heard of my enlisting from the stagedriver, and I found them all in tears. But when I made my appearance tears changed to laughter, for the sight of me I think was enough to give them hope. They didn't believe our government would have such a little, ill-dressed soldier. And father said, after looking me all over: "Well, if they have mustered you in, after they see you in that uniform it will be muster out, my boy."

In about ten days I received orders to report in Augusta. Then the family realized there was more in it than they at first thought, but consoled themselves with the belief that when I reached headquarters, I would be found useless, and sent home. I went away, leaving them with that feeling of hope struggling behind their copious tears. And the lingering kiss of my little step-sister, and her soft sobbing, "Don't, don't, please don't go," as she hung around my neck, ran constantly in my mind from that time till now. All through the nights, on the long marches, in all my troubles, that soft, sweet voice was calling, "George, please, please, don't go." And I could see her little form, and her ever-thoughtful face, a guiding star and a compass that ever guided me away from the shoals and quicksands. She was an angel companion to me all through the trials and hardships of that awful war.

Well, I arrived in Portland, was sent to the barracks with three or four thousand others, was allotted a hard bunk, and then for the first time did I realize what I was doing, what I had committed myself to, and I think if I could have caught that mustering officer I should have appealed to him just as hard to muster me out, as I did to muster me in; but I was in it and must stay. I will never forget the first day of my soldier experience. With what feeling of awe and thumping of my cowardly, timid heart, I heard the different commands of the officers. The disciplining began; the routine of a soldier's life had really started right in Portland, far away from the front where I had only expected to find it. I was detained in those barracks only a few days, and the tap of the drum, and the sound of the bugle as they sounded their different calls, had grown monotonous to me; I no longer regarded them with awe, but with mockery. I wanted to go to the front where the real life of a soldier was known, where glory could be won. I wanted the reality, not boy's play.

I was glad when I was numbered among a squad of about 200 who had orders to go to Washington. That night we marched down to the depot and were crowded into cars. I did not care; I was overjoyed: I was delighted at the prospects of going to the seat of war, near the front, where I thought I might hear the booming of the cannon, and to a place where I would soon be forwarded to my regiment. We arrived in Boston, and to my disappointment, were laid over. We were marched to the barracks on Beach street, which in early days was the "Beach Street Theater." The seats, benches, gallery, stage and scenery were all there, and we were crowded into this old, unused temple of Thespis to select a place to sleep where best we could, on the floor, or anywhere. Here I began to grow sick of soldiering; we were in this old musty theater with a guard over us, not allowed to go on the street, and unable to find out how long we were to be incarcerated there, for we were treated more like prisoners than men who had volunteered to serve their country.

I thought it a great hardship at that time, and kicked at it loud and hard, without any result that benefited us; but since I have been through it all, I can see where it was absolutely necessary to use the rigid and seemingly ungrateful discipline. Well, we were kept in the old theater for about a week; we were allowed out for two hours each day on passes, and in the evening we sang songs and "acted" on the stage. Each one who could recite or do anything did it, and it was appreciated by a deadhead audience, something unusual nowadays. It was here in this old Beach Street Theater that my future life was undoubtedly mapped out; from that time I was impressed with a desire to become an actor, and there is no doubt that the seed was planted then and grew and increased in after years.

On the 11th of November, we were ordered to Washington, and embarked on the steamboat train via Fall River, and I shall never forget when we arrived in New York, the demonstration, the greeting, the cheers, the God-speeds that we received as we marched through the city to the ferry, and it seemed to me that I was the one all this was meant for; I thought I was a hero. It seemed that all eyes were on me, and perhaps they were, for among all those Maine giants I belied my state, for I was a dot only, a pigmy beside those mighty woodsmen.

We arrived in Washington without mishap. I was granted permission to go over the city, and then to report to the commanding officer of the camp at Alexandria. My first desire when I found myself with a privilege in the great capital was to visit President Lincoln, have a talk with him and also with Secretary Stanton. My admiration for those two men was almost love, and I fancied, now that I was a soldier, that I could easily meet them; that they would grasp me by the hand, compliment and shower me with congratulations and advice. It is needless to say that I found out that I had overestimated my importance; I did not discuss the war situation with either of those gentlemen. I was a little crestfallen at not meeting them, but contented myself by looking over the city; and wherever I went I noticed I was scrutinized by everybody; soldiers on guard would come to a halt, hesitate and then present arms; some officers would pass me by, then turn and look me over from head to foot; others would touch their caps and then turn and watch me with a kind of wondering gaze, as much as to say, "What is it?"

I forgot to mention that while in Portland I had a tailor make me a very handsome suit of military clothes. He was as ignorant of the regulation style as I was. He only knew the colors and knew that I wanted it nice and handsome. He made it and so covered it over with gold braid and ornaments, that you could not tell whether I was a drum-major or a brigadier-general; that accounted for the salutations and looks of astonishment I received. The first night I was tired out and started for Alexandria; arrived at headquarters about midnight, and told the sentry I must see the colonel. He thought I had important messages, or was some officer, and escorted me to the colonel's quarters. I woke him up, told him I had reported and wanted a bed.

The colonel said, "Is that all you want? Corporal, put this man in the guard-house." He did!

That was my first experience, and I always after tried to avoid guard-houses. The next morning I was given a broom and put to sweeping around camp with about twenty tough-looking customers. The broom did not look well with my uniform, and as soon as an officer noticed me, I was summoned before the colonel in command. He asked, what I was? I told him I didn't know yet—would not know 'till I reached my regiment. He had a hearty laugh at my appearance; said I ought to be sent to some fair instead of the front. However, he detailed me as his orderly.

I held this position some time, until one day there was going to be a squad of recruits, and returned furloughed men sent on a steam-barge to the front at City Point, where Butler was bottled up. I asked to be one of them. The colonel told me I was foolish, and better stay with him, but I insisted; and he allowed me to go. The barge was a kind of an open double-deck boat without cabin or shelter, and they crowded us on to her as thick as we could stand; we were like sardines. I secured a position against the smoke-stack, and before we reached Chesapeake bay I was glad of it, for it became bitterly cold, and I curled down around this smoke-stack, went to sleep, and when I awoke in the morning I was crisp, dirty, and nearly roasted alive. We crossed the bay in the afternoon. Oh, wasn't it rough! This old river barge would roll and pitch out of sight at times, and we were all wet from head to foot. Then I began to wish myself home on the farm again; but I was in for it, and could not back out. I had one thought that buoyed me up, the thought of meeting my brother.

That evening we passed by Fortress Monroe, up the James river. There was not much transpired to relieve the monotony or appease our hunger or thirst; in fact, it began to look dubious as to reaching City Point. The monotony, however, was somewhat relieved in the morning. About daylight a commotion was caused by the sound of distant cannonading. Everyone crowded to the front of the boat; everybody was asking questions of everybody. Each one had some idea to offer as to the cause. Some ventured to say it was a gunboat up the river practising. One old chap, who had evidently been to the front, facetiously claimed that it was the corks out of Butler's bottles.

The river was very crooked at this point, and you could not see very far; but presently we rounded a bend in the river, which revealed to us where the cannonading came from, but for what, we could not make out. About a mile ahead of us lay a United States gunboat, and every few minutes a puff of smoke, and then a loud bang—erang—

erang—erang—with its long vibrations on that still morning, awoke a sense of fear in everyone aboard that boat. No one could account for the situation. Even the captain of the barge stood with pallid cheek, seemingly in doubt what to do as he rang the bell to slow down; but on—on we kept moving—nearer and nearer this most formidable war-ship, and as we did so the shots became more frequent. Then we noticed a man on the bank waving a flag back and forth, up and down in a wild, excited sort of a way. I asked what that meant. An old soldier said the man was signaling the boat to let them know they had hit the target. Suddenly we were brought to an understanding of what it all meant, for we could now hear the musketry very plain, and could even see the rebels on the banks of the river. At this point a "gig" from the gunboat pulled alongside and gave orders to the captain "to land those troops at once," telling him at the same time that this was Fort Powhatan landing; that Fitzhugh Lee with his cavalry had swooped down upon the garrison, which was only composed of two hundred [Black] troops, and that they must be re-enforced.

The captain protested, as the troops on board were all unarmed, being returned furloughed men and recruits; but it was no use, the order was imperative, and the captain headed his barge toward the shore. There was no wharf. That had been burnt, so he was obliged to run as far as he could onto the sand, then land us overboard. I tell you as that boat neared toward the shore, my face felt as if it were marbleized; sharp twinges ran up and down my whole body, and I'll bet that I was the picture of a coward. I was not the only one. I looked them all over, every one looked just as I felt. One man who stood near me, I know, was more frightened than I, for he was so frightened he smelt badly. But I didn't blame any of those poor men; it was not the pleasantest thing in the world to be placed before the enemy as we were. However, we all landed.

The firing above us on the bank became more intense. An officer who was on the boat with us, returning from a leave of absence, assumed command. He ordered us to fall into line, and marched us into a little ravine, halted, and told us the position and necessity of the occasion. He said the fort was a very important position, and must be held at all hazards; that there were only two hundred colored troops there, and they could not hold it.

Now, he proposed, as we had no arms, to go in with a rush and a yell, and make those rebels think that re-enforcements had arrived. All this time the musketry firing was increasing. The whizz of bullets through the air and about our heads were becoming too frequent. I was in the front rank, center of the line, and I tell you I think I had a little of that frightened smell about me at this time. Whether it was that or my looks or what, the officer probably took pity on me and told me to skirmish in the rear. I hardly knew where the rear was, but I thought it would be safer under the bank of the river, and there I hastened, and none too soon, for the rebels had made a break through the lines and poured several volleys into our poor, unarmed re-enforcements. The rebs became more cautious, and that was what was wanted, as the only hope we had was to hold them at bay until re-enforcements could arrive.

Well, I skirmished in the rear, and I found it hotter than the front, for the rebs would crawl to the bank at either end of the breastworks and kept a cross-fire up and down the river. Under and against the banking, there was a sort of old barn; this was filled with hay. The bullets were flying around so thickly that I squeezed myself behind this barn, and after I was well in, the bullets just rained against that old building; but I felt pretty secure till I looked up overhead—I saw that while I was in safety from bullets, a worse danger threatened me. The overhanging bank was liable to cave in and bury me alive.

The uncertainty of my position became more and more apparent. Each moment the increased storm of bullets on the barn prevented me from even looking out, and the constant rattling down of dirt and pebbles from above, told me plainly what a position I was in. I tell you I wished then I had never been mustered in. The uncertainty of my position was soon developed. I came to myself and found I was buried to my neck; my head and face were cut and bleeding, and a soldier was trying to wipe the sand from my eyes and ears. I found I had not been shot, but the banking had caved in and buried me. Gen. "Baldy" Smith, who was in command, happened to see me behind the barn just as the bank caved in. It was he who put the soldiers at work to rescue me. As soon as I was out, and the dust out of my eyes, the general rode down to the beach, leading an extra horse; he called to me. Ordered me to mount. I did so. He made me his orderly.

I was to carry dispatches across the field, but I did not now have the fear I did at first. I did not mind the sound of the bullets. I became accustomed to it, and I rode back and forth all day long without a scratch. I believe I was so small that I rode between those bullets, and from that time forth I had no fear. I felt as though I were bullet-proof. I felt as if it were ordained that I should go through the war unscathed and unscarred. It did seem so, for I would go through places where it rained bullets, and come out without a scratch. This was my experience all through, and was commented on by comrades, who said I had a charmed life.

Well, the day wore away the rebs making feints first at one point, then another. Finally they concentrated their forces against one point, and would have carried it, too, but just then a steamboat loaded with troops rounded the bend of the river. Well, the shouts that went up from the handful of brave soldiers at the sight of that boat I never can forget. The boys on the boat caught the sound. They took in the situation, and answered back the shout with three long, hearty cheers. It created consternation in the rebel lines. They knew the jig was up, but they drew up in line, like dare-devils that they were, and with a cool deliberation, poured volley after volley into the side of the steamer until her nose touched the shore.

Well, to see those soldiers leave that steamer was a sight never to be forgotten. They jumped overboard from every part of her. It did not seem five minutes from the time she touched shore until the banks were swarming with our boys in blue. The rebels had taken to flight—our boys followed some distance, and then returned, relieving us and allowing us to embark again for City Point. After the rebels had retreated, I went outside the breastworks, and the sight that met my eyes on every side would curdle the blood of stouter hearts than mine. It appeared that Lee, with his cavalry, had surprised the pickets, and being [Black], every one they captured they would hang up to a tree after they were mutilated. I saw several with fingers cut off in order to obtain a ring quickly, and many other sickening sights which tended to make me a hardened soldier. I was having lots of experience, even before I had really reached my regiment, and I tell you, the heroic ardor of my boyish dream was beginning to ooze out of me quite fast. I began to think I was not cut for a soldier.

Well, my first battle was over, my first experience before an enemy. The first sound of musketry had died away, and we were again steaming towards City Point to join our regiments. We arrived there the next night about ten o'clock. There didn't seem to be any one in command of us or any one to direct us. It was very dark on shore, but in the distance you could see a glaring light above the horizon, as if there was a long building on fire. But from the occasional sound of guns from that quarter, I made up my mind it was the advance line of our army. It was Butler's command, and our regiment, the Eighth Maine, must be there. The Eighth Maine, Company H, was the regiment and company to which my brother belonged, and in which I was enlisted.

I started out across the fields in the direction of the light—on, on I tramped, into ditches, through mires, over fences. The farther I went the faster I went. I was so impatient I could not hold myself to a walk; it was a dog-trot all the time. I was heedless of every obstacle, till I began to near the front. I realized the danger by the whizzing of shell, and the zip, zip of bullets. I found myself among lots of soldiers, and how ragged and dirty the poor fellows looked. I asked the first man I came to where the Eighth Maine was? He looked at me in perfect astonishment. "This is the Eighth, what's left of it." I asked him if he knew where my brother was—Charley Ulmer? "Oh, yes," he said, and pointing to a little group of men, who were round a wee bit of a fire; "there he is, don't you know him?" I hesitated, for really I could hardly tell one from the other. He saw my bewilderment, and took me by the arm and led me over to the fire. They all started and stared at me, and to save my life I could not tell which was my brother; but one more ragged than the rest uttered a suppressed cry, rushed forward, and throwing his arm about my neck, sobbed and cried like a child. "My God! my brother! Oh George, George, why did you come here?" His grief seemed to touch them all, for they all began to wipe their eyes with their ragged coat-sleeves. This began to tell on me, and for the next ten minutes it was a kind of a blubbering camp. After awhile they reconciled themselves, and began to ply me with questions faster than I could answer.

My brother sat down with me and lectured me very soundly for coming, as there was no need of it. He gave a graphic description of the hardships they had endured, and I can never obliterate the picture he presented that night. His clothes were ragged and patched, begrimed with smoke, grease and dirt; his hat an old soft one, with part of the rim gone and the crown perforated with bullet holes; his beard scraggly and dirty; his big toes peeping out of a pair of old boots with the heels all run down, in fact, he was a sight—a strong contrast to my tailor-made suit. I will never forget the expression on my brother's face when about half an hour after my arrival he looked up to me with his eyes half full of tears glistening on that dirty face, and with a kind of cynical smile, asked, after looking me over and over: "What are you, anyhow?"

I told him I didn't know.

"Well, after you have been here awhile, those pretty clothes won't look as they do now, and you will probably find out what you are after you have dodged a few shells."

Our conversation was brought to a climax by orders to break camp and fall in. We learned we were going to embark somewhere on a boat; everything was hustle-bustle now; little sheltered tents were struck, tin cups, canteens, knapsacks were made ready, and in about fifteen minutes that begrimed, dirty, hungry family of Uncle Sam's was on the march to the river. We were marched on board an old ferry-boat, and crowded so thickly that we could scarcely stand.

My brother seemed now to feel that he had the responsibility of my comfort, even my life, on his hands—and being a favorite he elbowed me a place at the end of the boat, where we could sit down by letting our feet hang over the end of the boat. In that position we remained. We didn't have room to stand up and turn around. I was awful sleepy, but dared not go to sleep for fear I would fall overboard. Finally my brother fixed me so I could lay my head back, and he held on to me while I slept. The next morning we landed at a place called West Point, on the York river; why we landed there we didn't know.

Of course soldiers never did know anything of the whys and wherefores; they only obeyed orders, stood up or laid down and got killed—they had no choice in the matter. Well, we landed, and I tell you, we were stiff and hungry. While they were unloading the horses, which was done by lowering them into the water and letting them swim ashore, which took some time, they allowed us a chance to skirmish for food.

I had to resort to pork and hard tack for my breakfast. About noon that day we began our march. Where we were going, everybody guessed, but none knew. I didn't care. I was now a kind of a half-settled soldier, but from the first, I was a kind of privileged character. No one gave me orders. No one seemed to claim me. I had never been assigned to any company. I never had to answer roll-call. I could go and come as I pleased. Once in awhile a guard would halt me, but not often. They didn't know what I was, and they didn't care. All the afternoon we marched. Our route was along the railroad, the rails of which had the appearance of being recently torn up by the rebels. About four o'clock I was becoming very tired. We came to a clearing, and some distance in the field was a [Black man] plowing with a mule. I made a break for him, and the rest of that march I rode. No one objected, but the boys shouted as I made my appearance on the mule; a mile or two further along we sighted a farm-house. I drew reins on my mule and made for the house; I made the boys glad on my return, for I secured a demijohn of applejack, a big bundle of tobacco, and a box of eggs. That successful raid gave me courage, and I began to think that was what I was destined for, and I liked it first-rate, for it was a pleasure to me to see those poor, hungry boys have any delicacy, or even enough of ordinary food.

That night we had to halt, for the rebs had burned the bridge, and we had to wait for pontoons. The boys were tired and hungry. A guard was posted to prevent any foraging, but I was a privileged character, and I bolted through the lines. I had seen some pigs and calves scamper into the swamp about half a mile back from where we halted, and thinking a bit of fresh meat would be nice for the boys, I determined to have some. Cautiously I stole away, till I arrived at the edge of the swamp; and such a jungle! It was almost impossible to penetrate it, so I skirted the edge, hoping to see a pig emerge. After tramping an hour I was rewarded by seeing a calf. I drew my revolver, sneaked up and fired at poor bossy. It dropped—I was a good shot— but when I reached the poor beast I found it was as poor as a rail and covered with sores as big as my hand.

I was disappointed, but cut off as much as I could that was not sore, and took it to camp. We put the kettles on the fires in short order, and my brother's company had fresh meat broth—the first fresh meat in a month—and I tell you it was good, even if it had been sore. After that episode Company H claimed me and dubbed me their mascot. I accepted the position, and from that time forth I devoted my time to foraging, stealing anything I could for my company, and I doubt if there was a company in the whole army that fared better than ours, for I was always successful in my expeditions.

After a long, tedious march across pontoons, over corduroy roads, we confronted the Johnnies at "Cold Harbor." It was here that I found myself in a real, genuine battle. I got lost in the scuffle. I found myself amidst bursting shell and under heavy musketry fire. I was bewildered and frightened. I did not know which way to go. I ran this way and that, trying to find my brother and regiment. Every turn I made it seemed I encountered more bullets and shells. Soldiers were shouting and running in every direction, artillery was galloping here and there, on every side it seemed they were fighting for dear life.

On one side of me I saw horses and men fall and pile up on top of each other. Cannon and caissons with broken wheels were turned upside down, riderless horses were scampering here and there, officers were riding and running in all directions, the shells were whizzing through the air, and soldiers shouting at the top of their voices. Everything seemed upside down. I thought the world had come to an end. I tried to find shelter behind a tree, away from the bullets, but as soon as I found shelter on one side it seemed as though the bullets and shells came from all sides, and I lay down in utter despair and fright.

I don't know how long I was there, but when I awoke I thought the war was over, it was so still. I thought every one had been killed on both sides, excepting myself. I was just thinking I would try and find a live horse, ride back to Washington and tell them that the war was over, everybody was killed, when my brother tapped me on the shoulder and asked me where I had been. He had gone through it all, escaped with the loss of one toe, and had come to the rear to have it dressed and find me.

The next morning I was sent with the "Stretcher Corps" under a flag of truce to the battle field to help take the wounded to the rear and bury the dead, and when we reached the scene, how well could I imagine what the awful struggle had been. The worst of the great conflict had occurred in an orchard, and there the sight was most appalling; dead and dying heroes were lying about as thick as a slumbering camp would be, sleeping with their guns for pillows the night before a battle; to many of those poor fellows it was that sleep that knows no waking, while to others it was the awaking from unconsciousness by the twinges of a mortal gaping wound, awake just long enough to get a glimpse of the Gates Ajar, sink back and start on that journey from which no traveler returns.

Blue and the gray were mingled together on this awful field of slaughter, and both sides seemed to respect the solemnity by a cessation of hostilities, and the hushed silence was only broken by the painful cry of some helpless wounded, or dying groans of others. The little white cloth we wore around our arms to denote, we belonged to the stretcher corps, seemed to add to the sadness of the occasion, for to those poor wounded souls we were like ministering angels, and as I moved from one to the other with tear dimmed eyes offering water and assistance to those who needed it I saw many incidents of bravery and self-sacrifice that went far toward ameliorating the suffering and obliterating the bitterness of the blue and the gray. I noticed one poor fellow who had spread his rubber blanket to catch the dew of the night sharing the moisture thus gathered with an unfortunate confederate who had lost a leg. Another, a confederate was staying the life-blood of a union officer by winding his suspenders around the mangled limb. Oh! the horror of such a picture can never be penned—or told, and contemplated only by soldiers who have been there.

One-half of our regiment had been killed or wounded. After this things settled down into a siege. I employed my time foraging for the company. One day I found an apple orchard, gathered as many apples as I could carry, took them to the company and made apple sauce without sweetening. They ate very heartily of it, poor fellows. It was a treat for them; but it was a bad find, for the next day the whole lot of them were unfit for duty. That nearly put a stop to my reconnoitering. Our regiment lay here in the advance line of breastworks for thirteen days. The sappers and miners were constantly working our breastworks towards the enemy, and every time I wanted to reach my company I found it in a new place and more difficult to reach. The rebel sharpshooters, with their deadly aim, were waiting for such chaps as me. However, under cover of night, I always managed to find and reach the company with some palatable relish.

I will never forget one night; four men were detailed to go to the rear for rations. The commissary was located about two miles to the rear, and the wagon could only haul the rations within one mile of us on account of jungle and rebel sharpshooters. Therefore these men were detailed to pack the rations the rest of the way. I was one of the detail from my company.

We went back to the covered wagons that were waiting for us. The boys said I was too small to walk, and they threw me into the rear end of one of the wagons. We got to the commissary tent—a long tent open at both ends—and from both ends they weighed out the rations of coffee, sugar, etc. While the soldier who was doing the weighing on one end had his back turned, I managed to fill my haversack from a full barrel of coffee that stood at the end of the tent. I had two haversacks for that purpose, for I went there with that intent; but I came away with only one filled. I could not get a chance for the other; it was on the wrong side. Finally the rations were all aboard, and we started back. The boys repeated the operation of throwing me into the wagon again, and there was my opportunity. I would fill my other haversack from the bags in the wagon; that's what the boys expected I would do, and I did from the first bag I could get into. Each company had its own bag.

When we arrived at the breastworks my company crowded around me for plunder. I divided it up, and was looked upon as quite a hero, but when the rations were issued it was found our company's bag was short about thirty rations of sugar, but no one said a word. It was surmised that it got spilled.

Day after day our regiment lay there and our army did not seem to gain anything. I was becoming disgusted and discouraged.

One night the Johnnies made a charge on us. That was the only time I ever fired a gun in the whole war, and I honestly believe I killed a dozen men, for immediately after they stopped firing. It was only a few moments, however; on they came, only to be repulsed. They kept that up nearly all night, and I served my country by standing down in the trench, loading a gun and passing it up to my brother to fire. I did this all night, but I didn't see any less rebels in the morning.

Our next order was to fall back, under cover of darkness. We fell back about a mile and halted for some reason, I thought to get breakfast. Anyway I built a little fire behind a stone wall, put my coffee-pot on and the remnants of a pot of beans. They were getting nice and hot; my brother and I stood waiting, smacking our lips in the anticipation of a feast, when whizz came one of those nasty little "Cohorn" mortor shells and it dropped right into our coffee and beans. Then the bugle sounded, "fall in," and we started with downcast hearts and empty stomachs, and a longing good-bye to the debris of beans and coffee. It was a tiresome march. Of course, we didn't know where we were going, and that made it all the longer.

We eventually brought up at White-House landing on the York river, where we were put on board of a steam transport without being given time to draw rations. From there we steamed down the York and up the James river to the Appomattox, and up the river to Point of Rocks. We landed here on the Bermuda Hundred side, in the rear of Butler's works, obtained some bread and coffee, and then crossed the Appomattox on pontoons and pushed on towards Petersburg. Our regiment belonged at that time to the 2nd brigade, 2nd division of the 18th corps, commanded by Major General "Baldy" Smith.

We soon met the enemy's pickets in front of Petersburg. They fled before that long, serpentine file of blue-coats like deer. On, on we went. We could see the rebels running in their shirt sleeves, throwing coats, guns and everything in their mad flight. I don't think there was a shot fired on either side 'till we reached a fort, Smith I think it was called. It was just at dusk. This fort was located on a mound or hill with a ravine in front of it. Our brigade was drawn up in line of battle in a wheat-field on the right. A colored brigade was ordered to charge the fort from the hill opposite, and across this ravine; then I beheld one of the grandest and most awful sights I ever saw; those colored troops started on a double quick, and as they descended the hill, the fort poured volley after volley into them. The men seemed to fall like blades of grass before a machine, but it did not stop them; they rallied and moved on; it was only the work of a few minutes. With a yell they were up and into that fort, and in less time than it takes to tell it, the guns were turned on the fleeing rebels.

Here was the greatest mistake of our greatest commander. All of our army was brought to a standstill by some one's foolish order. Not another move was made. We lay there waiting, and all night long we could hear the trains rumbling along on the other side of the Appomattox river. Lee had been outwitted. We had stolen a march on him. We had arrived in front of defenseless Petersburg, and could have gone right in and on to Richmond without a struggle. But that fatal order to halt gave him all night to hurry his forces from Cold Harbor, and in the morning we found plenty of determined rebels in front of us, and thereby the war was prolonged months and hundreds and thousands of lives lost. I swore all night. I kicked and condemned every general there was in the army for the blunder I saw they were making. I only wished I could be the general commanding for one hour. But it was no use; I couldn't be.

I was nothing but a boy. But I had my ideas. I thought, perhaps, more than some of the officers did. I kept myself posted on facts and the topography of the country. The dispositions of generals was a matter of grave importance to me. I believed generals should be selected to command, NOT for their qualifications in military tactics alone, NOT because they had graduated well-dressed from "West Point," but for their indomitable pluck, judgment and honesty of purpose. It did seem to me that some of our best officers were invariably placed in the most unimportant positions and commands.

Take, for instance, "Custer's" Brigade of daring men, headed by those intrepid officers, Alger and Towns, wasting their time and imperiling the lives of thousands of good soldiers around "Emettsburg," "Gordonsville," "Bottom Bridge," carrying out the foolish orders of superiors in command. Why could not these officers of cool judgment be with us at this critical moment?—they made THEIR victories, what would they have done had they the great opportunities that were presented to others who failed?

* * *

All night about the camp-fire the boys would delight in nagging me—getting me into arguments and debates. They called me the "midget orator of the Army of the Potomac." I will never forget one night soon after the advance on Petersburg; we were clustered about with coffee cups and pipes; an argument waxed warm in regard to the possibilities of the war lasting two more years; finally I was called upon for my views. "Midget," said Col. McArthur, "if you had supreme command of our army, what would you do?"

What would I do? If Uncle Sam would give me one regiment from each State in the Union—give me Grant, Burnside, Sherman, Sheridan, Custer, Alger, Hooker, Hancock, Thomas and Siegel to command them, I would take Richmond and settle the rebellion before they had time to wire and ask Stanton if I should. This was received with cheering and applause. But my boyish fancies and ideas were never gratified; I never had the pleasure of seeing my ideal army together, and Richmond was not taken for many months afterward. A few days after our regiment was drawn up in line of battle in a wheat-field. It was just nightfall. I was lying down on the bank of a ditch waiting for the moveforward. Suddenly a shell came over my head and bust right in the center of my company. I thought I saw legs and arms flying in all directions.

I started on the dead run for the rear. I believed I was going right, but it seemed as if the shells were coming from our own guns in the rear. I thought they had mistaken us for the enemy. I could see the shells coming, and every time they would fire, I would fall on my stomach, and thought they all went just over my head. I was soon, however, out of range, and began to feel easy, when a new fear took possession of me. What if I had, in my bewilderment, run into the rebel lines?

I saw just ahead of me an old-fashioned southern mansion, with a high board fence all around it, and in the inclosure several small cabins used for the slaves to live in. I could not remember seeing this before, so I made up my mind I was actually inside rebeldom. However, I decided to make the best of it, and if I were or were not I would see if I could find something to eat. With fear and faltering steps I moved toward the big gate, swung it open, and it gave an awful squeak as it swung on its old rusty hinges. There was not a sign of life in or about the place, and that gave me hope and courage. In the center of the yard was a large hen-house. Cautiously toward this I crawled, heard the cackle of fowl, went first on one side then on the other, looking for the door; and imagine my surprise, the fear that took possession of me—my hair stood on end; for sitting there on a bench back of this hen-house were two big Johnnies. I couldn't speak, I couldn't move, till one of them said, "Good evening, sar; got anything to eat?"

"Yes, yes," I stammered, "I have some hard tack." Finally, one of them seeing I was most scared to death, spoke up and said, "Don't be alarmed; we are only deserters and want to give ourselves up; show us to headquarters." I was brave now. I gave them what hard tack I had, and marched them ahead of me back to the rear, till we found headquarters.

Afterward, I was offered a furlough for capturing two of the enemy. I never told this before; I took the credit. But I was not satisfied; I'd rather have some of those chickens than live rebels. So back I went and I got five; started back to the rear, put a kettle on a fire and boiled them, kept them three days, till I found my brother and the remnant of the regiment.

* * *

This was on the day fixed for the great mine explosion, every soldier on the entire line was waiting with bated breath for the signal or pro-longed rumble of that expected explosion. It did not come, however. The suspense was broken by the appearance nearly a half a mile away, of a soldier with something white on his back, that made a good tar-get for the rebel sharpshooters. Down the railroad I came. I reached the first line of earthworks. For a short distance I would keep on top. In this way I kept on, on, first running one breastwork then another, till I reached the front line. On top of this I ran the whole length, heedless and unmindful of the rebel bullets that pelted about me. I almost flew along. The soldiers shouted to me to keep down, but I heeded them not. Finally I reached the place where my regiment was, jumped down as coolly as if I had run no risk, deposited my bag, received the congratulations of my company, who examined me all over to see if there were any wounds. They found none, however, but on opening the shirt every can of milk had a bullet hole through it, and con-densed milk, extract of beef, and tobacco had to be eaten as a soufflee.

There was a desperate fight going on at the right of our line. I was pressed into the service of the stretcher corps, which is usually composed of drummer boys. I did duty at this all the forenoon. The onslaught was terrible, and many poor fellows did I help carry off that field; some to live for an hour, others to lose a limb that would prove their valor and courage for the balance of their lives.

This day our regiment was relieved from the front and supposing they were going to City Point to recruit, they came back about a half a mile, halted for orders; I heard of it and concluded I would go with them and so hastened to where they were, and soon after my arrival the order came to "fall in." They did so with alacrity and bright hopes of much needed rest. I took my drum and place at the head of the regiment and started with them.

The road to the left led to City Point. Imagine their surprise when nearing it, the order came, "FILE RIGHT, BY COMPANY INTO LINE, DOUBLE QUICK MARCH."

The entire regiment seemed paralyzed for a moment, but only for a moment, the whizzing of the shells and the zip zip of the rebel bullets plainly told them what caused the sudden change. I was dumbfounded, I didn't know what to do. My brother yelled to me to go to the rear quick, but I didn't; I kept on with them until it seemed to rain bullets, but on, on they went unmindful of the awful storm of leaden messengers of death—on, on and into one of the fiercest charges of the entire war. I saw men fall so thick and fast that there didn't seem as if there was any of my regiment left, and I made up my mind it was too hot for me, so started on the dead run to the rear for a place of safety, and I didn't stop until I was pretty sure I was out of harm's way.

I came to a place about one mile back where evidently there had been a battery located; here I sat down to rest and meditate. I examined myself all over to see if I was hit, found I was unhurt but my drum had received several bullet holes in it.

Finding a green spot I stretched myself out and listened to the awful sound of musketry firing which was going on at the front, around me on all sides was the debris of a deserted camp, empty tin cans, broken bayonets, pieces of guns, fragments of bursted shell, and occasionally a whole one that had failed to explode. I had only sat here a few moments thinking which was the best way to go when I was joined by another Drummer Boy from a Pennsylvania regiment. We sat down and talked over our exploits, and I thought he was the most profane lad I had ever met. Most every other word he uttered was an oath.

I asked him if he wasn't afraid to talk so.

"What the h—l should I be afraid of?" he asked, at the same time picking up an old tent stake and sticking it into the ground, trying to drive it in with the heel of his boot. Failing in this he reached over and got hold of an unexploded shell and used this on the stake, but it was heavy and unwieldy.

"I wonder if this was fired by those d—d rebs," he asked.

"I guess it was," I replied, "and you better look out, or it might go off."

"Off be d—d, their shells were never worth the powder to blow 'em to h—l, see the hole in the butt of it, it would make a G—d—d good mawl, wouldn't it?" and looking round at the same time he found an old broom. Stripping the brush and wire from the handle he said, "I'll make a mawl of it and drive that d—d rebel stake into the ground with one of their own d—d shells, be d—d if I don't." Inserting the broom handle into the end of the shell he walked over to a stump, and taking the shell in both hands commenced pounding onto the stick against the stump; "d—d tight fit," he hollored to me, and the next instant I was knocked down by a terrific explosion. I came to my senses in a minute and hastened to where he had been standing. There the poor fellow lay unconscious and completely covered with blood, there was hardly a shred of clothes on him, his hair was all burned and both hands taken completely off, as if done by a surgeon's saw.

I was excited and horror stricken for a moment. The sight was horrible, but I quickly regained my composure, knowing that something must be done, and done quickly. So taking the snares from my drum I wound them tightly around his wrists to stop the flow of blood, then I hailed an ambulance, and we took him to the field hospital about a mile to the rear.

On the way the poor fellow regained consciousness, and looking at his mutilated wrists, and then with a quick and bewildered glance at me, "G—d—d tough, ain't it," then the tears started in his eyes, and he broke down and sobbed the rest of the way, "Oh, my God! What will my poor mother say? Oh, what will she do!"

We reached the field hospital, which is only a temporary place for the wounded where the wounds are hurriedly dressed, and then they are sent to regular hospitals, located in Baltimore, Philadelphia, Norfolk, Portsmouth, etc., where they have all the comforts possible.

We laid the little fellow down in one corner of the tent to wait his turn with the surgeon, and when I left him, he cried and begged for me to stay, but I couldn't stand his suffering longer, so I bade him good-bye with tears streaming down my own cheeks. I hurried out, and even after I reached the outside I could hear him cry, "Oh, my God! What will my poor mother say? Oh, what will she do!"

In the afternoon I was detailed to wait on the amputating tables at the field hospital. It was a horrible task at first. My duty was to hold the sponge or "cone" of ether to the face of the soldier who was to be operated on, and to stand there and see the surgeons cut and saw legs and arms as if they were cutting up swine or sheep, was an ordeal I never wish to go through again. At intervals, when the pile became large, I was obliged to take a load of legs or arms and place them in a trench near by for burial. I could only stand this one day, and after that I shirked all guard duty. The monotony, the routine of life, in front of Petersburg, was becoming distasteful to me. I had stolen everything I could. My district or territory had given out, so the next day I started for the front to bid my brother good-bye. Our regiment was sometimes relieved and ordered to the rear for rest; so it was on this occasion, they had fallen back and halted in a little ravine. I met my brother, who always expected me to bring him some stolen sweets or goodies of some kind, but unfortunately this time I came empty-handed. I had failed to find anything to steal. I was hungry myself, but when I looked at him I forgot my own hunger, for such a forlorn appearance as he presented almost broke my heart, and I determined to find him something to eat at all hazards. So off I started on an independent foraging expedition.

That night the regiment went into action, and my brother was slightly wounded several times. One shot would have proved fatal, but the watch received the bullet and the wound proved fatal only to the watch; it was smashed all to pieces. But my brother prizes the pieces now more than he ever did the whole watch.

The next day my regiment was ordered to the front again. I made up my mind I would not go with them. I concluded I needed rest in order to recuperate, so when the regiment started I bade my brother good-bye, gave him a parting kiss and God's blessings, so off I started.

About a half a mile from my regiment I came to one of those Virginia fences, got up on top of it, and sat thinking, and while sitting there the shells began to fly pretty thick. I thought I had better be moving, jumped down, and as I did so a shell struck one of the rails of the fence. A piece of the rail struck me and was harder than I was, for when I came to my senses I found I was in the hospital. I didn't think I was hurt very badly, but when I tried to get up, found I couldn't.

From there they moved me to "Balfour Hospital" at Portsmouth, Virginia. I never will forget the shame and mortification I felt at the sight I must have presented when the boat that conveyed us to Portsmouth arrived.

An old [Black man] came to my bunk and took me on his back, and with a boot in each hand dangling over his shoulder he carried me pickaback through the streets to the hospital, a large, fine building, formerly the "Balfour Hotel," and converted into a hospital after Portsmouth was captured. They took me up stairs into what was formerly the dining-room but now filled with over two hundred little iron beds, and each bed occupied by a wounded soldier. Everything in and about the place was as neat as wax. They carried me to a vacant bed near the center of the room, and I noticed the next bed to mine had several tin dishes hanging over it, suspended from the ceiling. These were filled with water, and from a small hole punctured in the bottom the water would slowly but constantly drip upon some poor fellow's wound to keep it moist. I had just sat down on the side of my bed, when I was startled by the sound of a familiar voice. "Hello, cully! What you been doin', playing with one of those d—d shells, too?"

No, I replied, the shells were playing with me. Then I recognized the occupant of the next bed as my drummer boy acquaintance who had his hands blown off a week ago. What a strange thing that we should be brought together side by side again, both wounded with a shell and nearly on the same spot.

He had changed wonderfully; his little white pinched face told too plainly the suffering he had endured. I asked him how he was getting along. "Oh I'm getting along pretty d—d fast. I guess I'll croak in a few days." "Oh you musn't talk that way, you'll be all right in a little while."

"Oh, no, cully, I know better. I'm a goner; I know it. I don't want to live, anyhow. What in h—l is the good of a man without hands?" Then turning his bandaged head towards me, his eyes filling with tears. "I aint afraid to die, cul., but I would like to see my old mother first. Do you think I will?"

Oh, yes, I said, no doubt of it; at the same time I felt that his days were numbered, but I wanted to make him feel as comfortable as possible. He was so much worse off than I, that I forgot my own injuries and was eager to assist him all I could. After a few minutes silence—

"Say, cully, reach under my pillow and find a little book there; it's a little Testament that my dear old mother gave me; read a little for me, will you please? You'll find a place mother marked for me, read that, please."

I turned the leaves over till I found a little white ribbon pinned to a leaf, marking the verse beginning, "Suffer little children to come unto me." I started to read for him, but the tears filled my eyes, I had to stop, and as I did so, I noticed he seemed very quiet. I glanced at him, and the open, staring eyes and the rigid drawn features told me too plainly that the little fellow was out of his sufferings—he was dead!

"Mother" was the countersign on his lips so thin, And the sentry in heaven must let him in.

I remained here three weeks, finally got up and around and began to think I had enough of soldier life. I had everything I wished for; some ladies in the town—God bless them, I never will forget them—visited the hospital occasionally, and they always took pains to bring me flowers or goodies of some kind. (Pardon me, but somehow I was always a favorite with ladies.) Well, after remaining there three or four weeks I concluded I didn't want to go to the front, so I sat down and wrote a personal letter to Secretary Stanton, told him who, how, and what I was, and asked him to advise me what to do; if I should go to the front or home. Soon after, a special order came back from him to have me transferred to the "2nd Battalion Veteran Reserve Corps." Let me here state to those who do not understand; all soldiers who were sick or wounded, unfit for field service were transferred to the Veteran Reserve Corps, for the purpose of doing light guard duty in camp, or at headquarters; they were divided into two battalions, 1st and 2nd. The 1st battalion was supposed to be able to carry a musket for duty, while the 2nd battalion was composed of one-armed men or totally disabled soldiers, and were supplied with a small sword; and thus I was condemned by special order; however I liked it. I had an easy time, nothing to do, and others to help me.

I continued here for about two months, until the hospital was ordered to be removed to Old Point Comfort. I had become a great favorite of Lieutenant Russell, the officer in charge of the hospital, and a nice man he was. When the order came to move, the fixtures, furniture, in fact everything in and about the building was ordered to be sold. I was detailed by Lieutenant Russell to remain behind and superintend the sale of the stuff, keep accounts, make a report when all was sold, and turn over the proceeds. That detained me there two weeks longer. I sold the beds, dishes, tables, everything. There remained about thirty tons of coal in the yard to be disposed of. I sold it in any quantity to poor people; took any price for it I could get, the same as everything else. Finally, everything was sold off, and I was ready to depart the next day for Old Point Comfort.

The next day I landed and reported to headquarters at Fortress Monroe. A day or two after, Lieutenant Russell sent for me; he wanted a foreman in the Government Printing Office. I was down for occupation on the pay-roll as a printer. He asked me if I understood the business. I said yes, I had some knowledge of it, so I was detailed with an extra eight dollars per month. I took charge of the office at once.

The first day I had orders to print fifty thousand official envelopes. The press-boy brought me the proof, I looked it over, and marked it correct; they were printed and sent to headquarters.

A few days after Lieutenant Russell sent for me to report at his office. I didn't know what was up. Thought perhaps I was going to be sent to Washington to take charge of the Government Printing Office there. As I went in, the lieutenant turned to me with a quizzical smile on his face:

"Young man, you told me you were a printer?"

"Yes, sir."

"Did you 'O. K.' this job?" passing one of the envelopes he held in his hand. "Yes sir," I answered.

"Umph! Is it correct?"

"Yes, sir."

"It is, eh!"

"Yes-s, sir."

"Umph! how do you spell business?"

"B-u-i-s-n-e-ss," said I.

"You do, eh?"

"Yes, sir."

"Well," said he in an imperative manner, "our government sees fit to differ with you. You will go to your office and print fifty thousand more, but see that you spell business right, and bring me the proof. The lot you have printed we will send to Washington, and recommend that they be made into a paper mache statue of yourself, and label it 'Buisness' or the only government printer."

I was a little chagrined at the mistake, but did not take it to heart; but I was soon relieved by a man who was more careful in his spelling. A week or so after leaving the printing office, I was sent to the fort to act as a kind of a companion to the confederate president, Jefferson

Davis. I was instructed to walk and talk with him. I presume I was intended for a sort of guard. Perhaps our government wished to make him feel as if he were not under surveillance, and so placed one whose insignificant appearance would put him at his ease. However, I found it a very agreeable occupation.

One of the most pleasant weeks I ever passed was with Mr. Jefferson Davis. He was a most agreeable man to me. He gave me lots of good advice, and I learned more from conversation with him about national affairs than I ever expected to know; and if I ever become president I will avail myself of the advice and teaching of that great man. He pointed out the right and wrong paths for young men; urged me above all things to adhere strictly to honesty and integrity; to follow these two principles, and I would succeed in business and become great and respected.

I thanked him for his kind advice, and pressed his hand good-bye. "Good-bye, my boy," said he. "You have been a comfort to me in my loneliness and sorrow. God bless you, my boy, God bless you!"

A great, big something came up in my throat as I turned and left him, and I have regretted all my life that I was not fortunate enough to have the pleasure of meeting him again before he passed away; for I assure you, indulgent readers and comrades, that no matter what he had done, or what mistakes he had made, his memory will always find a warm spot in the heart of that little Drummer Boy from Maine.

14

VERMONT SHARPSHOOTERS

BY WM. Y. W. RIPLEY

Unique rifles and special skills made them the forerunners of the elite Special Forces units so well known in today's military.

Very soon after the outbreak of the war for the Union, immediately, in fact, upon the commencement of actual operations in the field, it became painfully apparent that, however inferior the rank and file of the Confederate armies were in point of education and general intelligence to the men who composed the armies of the Union, however imperfect and rude their equipment and material, man for man they were the superiors of their northern antagonists in the use of arms.

Recruited mainly from the rural districts (for the South had but few large cities from which to draw its fighting strength), their armies were composed mainly of men who had been trained to the skillful use of the rifle in that most perfect school, the field and forest, in the pursuit of the game so abundant in those sparsely settled districts. These men, who came to the field armed at first, to a large extent, with their favorite sporting or target rifles, and with a training acquired in such a school, were individually more than the equals of the men of the North, who were, with comparatively few exceptions, drawn from the farm, the workshop, the office or the counter, and whose life-long occupations had been such as to debar them from those pursuits in which the men of the South had gained their skill. Indeed, there were in many regiments in the northern armies men who had never even fired a gun of any description at the time of their enlistment.

On the other hand, there were known to be scattered throughout the loyal states, a great number of men who had made rifle shooting a study, and who, by practice on the target ground and at the country shooting matches, had gained a skill equal to that of the men of the South in any kind of shooting, and in long range practice a much greater degree of excellency.

There were many of these men in the ranks of the loyal army, but their skill was neutralized by the fact that the arms put into their hands, although the most perfect military weapons then known, were not of the description calculated to show the best results in the hands of expert marksmen.

Occasionally a musket would be found that was accurate in its shooting qualities, and occasionally such a gun would fall into the hands of a man competent to appreciate and utilize its best features. It was speedily found that such a gun, in the hands of such a man, was capable of results not possible to be obtained from a less accurate weapon in the hands of a less skillful man. To remedy this state of affairs, and to make certain that the best weapons procurable should be placed in the hands of the men best fitted to use them effectively, it was decided by the war department, early in the summer of 1861, that a regiment should be organized, to be called the First Regiment of United States Sharp Shooters, and to consist of the best and most expert rifle shots in the Northern States. The detail of the recruiting and organization of this regiment was entrusted to Hiram Berdan, then a resident of the city of New York, himself an enthusiastic lover of rifle shooting, and an expert marksman.

Col. Berdan set himself earnestly at work to recruit and organize such a body of men as should, in the most perfect manner, illustrate the capacity for warlike purposes of his favorite weapon.

It was required that a recruit should possess a good moral character, a sound physical development, and in other respects come within the usual requirements of the army regulations; but, as the men were designed for an especial service, it was required of them that before enlistment they should justify their claim to be called "sharp shooters" by such a public exhibition of their skill as should fairly entitle them to the name, and warrant a reasonable expectation of usefulness in the field. To insure this it was ordered that no recruit be enlisted who could not, in a public trial, make a string of ten shots at a distance of two hundred yards, the aggregate measurement of which should not exceed fifty inches. In other words, it was required that the recruit should, in effect, be able to place ten bullets in succession within a ten-inch ring at a distance of two hundred yards.

Any style of rifle was allowed—telescopic sights, however, being disallowed—and the applicant was allowed to shoot from any position he chose, only being required to shoot from the shoulder.

Circular letters setting forth these conditions, and Col. Berdan authority, were issued to the governors of the loyal states, and, as a first result from the state of Vermont, Capt. Edmund Weston of Randolph applied for and received of Gov. Holbrook authority to recruit one company of sharp shooters, which was mustered into the service as Co. F, First United States Sharp Shooters, and is the subject of this history.

Capt. Weston at once put himself in communication with well known riflemen in different parts of the state and appointed recruiting officers in various towns to receive applications and superintend the trials of skill, without which no person could be accepted.

The response was more hearty and more general than could have been expected, and many more recruits presented themselves than could be accepted—many of whom, however, failed to pass the ordeal of the public competition—and, as the event proved, more were accepted than could be legally mustered into the service.

All who were accepted, however, fully met the rigid requirements as to skill in the use of the rifle.

The company rendezvoused at Randolph early in September, 1861, and on the 13th of that month were mustered into the state service by Charles Dana.

Thus organized, the company, with one hundred and thirteen enlisted men, left the state on the same day on which they were mustered, and proceeded via New Haven and Long Island Sound to the rendezvous of the regiment at Weehawken Heights, near New York, where they went into camp with other companies of the regiment which had preceded them. On or about the 24th of September the regiment proceeded under orders from the war department to Washington, arriving at that city at a late hour on the night of the twenty-fifth, and were assigned quarters at the Soldiers' Rest, so well known to the troops who arrived at Washington at about that time. On the twenty-sixth they were ordered to a permanent camp of instruction well out in the country and near the residence and grounds of Mr. Corcoran, a wealthy resident of Washington of supposed secession proclivities, where they were for the first time in a regularly organized camp, and could begin to feel that they were fairly cut off at last from the customs and habits of civil life. Here they were regularly mustered into the service of the United States, thirteen enlisted men being rejected, however, to reduce the company to the regulation complement of one hundred enlisted men; so that of the one hundred and thirteen men charged to the company on the rolls of the Adjt. and Ins.-Gen. of Vermont, only one hundred took the field. Other companies from different states arrived at about the same time, and the regiment was at last complete, having its full complement of ten companies of one hundred men each.

Only one of the field officers had had a military education or military experience. Lieutenant-Colonel Mears was an officer of the regular army, a thorough drill master and a strict disciplinarian. Under his efficient command the regiment soon began to show a marked and daily improvement that augured well for its future usefulness. The officers of the regimental staff were, each in his own department, able and painstaking men. The chaplain alone was not quite popular among the rank and file, and they rather envied the Second Regiment of Sharp Shooters who were encamped near them, and whose chaplain, the Rev. Lorenzo Barber, was the beau ideal of an army chaplain. Tender hearted and kind, he was ever ready to help the weak and the suffering; now dressing a wound and now helping along a poor fellow, whose fingers were all thumbs and whose thoughts were too big for utterance (on paper), with his letter to the old mother at home; playing ball or running a foot race, beating the best marksmen at the targets, and finally preaching a rousing good sermon which was attentively listened to on Sunday. His *faith* was in the "Sword of the Lord and of Gideon," but his best *work* was put in with a twenty pound telescopic rifle which he used with wonderful effect. The original plan of armament contemplated the use exclusively of target or sporting rifles. The men had been encouraged to bring with them their favorite weapons, and had been told that the government would pay for such arms at the rate of sixty dollars each, while those who chose to rely upon the United States armories for their rifles were to be furnished with the best implements procurable. The guns to be so furnished were to be breach loaders, to have telescopic sights, hair triggers, and all the requisites for the most perfect shooting that the most skillful marksman could desire.

Many of the men had, with this understanding, brought with them their own rifles, and with them target shooting became a pastime, and many matches between individuals and companies were made and many very short strings were recorded.

Under the stimulus of competition and organized practice great improvement was noted in marksmanship, even among those who had been considered almost perfect marksmen before. On one occasion President Lincoln, accompanied by Gen. McClellan, paid a visit to the camp and asked to be allowed to witness some of the sharp shooting of which he had heard so much.

A detail of the best men was made and a display of skill took place which, perhaps, was never before equalled. President Lincoln himself, as did Gen. McClellan, Col. Hudson and others of the staff, took part in the firing, the President using a rifle belonging to Corporal H. J. Peck of the Vermont company.

At the close of the exhibition Col. Berdan, being asked to illustrate the accuracy of his favorite rifle, fired three shots at different portions of the six hundred yard target; when having satisfied himself that he had the proper range, and that both himself and rifle could be depended upon, announced that at the next shot he would strike the right eye of the gaily colored Zouave which, painted on the half of an A tent, did duty for a target at that range. Taking a long and careful aim, he fired, hitting the exact spot selected and announced beforehand. Whether partly accidental or not it was certainly a wonderful performance and placed Col. Berdan at once in the foremost rank of rifle experts. On the 28th of November, the day set apart by the governors of the loyal states as Thanksgiving Day, shooting was indulged by in different men of Co. F and other companies for a small prize offered by the field officers, the terms being two hundred yards, off hand, the shortest string of two shots to win. The prize was won from a large number of skillful contestants by Ai Brown of Co. F—his two shots measuring 4-1/4 inches, or each within 2-1/8 inches of the center.

On the 7th of December another regimental shooting match took place; the prize going this time to a Michigan man, his string of three shots, fired off hand at two hundred yards, measuring six inches. These records are introduced here simply for the purpose of showing the wonderful degree of skill possessed by these picked marksmen in the use of the rifle. But it was soon found that there were objections to the use in the field of the fine guns so effective on the target ground. The great weight of some of them was of itself almost prohibitory, for, to a soldier burdened with the weight of his knapsack, haversack and canteen, blanket and overcoat, the additional weight of a target rifle—many of which weighed fifteen pounds each, and some as much as thirty pounds—was too much to be easily borne.

It was also found difficult to provide the proper ammunition for such guns in the field, and finally, owing to the delicacy of the construction of the sights, hair triggers, etc., they were constantly liable to be out of order, and when thus disabled, of even less use than the smooth-bore musket, with buck and ball cartridge of fifty years before. Manufacturers of fine guns from all parts of our own country, and many from Europe, flocked to the camp of the sharp shooters offering their goods, each desirous of the credit of furnishing arms to a body of men so well calculated to use them effectively, and many fine models were offered. The choice of the men, however, seemed to be a modified military rifle made by the Sharpe Rifle Manufacturing Co., and a request was made to the war department for a supply of these arms. At this early day, however, the departments were full of men whose ideas and methods were those of a half a century gone by; and at the head of the ordinance department was a man who, in addition to being of this stamp, was the father of the muzzle loading Springfield rifle, then the recognized arm of the United States Infantry, and from him came the most strenuous opposition to the proposal to depart from the traditions of the regular army.

Gen. McClellan, and even the President himself, were approached on this subject, and both recognized the propriety of the proposed style of armament and the great capacity for efficient service possessed by the regiment when it should be once satisfactorily armed and fairly in front of the enemy. But the ordinance department was ever a block in the way; its head obstinately and stubbornly refusing to entertain any proposition other than to arm the regiment with the ordinary army musket; and, to add to the growing dissatisfaction among the men over the subject of arms, it became known that the promises made to them at the time of enlistment, that the government would pay them for their rifles at the rate of sixty dollars each, was unauthorized and would not be fulfilled; and also that the representations made to them with respect to telescopic breech loaders were likewise unauthorized. Discontent became general and demoralization began to show itself in an alarming form.

Some of the field officers were notoriously incompetent; the Major, one of those military adventurers who floated to the surface during the early years of the war, particularly so; he was a kind of a modern Dalgetty without the courage or skill of his renowned prototype, rarely present in camp, and when there of little or no service. The Lieutenant-Colonel, a man of rare energy and skill in his profession, and whose painstaking care had made the regiment all that it was at that time, fearing the after effects of this demoralization on the efficiency of the command, and seeing opportunity for his talents in other fields, resigned; and on the 29th of November, 1861, Wm. Y. W. Ripley of Rutland, Vt., was appointed Lieutenant-Colonel, and Caspar Trepp, Captain of Co. A., was made Major. Lieutenant-Colonel Ripley had seen service only as Captain of Co. K, First Vermont Volunteers. Major Trepp had received a thorough military training in the army of his native Switzerland, and had seen active service in European wars. The regiment remained at camp of instruction under the immediate command of Lieut.-Col. Ripley, employed in the usual routine of camp duty, drills, etc., during the whole of the winter of 1861–62, particular attention being paid to the skirmish drill, in which the men became wonderfully proficient; and it is safe to say that for general excellence in drill, except the manual of arms, they were excelled by few volunteer regiments in the service. All orders were given by the sound of the bugle, and the whole regiment deployed as skirmishers could be as easily maneuvered as a single company could be in line of battle. The bugle corps was under the charge of Calvin Morse of Co. F as chief bugler, and under his careful instruction attained to an unusual degree of excellence. All camp and other calls were sounded on the bugle, and the men found them pleasant little devices for translating curt and often rough English into music. They were bugled to breakfast and to dinner, bugled to guard mounting and bugled to battle, brigades moved and cavalry charged to the sound of the bugle.

The winter was an unusually severe one, and, as the enemy maintained a strict blockade of the Potomac, the supply of wood was often short, and some suffering was the result. The health of the regiment remained fairly good; measles, small pox, and other forms of camp diseases appeared, however, and Co. F, of course, suffered its share, losing by death from disease during the winter, Wm. T. Battles, Edward Fitz, Sumner E. Gardner and Geo. H. Johnson.

On the 20th of March, 1862, the regiment received orders to report to Major-Gen. Fitz John Porter, whose division then lay at Alexandria, Va., awaiting transportation to Fortress Monroe to join the army under McClellan. At this time the regiment was without arms of any kind, except for the few target rifles remaining in the hands of their owners, and a few old smooth bore muskets which had been used during the winter for guard duty. Shortly before this time the war department, perhaps wearied by constant importunity, perhaps recognizing the importance of the subject, had so far receded from its former position as to offer to arm the regiment with revolving rifles of the Colt pattern, and had sent the guns to the camp for issue to the men with promise of exchanging them for Sharpe's rifles at a later day. They were five chambered breech loaders, very pretty to look at, but upon examination and test they were found inaccurate and unreliable, prone to get out of order and even dangerous to the user. They were not satisfactory to the men, who knew what they wanted and were fully confident of their ability to use such guns as they had been led by repeated promises to expect, to good advantage. When, however, news came that the rebels had evacuated Manassas, and that the campaign was about to open in good earnest, they took up these toys, for after all they were hardly more, and turned their faces southward. Co. F was the first company in the regiment to receive their arms, and to the influence of their patriotic example the regiment owes its escape from what at one time appeared to be a most unfortunate embarrassment.

The march to Alexandria over Long Bridge was made in the midst of a pouring rain and through such a sea of mud as only Virginia can afford material for. It was the first time the regiment had ever broken camp, and its first hard march. It was long after dark when the command arrived near Cloud's mills; the headquarters of Gen. Porter could not be found, and it became necessary for the regiment to camp somewhere for the night. At a distance were seen the lights of a camp, which was found upon examination to be the winter quarters of the 69th New York in charge of a camp guard, the regiment having gone out in pursuit of the enemy beyond Manassas. A few persuasive words were spoken to the sergeant in command, and the tired and soaked sharp shooters turned into the tents of the absent Irishmen.

★   ★   ★

CHANCELLORSVILLE.

On the 25th of January Gen. Burnside was relieved from the command and Gen. Hooker appointed to succeed him. The army accepted the change willingly, for although they recognized the many manly and soldierly qualities possessed by Gen. Burnside, and in a certain way respected and even sympathized with him, they had lost confidence in his ability to command so large an army in the presence of so astute a commander as Lee. His manly avowal of his sole responsibility for the terrible slaughter at Fredericksburgh commended him to their hearts and understandings as an honest and generous man; but they had no wish to repeat the experience for the sake of even a more generous acknowledgement after another Fredericksburgh.

The remainder of the winter of 1862–3 was spent by the men of Co. F in comparative comfort, although severe snow storms were of frequent occurrence, and occasional periods of exceedingly cold weather were experienced, to the great discomfort of the men in their frail canvas tents. Both armies seemed to have had enough of marching and fighting to satisfy them for the time being, and even picket firing ceased by tacit agreement and consent.

Soon after assuming command, Gen. Hooker reorganized the army on a plan more consistent with his own ideas than the one adopted by his predecessor. The system of Grand Divisions was abandoned and corps were reorganized; some corps commanders were relieved and others appointed to fill the vacancies. The cavalry, which up to this time had had no organization as a corps, was consolidated under Gen. Stoneman, and soon became, under his able leadership, the equals, if not the superiors, of the vaunted horsemen of the South. In these changes the sharp shooters found themselves assigned to the first division of the Third Corps, under Gen. Sickles. The division was commanded by Gen. Whipple, and the brigade by Gen. De Trobriand. The detachments were called in and the regiment was once more a unit.

Under Gen. Hooker's system the army rapidly improved in morale and spirit; he instituted a liberal system of furloughs to deserving men, and took vigorous measures against stragglers and men absent without leave, of whom there were at this time an immense number—shown by the official rolls to be above eighty thousand. Desertion, which under Burnside had become alarmingly prevalent, was substantially stopped; and by the 1st of April the tone and discipline of the army was such as to fairly warrant Hooker's proud boast that it was "the grandest army on the planet."

The winter was not altogether devoted to sober work. Sports of various kinds were indulged in, one of the most popular being snowball fights between regiments and brigades. Upon one occasion after a sharp conflict between the first and second regiments of sharp shooters, the former captured the regimental colors of the latter, and for a short time some little ill feeling between the regiments existed, a feeling which soon wore away, however, with the opening of the spring campaign.

As the season advanced and the roads became settled and passable, preparations began on all sides for an active campaign against the enemy. "Fighting Joe Hooker" had inspired the army with much of his own confidence and faith in the future, and it was believed by the troops that at last they had a commander worthy in every respect of the magnificent army he was called to command.

On the 28th of April the Third Corps, to which the sharp shooters were now attached, moved down the river to a point some five miles below Falmouth to support Sedgwick's command which was ordered to cross the Rappahannock at or near the point at which Gen. Franklin had crossed his Grand Division at the battle of Fredericksburgh.

Some days prior to this all surplus clothing and baggage had been turned in. Eight days rations and sixty rounds of ammunition were now issued, and the "finest army on the planet" was foot loose once more. Sedgwick's crossing was made, however, without serious opposition, and on the thirtieth the Third Corps, making a wide detour to the rear to avoid the notice of the watchful enemy, turned northward and on the next day crossed the river at United States ford and took its place in the lines of Chancellorsville with the rest of the army.

This great battle has been so often described and in such minute detail that it is not necessary for us to attempt a detailed description of the movements of the different corps engaged, or indeed proper, since this purports to be a history of the marches and battles of only one small company out of the thousands there engaged. It will be remembered that the regiment was now attached to the Third Corps, commanded by Gen. Sickles, the First Division under Gen. Whipple and the Third Brigade, Gen. De Trobriand. At eleven o'clock A. M. on this day, being the first of May, the battle proper commenced, although severe and continuous skirmishing had been going on ever since the first troops crossed the river on the 29th of April. The Third Corps was held in reserve in rear of the Chancellorsville house, having arrived at that point at about the time that the assaulting columns moved forward to the attack.

Almost instantly the fighting became furious and deadly. The country was covered with dense undergrowth of stunted cedars, among and over which grew heavy masses of the trailing vines which grow so luxuriantly in that portion of Virginia, and which renders the orderly passage of troops well nigh impossible. To add to the difficulties which beset the attacking forces, it was impossible to see what was in front of them; hence the first notice of the presence of a rebel line of battle was a volley delivered at short range directly in the faces of the Union soldiers, whose presence and movements were unavoidably made plain to the concealed enemy by the noise made in forcing a passage through the tangled forest. Notwithstanding these disadvantages the Fifth Corps, with which the sharp shooters had so recently parted, struck the enemy at about a mile distant from the position now held by the Third Corps, and drove them steadily back for a long distance until, having passed far to the front of the general line, Meade found his flank suddenly attacked and was forced to retire. Other columns also met the enemy at about the same distance to the front and met with a like experience, gaining, however, on the whole, substantial ground during the afternoon; and so night closed down on the first day of the battle.

On the morning of the 2d of May a division of the Third Corps was detached to hold a gap in the lines between the Eleventh and Twelfth Corps which Gen. Hooker thought too weak. The sharp shooters, however, remained with the main column near the Chancellorsville house. Early on this day the Confederate Gen. Jackson commenced that wonderful flank march which resulted in the disaster to the Eleventh Corps on the right, later in the day. This march, carefully masked as it was, was, nevertheless, observed by Hooker, who at first supposed it the commencement of a retreat on the part of Lee to Gordonsville, and Gen. Sickles was ordered with the two remaining divisions of his corps to demonstrate in that direction and act as circumstances should determine. In this movement Birney's division had the advance, the first division, under Whipple, being in support of Birney's left flank. The sharp shooters were, however, ordered to report to Gen. Birney, and were by him placed in the front line as skirmishers, although their deployment was at such short intervals that it was more like a single rank line of battle than a line of skirmishers.

Sickles started on his advance at about one o'clock P. M., his formation being as above described. Rapidly pressing forward, the sharp shooters passed out of the dense thickets into a comparatively open country, where they could at least breathe more freely and see a little of what was before them. They soon struck a line of rebels in position on the crest of a slight elevation, and brisk firing commenced; the advance, however, not being checked, they soon cleared the hill of the enemy and occupied it themselves. Changing front to the left, the regiment moved from this position obliquely to the southeast, and soon found themselves opposed to a line which had evidently come to stay. The fighting here was very severe and lasted for a considerable time. The rebels seemed to have a desire to stay the advance of the Union troops at that particular point, and for some particular reason, which was afterwards made apparent.

After some minutes of brisk firing, the sharp shooters, by a sudden rush on their flank, succeeded in compelling the surrender of the entire force, which was found to consist of the Twenty-third Georgia regiment, consisting of three hundred and sixty officers and men, which had been charged by Jackson with the duty of preventing any advance of the Union troops at this point which might discover his march towards Hooker's right, hence the tenacity with which they clung to the position. The obstruction having been thus removed, the Third Corps, led by the sharp shooters, pressed rapidly forward to the southward as far as Hazel Grove, or the old furnace, some two miles from the place of starting, and far beyond any supporting column which could be depended on for early assistance should such be needed. It had now become apparent to all that Jackson, instead of being in full retreat as had been supposed, was in the full tide of one of the most violent offensives on record; and at five o'clock P. M. Sickles was ordered to attack his right flank and thus check his advance on the exposed right of the army. But at about the same time Sickles found that he was himself substantially cut off from the army, and that it would require the most strenuous efforts to prevent the capture or destruction of his own command. Furthermore, before he could make his dispositions and march over the ground necessary to be traversed before he could reach Jackson's right, that officer had struck his objective point, and the rout of the Eleventh Corps was complete.

The most that Sickles could now do, under the circumstances, was to fight his own way back to his supports, and to choose, if possible, such a route as would place him, on his arrival, in a position to check Jackson's further advance and afford the broken right wing an opportunity to rally and regain their organization, which was hopelessly, as it appeared, lost. In the darkness and gloom of the falling night, with unloaded muskets (for in this desperate attempt the bayonet only was to be depended upon), the two divisions of the Third Corps set their faces northwardly, and pressed their way through the tangled undergrowth to the rescue of the endangered right wing.

As usual, the sharp shooters had the advance, and received the first volley from the concealed enemy. They had received no especial orders concerning the use, solely, of the bayonet, and were at once engaged in a close conflict under circumstances in which their only superiority over troops of the line consisted in the advantage of the rapidity of fire afforded by their breech loaders over the muzzle loading rifles opposed to them. Closely supported by the line of Birney's division, and firing as they advanced at the flashes of the opposing guns (for they could see no more), they pushed on until they were fairly intermingled with the rebels, and in many individual instances, a long distance inside the enemy's line, every man fighting for himself—for in this confused melee, in the dense jungle and in the intense darkness of the night, no supervision could be exercised by officers and many shots were fired at distances no greater than a few feet. So they struggled on until, with a hurrah and a grand rush, Birney's gallant men dashed forward with the bayonet alone, and after ten minutes of hand to hand fighting, they succeeded in retaking the plank road, and a considerable portion of the line held by the left of the Eleventh Corps in the early portion of the day and lost in the tremendous charge of Jackson's corps in the early evening. Sickles had cut his way out, and more, he was now in a position to afford the much needed aid to those who so sorely required it. Both parties had fought to the point of exhaustion, and were glad to suspend operations for a time for this cause alone, even had no better reasons offered. But the Union army was no longer in a position for offense; the extreme left, with which we have had nothing to do, had been so heavily pressed during the afternoon that it had been with difficulty that a disaster similar to the one which had overtaken the right had been prevented on that flank, and in the center, at and about Hazel Grove and the furnace, which had been held by Sickles, and from which he had been ordered to the support of the right as we have seen, an absolute gap existed, covered by no force whatever. This, then, was the situation, briefly stated.

The left was barely able to hold its own, the center was absolutely abandoned, and the right had been utterly routed. In this state of affairs the Union commander was in no mood for a further offense at that time. On the other hand, the controlling mind that had conceived, and thus far had successfully carried out this wonderful attack which had been so disastrous to the Union army, and which bade fair to make the Southern Confederacy a fact among the nations, had been stricken down in the full tide of its success. Stonewall Jackson had been wounded at about nine o'clock by the fire of his own men. He had passed beyond the lines of his pickets to reconnoiter the Union position, and on his return with his staff they were mistaken by his soldiers for a body of federal cavalry and he received three wounds from the effects of which he died about a week later. So fell a man who was perhaps as fine a type of stout American soldiership as any produced on either side during the war.

The sharp shooters, with the remnant of the Third Corps, passed the remainder of the night on the plank road near Dowdall's tavern. Co. F had left their knapsacks and blankets under guard near the Chancellorsville house when they advanced from that point in the morning, as had the rest of the regiment. Under these circumstances little sleep or rest could be expected even had the enemy been in less close proximity. But with the rebel pickets hardly thirty yards distant, and firing at every thing they saw or heard, sleep was out of the question. So passed the weary night of the disastrous 2d of May at Chancellorsville.

During the night Gen. Hooker, no longer on the offensive, had been busily engaged in laying out and fortifying a new line on which he might hope more successfully to resist the attack which all knew must come at an early hour on the morning of the third. On the extreme left the troops were withdrawn from their advanced positions to a more compact and shorter line in front of, and to the south and east of the Chancellorsville house. The center, which at sunset was unoccupied by any considerable body of Union troops, was made secure; and at daylight Sickles, with the Third Corps, was ordered to withdraw to a position indicated immediately in front of Fairview, a commanding height of land now strongly occupied by the Union artillery.

It was not possible, however, to withdraw so large a body of troops from their advanced position, in the face of so watchful an enemy, without interruption. In fact, even before the movement had commenced, the enemy took the initiative and commenced the battle of that day by a furious attack upon the heights of Hazel Grove, the position so handsomely won by the Third Corps on the previous day and from which they were ordered to the relief of the Eleventh Corps at five o'clock on the preceding afternoon, as we have seen.

This height of land commanded almost every portion of the field occupied by the Union army, and from it Sickles' line, as it stood at daybreak, could be completely enfiladed. This position was held by an inadequate force for its defense; indeed, as it was far in advance of the new line of battle it may be supposed that observation, rather than defense, was the duty of its occupants. They made a gallant fight, however, but were soon compelled to retire with the loss of four guns. The rebel commander, quick to see the great importance of the position, crowned the hill with thirty guns which, with the four taken from the Unionists, poured a heavy fire on all parts of the line, devoting particular attention to Sickles' exposed left and rear.

At almost the same period of time the rebels in Sickles' front made a savage attack on his line. The men of the Third Corps fought, as they always fought, stubbornly and well, but, with a force more than equal to their own in point of numbers, flushed with their success of the previous afternoon and burning to avenge the fall of Jackson, in their front, and this enormous concentration of artillery hammering away on their defenseless left, they were at last forced back to the new line in front of Fairview.

In preparation for the withdrawal contemplated, and before the rebel attack developed itself, the sharp shooters had been deployed to the front and formed a skirmish line to the north of the plank road with their left on that highway, and thus received the first of the rebel attack. They succeeded in repulsing the advance of the first line and for half an hour held their ground against repeated attempts of the rebel skirmishers to dislodge them. The position they held was one of the utmost importance since it commanded the plank road which must be the main line of the rebel approach to Fairview, the key to the new Union line, and aware of this the men fought on with a courage and determination seldom witnessed even in the ranks of that gallant regiment. After half an hour of this perilous work, the regiment on their right having given way, the sharp shooters were ordered to move by the right flank to cover the interval thus exposed, their own place being taken by still another body of infantry.

Steadily and coolly the men faced to the right at the sound of the bugle, and commenced their march, still firing as they advanced. Necessarily, however, the men had to expose themselves greatly in this movement, and as necessarily their own fire was less effective than when delivered coolly from the shelter of some friendly tree, log or bank which skirmishers are so prone to seek and so loath to leave. Still the march was made in good order and in good time, for the sharp shooters had only just time to fill the gap when the rebels came on for a final trial for the mastery.

For a long time the green coated riflemen clung to their ground and gave, certainly as good, as they received. But the end of the long struggle was at hand; the regiment which had taken the position just vacated by the sharp shooters was driven in confusion, and to cap the climax of misfortune, the Union artillery, observing the withdrawal of other troops, and supposing that all had been retired, opened a furious fire of canister into the woods. The sharp shooters were now in a sad case—before them a furious crowd of angry enemies, on the left the rebel artillery at Hazel Grove sweeping their lines from left to right at every discharge, while, worst of all, from the rear came the equally dangerous fire of their own friends.

To retreat was as bad as to advance. The ground to their right was an unknown mystery and no hopeful sign came from the left; so taking counsel from their very desperation they concluded to remain just there, at least until some reasonable prospect of escape should present itself. Taking such cover as they could get, some from the fire of our own guns and some from those of the rebels, shifting from side to side of the logs and trees as the fire came hotter from the one side or from the other, but always keeping up their own fire in the direction of the enemy, they maintained the unequal fight until an officer, sent for the purpose, succeeded in stopping the fire of our own guns, and the sharp shooters willingly withdrew from a position such as they had never found themselves in before, and from a scene which no man present will ever forget.

They were sharply pressed by the advancing enemy, but now, being out of the line of the enfilading fire from Hazel Grove, and no longer subject to the fire of their own friends, the withdrawal was made in perfect order, the line halting at intervals at the sound of the bugle and delivering well aimed volleys at the enemy, now fully exposed, and even at times making countercharges to check their too rapid advance.

In one of these rallies there fell a man from another company whose death as well deserves to be remembered in song as that of the "Sleeping Sentinel." He had been condemned to death by the sentence of a court martial, and was in confinement awaiting the execution of the sentence when the army left camp at Falmouth at the outset of the campaign. In some manner he managed to escape from his guards, and joined his company on the evening of the second day's light.

Of course it was irregular, and no precedent for it could possibly be found in the army regulations, but men were more valuable on that field than in the guard house; perhaps, too, his captain hoped that he might, in the furor of the battle, realize his own expressed wish that he might meet his fate there instead of at the hands of a firing party of the provost guard, and thus, by an honorable death on the battle field, efface to some extent the stain on his character.

However it was, a rifle was soon found for him (rifles without owners were plenty on that field), and he took his place in the ranks. During all of that long forenoon's fighting he was a marked man. All knew his history, and all watched to see him fall; for while others carefully availed themselves of such shelter as the field afforded, he alone stood erect and in full view of the enemy. Many times he exhausted the cartridges in his box, each time replenishing it from the boxes of his dead or wounded companions. He seemed to bear a charmed life; for, while death and wounds came to many who would have avoided either, the bullets passed him harmless by. At last, however, in one of the savage conflicts when the sharp shooters turned on the too closely following enemy, this gallant soldier, with two or three of his companions, came suddenly upon a small party of rebels who had outstripped their fellows in the ardor of the pursuit; he, being in the advance, rushed upon them, demanding their surrender. "Yes," said one, "we surrender," but at the same time, as —— lowered his gun, the treacherous rebel raised his, and the sharp shooter fell, shot through the heart.

He spoke no word, but those who caught the last glimpse of his face, as they left him lying where he fell, knew that he had realized his highest hope and wish, and that he died content. The sequel to this sad personal history brings into tender recollection the memory of that last and noblest martyr to the cause of the Union, President Lincoln. The case was brought to his notice by those who felt that the stain upon the memory of this gallant, true hearted soldier was not fully effaced, even by his noble self-sacrifice, and would not be while the records on the books stood so black against him. The President was never appealed to in vain when it was possible for him to be merciful, and, sitting down, he wrote with his own hand a full and free pardon, dating it as of the morning of that eventful 3d of May, and sent it to the widow of the dead soldier in a distant state. It was such acts as this that made Abraham Lincoln so loved by the soldiers of the Union. They respected the President, but Abraham Lincoln—the man—was *loved*.

Upon the arrival of the retreating riflemen at the new line in front of Fairview, they found their division, the main portion of which had, of course, preceded them, in line of battle in rear of the slight defenses which had been thrown up at that point, where they enjoyed a brief period of much needed repose, if a short respite from actual personal encounter could be called repose. They were still under heavy artillery fire, while musketry was incessant and very heavy only a short distance away, the air above their heads being alive, at times, with everything that kills. Yet so great was their fatigue, and so quiet and restful their position in comparison with what it had been for so long a time, that, after receiving rations and a fresh supply of ammunition for their exhausted boxes, officers and men alike lay down on the ground, and most of them enjoyed an hour of refreshing sleep. Their rest was not of long duration, however, for the rebels made a desperate and savage attack on the line in their front and the Third Corps soon found itself again engaged. The enemy, under cover of their artillery on the high ground at Hazel Grove, made an assault on what was now the front of the Union line (if it could be said to have a front) while the force which the sharp shooters had so long held in check during the early part of the day made a like attack on that line now the right of the entire army.

So heavy was the attack, and so tenaciously sustained, that the Union troops were actually forced from their lines in front and on the flank of Fairview, and the hill was occupied by the rebels, who captured, and held for a time, all the Union guns on that eminence. It was at this stage of affairs that the Third Corps was again called into action, and charging the somewhat disorganized enemy they retook the hill with the captured guns, and following up the flying rebels, they drove them to, and beyond the position they had occupied in the morning. Here, however, meeting with a fresh line of the enemy and being brought to a check, they were ordered again to retire; for Hooker, by this time intent only upon getting his army safely back across the river, had formed still another new line near to, and covering, the bridges and fords by which alone could he place his forces in a position of even comparative safety.

To this line then the Third Corps, with the tired and decimated sharp shooters, retired late in the afternoon, hoping and praying for a respite from their terrible labors. For a little time it looked, indeed, as if their hopes would be realized, but as darkness drew on the corps commander, desiring to occupy a wooded knoll at some little distance from his advanced picket line, and from which he anticipated danger, ordered Gen. Whipple, to whose division the sharp shooters had been returned, to send a brigade to occupy it. Gen. Whipple replied that he had one regiment who were alone equal to the task and to whom he would entrust it, and ordered the sharp shooters to attempt it.

Between this wooded hill and the position from which the regiment must charge was an open field about one hundred yards in width which was to be crossed under what might prove a destructive fire from troops already occupying the coveted position. It was a task requiring the most undaunted courage and desperate endeavor on the part of men who had already been for two full days and nights in the very face of the enemy, and they felt that the attempt might fairly have been assigned to a portion of the forty thousand men who, up to that time, had been held in reserve by Gen. Hooker for some inscrutable purpose, and who had not seen the face of an enemy, much less fired a shot at them; but they formed for the assault with cheerful alacrity.

To Co. F was assigned the lead, and marching out into the open field they deployed as regularly as though on their old drill ground at camp of instruction. Corps, brigade and division commanders were looking on, and the men felt that now, if never before, they must show themselves worthy sons of the Green Mountain state. Led by their officers, they dashed out into the plain closely supported by the rest of the regiment. Night was rapidly coming on, and in the gathering gloom objects could hardly be distinguished at a distance of a hundred yards.

Half the open space was crossed, and it seemed to the rushing men that their task was to be accomplished without serious obstructions, when, from the edge of the woods in front, came a close and severe volley betraying the presence of a rebel line of battle; how strong could only be judged by the firing, which was so heavy, however, as to indicate a force much larger than the attacking party. On went the brave men of Co. F, straight at their work, and behind them closely followed the supporting force. In this order they reached the edge of the forest when the enemy, undoubtedly supposing from the confidence with which the sharp shooters advanced that the force was much larger than it really was, broke and fled and the position was won.

From prisoners and wounded rebels captured in that night attack it was learned that the force which had thus been beaten out of a strong position by this handful of men was a portion of the famous Stonewall brigade, Jackson's earliest command, and they asserted that it was the first time in the history of the brigade that it had ever been driven from a chosen position. The sharp shooters were justly elated at their success and the more so when Gen. Whipple, riding over to the point so gallantly won, gave them unstinted praise for their gallant action. In this affair the regiment lost many gallant officers and men, among whom were Lieut. Brewer of Co. C and Capt. Chase, killed, and Major Hastings and Adjt. Horton, wounded. In Co. F Michael Cunningham, J. S. Bailey and E. M. Hosmer were wounded.

Major Hastings had not been a popular officer with the command. Although a brave and capable man, he was of a nervous temperament, and in the small details of camp discipline was apt to be over zealous at times. He had, therefore, incurred the dislike of many men, who were wont to apply various opprobrious epithets to him at such times and under such circumstances as made it extremely unpleasant for him. Such were the methods adopted by some soldiers to make it comfortable for officers to whom they had a dislike.

In the case of the Major, however, this was a thing of the past. On this bloody field the men learned to respect their officer, and he, as he was borne from the field, freely forgave the boys all the trouble and annoyance they had caused him, in consideration of their gallant bearing on that day. Adjt. Horton, also a brave and efficient officer, received a severe wound—which afterwards cost him his good right arm—while using the rifle of J. S. Bailey of Co. F, who had been wounded.

Co. F, which, it will be remembered, had been acting as skirmishers, were pushed forward in advance of the main portion of the regiment to further observe the movements of the enemy and to guard against a surprise, and shortly afterwards were moved by the flank some two hundred yards to the right, and were soon after relieved by a force of infantry of the line which had been sent up for that purpose. While retiring toward the position to which they were directed, they passed nearly over the same ground which they had just vacated when they moved by the right flank, as previously mentioned, and received from the concealed rebels, who had reoccupied the line, a severe volley at close range. Facing to the right, Co. F at once charged this new enemy and drove them in confusion from the field. Lying down in this advanced position they passed the remainder of the night in watchful suspense.

At day break on the fourth day of the battle, Co. F was relieved from its position on the picket line and returned to the regiment, which was deployed as skirmishers, and led the van of Whipple's division in a charge to check movements of the enemy which had for their apparent object the interposition of a rebel force between the right wing of the army and its bridges. Firing rapidly as they advanced, and supported by the division close on their heels, they drove the enemy from their rifle pits, which were occupied by the infantry of the Third Corps, the sharp shooters being still in front. Here they remained, exchanging occasional shots with the rebel sharp shooters as occasion offered, for some hours. Hooker was not minded to force the fighting at Chancellorsville; preferring to await the result of Sedgwick's battle at Salem Church, which had raged furiously on the preceding afternoon until darkness put an end to the strife, and the tell tale guns of which even now gave notice of further effort.

Lee, however, pugnacious and aggressive, determined to renew his attack on the right, and, if possible, secure the roads to the fords and bridges by which alone could the defeated army regain the north bank of the river. With this view he reenforced Jackson's (now Stuart's) corps, and organized a powerful attack on the position of the Third Corps. The force of the first onset fell on the sharp shooters, who fought with their accustomed gallantry, but were forced by the weight of numbers back to the main line. Here the fighting was severe and continuous. The one party fighting for a decisive victory, and the other, alas, only bent on keeping secure its last and only line of retreat; but the incentive, poor as it was, was sufficient, and the rebels were unable to break the line. After four hours of continued effort they abandoned the assault and quiet once more prevailed. In this fight Gen. Whipple, the division commander, was killed. He was a gallant and an able soldier, greatly beloved by his men for the kindliness of his disposition. He had an especial liking for and confidence in the sharp shooters, which was fully understood and appreciated by them, and they felt his death as a personal loss.

To add to the horrors of this bloody field, on which lay nearly nine thousand dead and wounded Union soldiers and nearly or quite as many rebels, the woods took fire and hundreds of badly wounded men, unable to help themselves, and hopeless of succor, perished miserably in the fierce flames. Nothing in the whole history of the war is more horrible than the recollection of those gallant men, who had been stricken down by rebel bullets, roasted to death in the very presence of their comrades, impotent to give them aid in their dire distress and agony.

It was reserved for the *wounded* to experience the agonies of a ten-fold death. Hour after hour the conflagration raged, until a merciful rain quenched it and put an end to the horrible scene. The Third Corps remained in their position during the night, the sharp shooters, oddly enough as it seemed to them, with a strong line of infantry behind works between them and the enemy. Nothing occurred to break their repose, and for the first time for seven days they enjoyed eight hours of solid sleep unbroken by rebel alarms.

At day break on the morning of the 5th of May they were aroused by the usual command of "sharp shooters to the front," and again found themselves on the picket line confronting the enemy. The day passed, however, without serious fighting, one or two attacks being made by rebel skirmishers, more, apparently, to ascertain if the Union troops were actually there than for any more serious business.

These advances were easily repulsed by the sharp shooters with-out other aid, and at nine o'clock P. M., after seventeen hours of continuous duty without rations—for the eight days rations with which they started from their camp at Falmouth had long since been exhausted, and the scanty supply they had received on the afternoon of the third was barely enough for one meal—they were relieved and retired to the main line. The company lost on this day but one man, Martin C. Laffie, shot through the hand. Laffie was perma-nently disabled by his wound, and on the 1st of the following August was transferred to the Invalid Corps and never rejoined the company.

Several prisoners were captured by the men of Co. F on that day, but on the whole it was, as compared with the days of the preceding week, uneventful. On the 6th the army recrossed the Rappahannock by the bridges which had been preserved by the stubborn courage of the Third Corps, and the battle of Chancellorsville passed into history. The sharp shooters returned to their old camp at Falmouth as they had returned to the same camp after the disastrous battle of Fredericksburgh. It seemed as though they were fated never to leave that ground to fight a successful battle. Only eight days before they had marched out with buoyant anticipations, full of courage and full of hope. They returned discouraged and dispirited beyond description.

At Fredericksburgh the army had marched to the attack without hope or expectation of victory, for their soldiers' instinct told them that that was impossible. At Chancellorsville, however, they felt that they had everything to hope for—a magnificent army in full health and high spirits, an able and gallant commander, for such he had always shown himself to be, and a fair field. The thickets of the wilderness, it is true, were dense and well nigh impassable for them, but they were as bad for the enemy as for themselves, and they had felt that on anything like a fair field they ought to win. Now they found themselves just where they started; they had left seventeen thousand of their comrades dead, or worse than dead, on the field, and fourteen guns remained in the hands of the rebels as trophies of their victory; guns, too, that were sure to be turned against the federals in the very next battle. Twenty thousand stand of small arms were also left on the field to be gathered up by the victors. It was a disheartening reflection, but soldier-like the men put it from their thoughts and turned their minds and hands to the duties and occupations of the present.

15

VICKSBURG DURING THE TROUBLE

BY MARK TWAIN

There seem to be few subjects about which Mark Twain did not take up pen,
and the Civil War was no exception. In his classic Life on the Mississippi, *as*
he steams past Vicksburg, Mississippi—well known for its famous caves—he
recounts the story of a couple who lived through the city's shelling between
May and July 1863.

We used to plow past the lofty hill-city, Vicksburg, down-stream; but we cannot do that now. A cut-off has made a country town of it, like Osceola, St. Genevieve, and several others. There is currentless water—also a big island—in front of Vicksburg now. You come down the river the other side of the island, then turn and come up to the town; that is, in high water: in low water you can't come up, but must land some distance below it.

Signs and scars still remain, as reminders of Vicksburg's tremendous war experiences; earthworks, trees crippled by the cannon balls, cave-refuges in the clay precipices, etc. The caves did good service during the six weeks' bombardment of the city—May 8 to July 4, 1863. They were used by the non-combatants—mainly by the women and children; not to live in constantly, but to fly to for safety on occasion. They were mere holes, tunnels, driven into the perpendicular clay bank, then branched Y shape, within the hill. Life in Vicksburg, during the six weeks was perhaps—but wait; here are some materials out of which to reproduce it:

Population, twenty-seven thousand soldiers and three thousand non-combatants; the city utterly cut off from the world—walled solidly in, the frontage by gunboats, the rear by soldiers and batteries; hence, no buying and selling with the outside; no passing to and fro; no God-speeding a parting guest, no welcoming a coming one; no printed acres of world-wide news to be read at breakfast, mornings—a tedious dull absence of such matter, instead; hence, also, no running to see steamboats smoking into view in the distance up or down, and plowing toward the town—for none came, the river lay vacant and undisturbed; no rush and turmoil around the railway station, no struggling over bewildered swarms of passengers by noisy mobs of hackmen—all quiet there; flour two hundred dollars a barrel, sugar thirty, corn ten dollars a bushel, bacon five dollars a pound, rum a hundred dollars a gallon; other things in proportion: consequently, no roar and racket of drays and carriages tearing along the streets; nothing for them to do, among that handful of non-combatants of exhausted means; at three o'clock in the morning, silence; silence so dead that the measured tramp of a sentinel can be heard a seemingly impossible distance; out of hearing of this lonely sound, perhaps the stillness is absolute: all in a moment come ground-shaking thunder-crashes of artillery, the sky is cobwebbed with the crisscrossing red lines streaming from soaring bomb-shells, and a rain of iron fragments descends upon the city; descends upon the empty streets: streets which are not empty a moment later, but mottled with dim figures of frantic women and children scurrying from home and bed toward the cave dungeons—encouraged by the humorous grim soldiery, who shout "Rats, to your holes!" and laugh. The cannon-thunder rages, shells scream and crash overhead, the iron rain pours down, one hour, two hours, three, possibly six, then stops; silence follows, but the streets are still empty; the silence continues; by-and-bye a head projects from a cave here and there and yonder, and reconnoitres, cautiously; the silence still continuing, bodies follow heads, and jaded, half smothered creatures group themselves about, stretch their cramped limbs, draw in deep draughts of the grateful fresh air, gossip with the neighbors from the next cave; maybe straggle off home presently, or take a lounge through the town, if the stillness continues; and will scurry to the holes again, by-and-bye, when the war-tempest breaks forth once more.

There being but three thousand of these cave-dwellers—merely the population of a village—would they not come to know each other, after a week or two, and familiarly; insomuch that the fortunate or unfortunate experiences of one would be of interest to all? Those are the materials furnished by history. From them might not almost anybody reproduce for himself the life of that time in Vicksburg? Could you, who did not experience it, come nearer to reproducing it to the imagination of another non-participant than could a Vicksburger who did experience it? It seems impossible; and yet there are reasons why it might not really be. When one makes his first voyage in a ship, it is an experience which multitudinously bristles with striking novelties; novelties which are in such sharp contrast with all this person's former experiences that they take a seemingly deathless grip upon his imagination and memory. By tongue or pen he can make a landsman live that strange and stirring voyage over with him; make him see it all and feel it all. But if he wait? If he make ten voyages in succession—what then? Why, the thing has lost color, snap, surprise; and has become commonplace. The man would have nothing to tell that would quicken a landsman's pulse.

Years ago, I talked with a couple of the Vicksburg non-combatants—a man and his wife. Left to tell their story in their own way, those people told it without fire, almost without interest.

A week of their wonderful life there would have made their tongues eloquent forever perhaps; but they had six weeks of it, and that wore the novelty all out; they got used to being bomb-shelled out of home and into the ground; the matter became commonplace. After that, the possibility of their ever being startlingly interesting in their talks about it was gone. What the man said was to this effect:

"It got to be Sunday all the time. Seven Sundays in the week—to us, anyway. We hadn't anything to do, and time hung heavy. Seven

Sundays, and all of them broken up at one time or another, in the day or in the night, by a few hours of the awful storm of fire and thunder and iron. At first we used to shin for the holes a good deal faster than we did afterwards. The first time, I forgot the children, and Maria fetched them both along. When she was all safe in the cave she fainted. Two or three weeks afterwards, when she was running for the holes, one morning, through a shell-shower, a big shell burst near her, and covered her all over with dirt, and a piece of the iron carried away her game-bag of false hair from the back of her head. Well, she stopped to get that game-bag before she shoved along again! Was getting used to things already, you see. We all got so that we could tell a good deal about shells; and after that we didn't always go under shelter if it was a light shower. Us men would loaf around and talk; and a man would say, 'There she goes!' and name the kind of shell it was from the sound of it, and go on talking—if there wasn't any danger from it. If a shell was bursting close over us, we stopped talking and stood still;—uncomfortable, yes, but it wasn't safe to move. When it let go, we went on talking again, if nobody hurt—maybe saying, 'That was a ripper!' or some such commonplace comment before we resumed; or, maybe, we would see a shell poising itself away high in the air over-head. In that case, every fellow just whipped out a sudden, 'See you again, gents!' and shoved. Often and often I saw gangs of ladies prom-enading the streets, looking as cheerful as you please, and keeping an eye canted up watching the shells; and I've seen them stop still when they were uncertain about what a shell was going to do, and wait and make certain; and after that they sa'ntered along again, or lit out for shelter, according to the verdict. Streets in some towns have a litter of pieces of paper, and odds and ends of one sort or another lying around. Ours hadn't; they had iron litter. Sometimes a man would gather up all the iron fragments and unbursted shells in his neighborhood, and pile them into a kind of monument in his front yard—a ton of it, sometimes. No glass left; glass couldn't stand such a bombardment; it was all shivered out. Windows of the houses vacant—looked like eye-holes in a skull. Whole panes were as scarce as news. "We had church Sundays. Not many there, along at first; but by-and-bye pretty good turnouts. I've seen service stop a minute, and everybody sit quiet—no voice heard, pretty funeral-like then—and all the more so on account of the awful boom and crash going on outside and overhead; and pretty soon, when a body could be heard, service would go on again. Organs and church-music mixed up with a bombardment is a powerful queer combination—along at first. Coming out of church, one morning, we had an accident—the only one that happened around me on a Sunday. I was just having a hearty handshake with a friend I hadn't seen for a while, and saying, 'Drop into our cave to-night, after bombardment; we've got hold of a pint of prime wh—.' Whiskey, I was going to say, you know, but a shell interrupted. A chunk of it cut the man's arm off, and left it dangling in my hand. And do you know the thing that is going to stick the longest in my memory, and outlast everything else, little and big, I reckon, is the mean thought I had then? It was 'the whiskey is saved.' And yet, don't you know, it was kind of excusable; because it was as scarce as diamonds, and we had only just that little; never had another taste during the siege.

"Sometimes the caves were desperately crowded, and always hot and close. Sometimes a cave had twenty or twenty-five people packed into it; no turning-room for anybody; air so foul, sometimes, you couldn't have made a candle burn in it. A child was born in one of those caves one night. Think of that; why, it was like having it born in a trunk.

"Twice we had sixteen people in our cave; and a number of times we had a dozen. Pretty suffocating in there. We always had eight; eight belonged there. Hunger and misery and sickness and fright and sorrow, and I don't know what all, got so loaded into them that none of them were ever rightly their old selves after the siege. They all died but three of us within a couple of years. One night a shell burst in front of the hole and caved it in and stopped it up. It was lively times, for a while, digging out. Some of us came near smothering. After that we made two openings—ought to have thought of it at first.

"Mule meat. No, we only got down to that the last day or two. Of course it was good; anything is good when you are starving."

This man had kept a diary during—six weeks? No, only the first six days. The first day, eight close pages; the second, five; the third, one—loosely written; the fourth, three or four lines; a line or two the fifth and sixth days; seventh day, diary abandoned; life in terrific Vicksburg having now become commonplace and matter of course.

The war history of Vicksburg has more about it to interest the general reader than that of any other of the river-towns. It is full of variety, full of incident, full of the picturesque. Vicksburg held out longer than any other important river-town, and saw warfare in all its phases, both land and water—the siege, the mine, the assault, the repulse, the bombardment, sickness, captivity, famine.

The most beautiful of all the national cemeteries is here. Over the great gateway is this inscription:

"*Here Rest In Peace 16,600 Who Died For Their Country In The Years 1861 To 1865*"

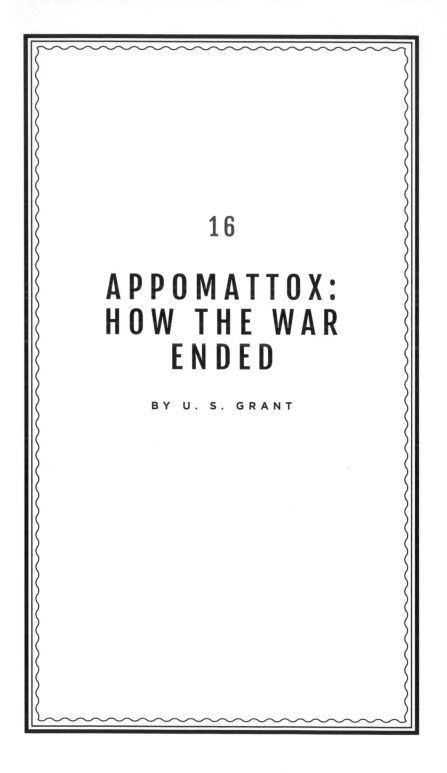

16

APPOMATTOX: HOW THE WAR ENDED

BY U. S. GRANT

Here are details and facts—not myths—on Lee's surrender, by the man who made it happen and was there. (Myth: Lee presenting sword; Grant handing it back. It never happened.)

This stoppage of Lee's column no doubt saved to us the trains following. Lee himself pushed on and crossed the wagon road bridge near the High Bridge, and attempted to destroy it. He did set fire to it, but the flames had made but little headway when Humphreys came up with his corps and drove away the rear-guard which had been left to protect it while it was being burned up. Humphreys forced his way across with some loss, and followed Lee to the intersection of the road crossing at Farmville with the one from Petersburg. Here Lee held a position which was very strong, naturally, besides being intrenched. Humphreys was alone, confronting him all through the day, and in a very hazardous position. He put on a bold face, however, and assaulted with some loss, but was not assaulted in return.

Our cavalry had gone farther south by the way of Prince Edward's Court House, along with the 5th corps (Griffin's), Ord falling in between Griffin and the Appomattox. Crook's division of cavalry and Wright's corps pushed on west of Farmville. When the cavalry reached Farmville they found that some of the Confederates were in ahead of them, and had already got their trains of provisions back to that point; but our troops were in time to prevent them from securing anything to eat, although they succeeded in again running the trains off, so that we did not get them for some time. These troops retreated to the north side of the Appomattox to join Lee, and succeeded in destroying the bridge after them. Considerable fighting ensued there between Wright's corps and a portion of our cavalry and the Confederates, but finally the cavalry forded the stream and drove them away. Wright built a foot-bridge for his men to march over on and then marched out to the junction of the roads to relieve Humphreys, arriving there that night. I had stopped the night before at Burkesville Junction. Our troops were then pretty much all out of the place, but we had a field hospital there, and Ord's command was extended from that point towards Farmville.

Here I met Dr. Smith, a Virginian and an officer of the regular army, who told me that in a conversation with General Ewell, one of the prisoners and a relative of his, Ewell had said that when we had got across the James River he knew their cause was lost, and it was the duty of their authorities to make the best terms they could while they still had a right to claim concessions. The authorities thought differently, however. Now the cause was lost and they had no right to claim anything. He said further, that for every man that was killed after this in the war somebody is responsible, and it would be but very little better than murder. He was not sure that Lee would consent to surrender his army without being able to consult with the President, but he hoped he would.

I rode in to Farmville on the 7th, arriving there early in the day. Sheridan and Ord were pushing through, away to the south. Meade was back towards the High Bridge, and Humphreys confronting Lee as before stated. After having gone into bivouac at Prince Edward's Court House, Sheridan learned that seven trains of provisions and forage were at Appomattox, and determined to start at once and capture them; and a forced march was necessary in order to get there before Lee's army could secure them. He wrote me a note telling me this. This fact, together with the incident related the night before by Dr. Smith, gave me the idea of opening correspondence with General Lee on the subject of the surrender of his army. I therefore wrote to him on this day, as follows:

HEADQUARTERS ARMIES OF THE U. S., 5 P.M., April 7, 1865. GENERAL R. E. LEE Commanding C. S. A.

The result of the last week must convince you of the hopelessness of further resistance on the part of the Army of Northern Virginia in this struggle. I feel that it is so, and regard it as my duty to shift from myself the responsibility of any further effusion of blood, by asking of you the surrender of that portion of the Confederate States army known as the Army of Northern Virginia.

U. S. GRANT, Lieut.-General.

Lee replied on the evening of the same day as follows:

April 7, 1865.

GENERAL: I have received your note of this day. Though not entertaining the opinion you express on the hopelessness of further resistance on the part of the Army of Northern Virginia, I reciprocate your desire to avoid useless effusion of blood, and therefore before considering your proposition, ask the terms you will offer on condition of its surrender.

R. E. LEE, General.

LIEUT.-GENERAL U. S. GRANT, Commanding Armies of the U. S.

This was not satisfactory, but I regarded it as deserving another letter and wrote him as follows:

April 8, 1865.

GENERAL R. E. LEE, Commanding C. S. A.

Your note of last evening in reply to mine of same date, asking the condition on which I will accept the surrender of the Army of Northern Virginia is just received. In reply I would say that, peace being my great desire, there is but one condition I would insist upon, namely: that the men and officers surrendered shall be disqualified for taking up arms again against the Government of the United States until properly exchanged. I will meet you, or will designate officers to meet any officers you may name for the same purpose, at any point agreeable to you, for the purpose of arranging definitely the terms upon which the surrender of the Army of Northern Virginia will be received.

U. S. GRANT, Lieut.-General.

Lee's army was rapidly crumbling. Many of his soldiers had enlisted from that part of the State where they now were, and were continually dropping out of the ranks and going to their homes. I know that I occupied a hotel almost destitute of furniture at Farmville, which had probably been used as a Confederate hospital. The next morning when I came out I found a Confederate colonel there, who reported to me and said that he was the proprietor of that house, and that he was a colonel of a regiment that had been raised in that neighborhood. He said that when he came along past home, he found that he was the only man of the regiment remaining with Lee's army, so he just dropped out, and now wanted to surrender himself. I told him to stay there and he would not be molested. That was one regiment which had been eliminated from Lee's force by this crumbling process.

Although Sheridan had been marching all day, his troops moved with alacrity and without any straggling. They began to see the end of what they had been fighting four years for. Nothing seemed to fatigue them. They were ready to move without rations and travel without rest until the end. Straggling had entirely ceased, and every man was now a rival for the front. The infantry marched about as rapidly as the cavalry could.

Sheridan sent Custer with his division to move south of Appomattox Station, which is about five miles south-west of the Court House, to get west of the trains and destroy the roads to the rear. They got there the night of the 8th, and succeeded partially; but some of the train men had just discovered the movement of our troops and succeeded in running off three of the trains. The other four were held by Custer.

The head of Lee's column came marching up there on the morning of the 9th, not dreaming, I suppose, that there were any Union soldiers near. The Confederates were surprised to find our cavalry had possession of the trains. However, they were desperate and at once assaulted, hoping to recover them. In the melee that ensued they succeeded in burning one of the trains, but not in getting anything from it. Custer then ordered the other trains run back on the road towards Farmville, and the fight continued.

So far, only our cavalry and the advance of Lee's army were engaged. Soon, however, Lee's men were brought up from the rear, no doubt expecting they had nothing to meet but our cavalry. But our infantry had pushed forward so rapidly that by the time the enemy got up they found Griffin's corps and the Army of the James confronting them. A sharp engagement ensued, but Lee quickly set up a white flag.

★　★　★

On the 8th I had followed the Army of the Potomac in rear of Lee. I was suffering very severely with a sick headache, and stopped at a farmhouse on the road some distance in rear of the main body of the army. I spent the night in bathing my feet in hot water and mustard, and putting mustard plasters on my wrists and the back part of my neck, hoping to be cured by morning. During the night I received Lee's answer to my letter of the 8th, inviting an interview between the lines on the following morning. But it was for a different purpose from that of surrendering his army, and I answered him as follows:

HEADQUARTERS ARMIES OF THE U. S., April 9, 1865.
GENERAL R. E. LEE, Commanding C. S. A.

Your note of yesterday is received. As I have no authority to treat on the subject of peace, the meeting proposed for ten A.M. to-day could lead to no good. I will state, however, General, that I am equally anxious for peace with yourself, and the whole North entertains the same feeling. The terms upon which peace can be had are well understood. By the South laying down their arms they will hasten that most desirable event, save thousands of human lives and hundreds of millions of property not yet destroyed. Sincerely hoping that all our difficulties may be settled without the loss of another life, I subscribe myself, etc.,

U. S. GRANT, Lieutenant-General.

I proceeded at an early hour in the morning, still suffering with the headache, to get to the head of the column. I was not more than two or three miles from Appomattox Court House at the time, but to go direct I would have to pass through Lee's army, or a portion of it. I had therefore to move south in order to get upon a road coming up from another direction.

When the white flag was put out by Lee, as already described, I was in this way moving towards Appomattox Court House, and consequently could not be communicated with immediately, and be informed of what Lee had done. Lee, therefore, sent a flag to the rear to advise Meade and one to the front to Sheridan, saying that he had sent a message to me for the purpose of having a meeting to consult about the surrender of his army, and asked for a suspension of hostilities until I could be communicated with.

As they had heard nothing of this until the fighting had got to be severe and all going against Lee, both of these commanders hesitated very considerably about suspending hostilities at all. They were afraid it was not in good faith, and we had the Army of Northern Virginia where it could not escape except by some deception. They, however, finally consented to a suspension of hostilities for two hours to give an opportunity of communicating with me in that time, if possible. It was found that, from the route I had taken, they would probably not be able to communicate with me and get an answer back within the time fixed unless the messenger should pass through the rebel lines.

Lee, therefore, sent an escort with the officer bearing this message through his lines to me.

> April 9, 1865.
>
> GENERAL: I received your note of this morning on the picket-line whither I had come to meet you and ascertain definitely what terms were embraced in your proposal of yesterday with reference to the surrender of this army. I now request an interview in accordance with the offer contained in your letter of yesterday for that purpose.
>
> R. E. LEE, General.
>
> LIEUTENANT-GENERAL U. S. GRANT Commanding U. S. Armies.

When the officer reached me I was still suffering with the sick headache, but the instant I saw the contents of the note I was cured. I wrote the following note in reply and hastened on:

April 9, 1865.

GENERAL R. E. LEE, Commanding C. S. Armies.

Your note of this date is but this moment (11.50 A.M.) received, in consequence of my having passed from the Richmond and Lynchburg road to the Farmville and Lynchburg road. I am at this writing about four miles west of Walker's Church and will push forward to the front for the purpose of meeting you. Notice sent to me on this road where you wish the interview to take place will meet me.

U. S. GRANT, Lieutenant-General.

I was conducted at once to where Sheridan was located with his troops drawn up in line of battle facing the Confederate army near by. They were very much excited, and expressed their view that this was all a ruse employed to enable the Confederates to get away. They said they believed that Johnston was marching up from North Carolina now, and Lee was moving to join him; and they would whip the rebels where they now were in five minutes if I would only let them go in. But I had no doubt about the good faith of Lee, and pretty soon was conducted to where he was. I found him at the house of a Mr. McLean, at Appomattox Court House, with Colonel Marshall, one of his staff officers, awaiting my arrival. The head of his column was occupying a hill, on a portion of which was an apple orchard, beyond a little valley which separated it from that on the crest of which Sheridan's forces were drawn up in line of battle to the south.

Before stating what took place between General Lee and myself, I will give all there is of the story of the famous apple tree.

Wars produce many stories of fiction, some of which are told until they are believed to be true. The war of the rebellion was no exception to this rule, and the story of the apple tree is one of those fictions based on a slight foundation of fact. As I have said, there was an apple orchard on the side of the hill occupied by the Confederate forces. Running diagonally up the hill was a wagon road, which, at one point, ran very near one of the trees, so that the wheels of vehicles had, on that side, cut off the roots of this tree, leaving a little embankment. General Babcock, of my staff, reported to me that when he first met General Lee he was sitting upon this embankment with his feet in the road below and his back resting against the tree. The story had no other foundation than that. Like many other stories, it would be very good if it was only true.

I had known General Lee in the old army, and had served with him in the Mexican War; but did not suppose, owing to the difference in our age and rank, that he would remember me, while I would more naturally remember him distinctly, because he was the chief of staff of General Scott in the Mexican War.

When I had left camp that morning I had not expected so soon the result that was then taking place, and consequently was in rough garb. I was without a sword, as I usually was when on horseback on the field, and wore a soldier's blouse for a coat, with the shoulder straps of my rank to indicate to the army who I was. When I went into the house I found General Lee. We greeted each other, and after shaking hands took our seats. I had my staff with me, a good portion of whom were in the room during the whole of the interview.

What General Lee's feelings were I do not know. As he was a man of much dignity, with an impassible face, it was impossible to say whether he felt inwardly glad that the end had finally come, or felt sad over the result, and was too manly to show it. Whatever his feelings, they were entirely concealed from my observation; but my own feelings, which had been quite jubilant on the receipt of his letter, were sad and depressed. I felt like anything rather than valiantly, and had suffered so much for a cause, though that cause was, I believe, one of the worst for which a people ever fought, and one for which there was the least excuse. I do not question, however, the sincerity of the great mass of those who were opposed to us.

General Lee was dressed in a full uniform which was entirely new, and was wearing a sword of considerable value, very likely the sword which had been presented by the State of Virginia; at all events, it was an entirely different sword from the one that would ordinarily be worn in the field. In my rough traveling suit, the uniform of a private with the straps of a lieutenant-general, I must have contrasted very strangely with a man so handsomely dressed, six feet high and of faultless form. But this was not a matter that I thought of until afterwards.

We soon fell into a conversation about old army times. He remarked that he remembered me very well in the old army; and I told him that as a matter of course I remembered him perfectly, but from the difference in our rank and years (there being about sixteen years' difference in our ages), I had thought it very likely that I had not attracted his attention sufficiently to be remembered by him after such a long interval. Our conversation grew so pleasant that I almost forgot the object of our meeting. After the conversation had run on in this style for some time, General Lee called my attention to the object of our meeting, and said that he had asked for this interview for the purpose of getting from me the terms I proposed to give his army. I said that I meant merely that his army should lay down their arms, not to take them up again during the continuance of the war unless duly and properly exchanged. He said that he had so understood my letter.

Then we gradually fell off again into conversation about matters foreign to the subject which had brought us together. This continued for some little time, when General Lee again interrupted the course of the conversation by suggesting that the terms I proposed to give his army ought to be written out. I called to General Parker, secretary on my staff, for writing materials, and commenced writing out the following terms:

APPOMATTOX C. H., VA., Ap 19th, 1865.
GEN. R. E. LEE, Comd'g C. S. A.

GEN: In accordance with the substance of my letter to you of the 8th inst., I propose to receive the surrender of the Army of N. Va. on the following terms, to wit: Rolls of all the officers and men to be made in duplicate. One copy to be given to an officer designated by me, the other to be retained by such officer or officers as you may designate. The officers to give their individual paroles not to take up arms against the Government of the United States until properly exchanged, and each company or regimental commander sign a like parole for the men of their commands. The arms, artillery and public property to be parked and stacked, and turned over to the officer appointed by me to receive them. This will not embrace the side-arms of the officers, nor their private horses or baggage. This done, each officer and man will be allowed to return to their homes, not to be disturbed by United States authority so long as they observe their paroles and the laws in force where they may reside.

Very respectfully, U. S. GRANT, Lt. Gen.

When I put my pen to the paper I did not know the first word that I should make use of in writing the terms. I only knew what was in my mind, and I wished to express it clearly, so that there could be no mistaking it. As I wrote on, the thought occurred to me that the officers had their own private horses and effects, which were important to them, but of no value to us; also that it would be an unnecessary humiliation to call upon them to deliver their side arms.

No conversation, not one word, passed between General Lee and myself, either about private property, side arms, or kindred subjects. He appeared to have no objections to the terms first proposed; or if he had a point to make against them he wished to wait until they were in writing to make it. When he read over that part of the terms about side arms, horses and private property of the officers, he remarked, with some feeling, I thought, that this would have a happy effect upon his army.

Then, after a little further conversation, General Lee remarked to me again that their army was organized a little differently from the army of the United States (still maintaining by implication that we were two countries); that in their army the cavalrymen and artillerists owned their own horses; and he asked if he was to understand that the men who so owned their horses were to be permitted to retain them. I told him that as the terms were written they would not; that only the officers were permitted to take their private property. He then, after reading over the terms a second time, remarked that that was clear.

I then said to him that I thought this would be about the last battle of the war—I sincerely hoped so; and I said further I took it that most of the men in the ranks were small farmers. The whole country had been so raided by the two armies that it was doubtful whether they would be able to put in a crop to carry themselves and their families through the next winter without the aid of the horses they were then riding. The United States did not want them and I would, therefore, instruct the officers I left behind to receive the paroles of his troops to let every man of the Confederate army who claimed to own a horse or mule take the animal to his home. Lee remarked again that this would have a happy effect.

He then sat down and wrote out the following letter:

HEADQUARTERS ARMY OF NORTHERN VIRGINIA,
April 9, 1865.

GENERAL:—I received your letter of this date containing the terms of the surrender of the Army of Northern Virginia as proposed by you. As they are substantially the same as those expressed in your letter of the 8th inst., they are accepted. I will proceed to designate the proper officers to carry the stipulations into effect.

R. E. LEE, General. LIEUT.-GENERAL U. S. GRANT.

While duplicates of the two letters were being made, the Union generals present were severally presented to General Lee.

The much talked of surrendering of Lee's sword and my handing it back, this and much more that has been said about it is the purest romance. The word sword or side arms was not mentioned by either of us until I wrote it in the terms. There was no premeditation, and it did not occur to me until the moment I wrote it down. If I had happened to omit it, and General Lee had called my attention to it, I should have put it in the terms precisely as I acceded to the provision about the soldiers retaining their horses.

General Lee, after all was completed and before taking his leave, remarked that his army was in a very bad condition for want of food, and that they were without forage; that his men had been living for some days on parched corn exclusively, and that he would have to ask me for rations and forage. I told him "certainly," and asked for how many men he wanted rations. His answer was "about twenty-five thousand;" and I authorized him to send his own commissary and quartermaster to Appomattox Station, two or three miles away, where he could have, out of the trains we had stopped, all the provisions wanted. As for forage, we had ourselves depended almost entirely upon the country for that.

Generals Gibbon, Griffin and Merritt were designated by me to carry into effect the paroling of Lee's troops before they should start for their homes—General Lee leaving Generals Longstreet, Gordon and Pendleton for them to confer with in order to facilitate this work. Lee and I then separated as cordially as we had met, he returning to his own lines, and all went into bivouac for the night at Appomattox.

Soon after Lee's departure I telegraphed to Washington as follows:

HEADQUARTERS APPOMATTOX C. H., VA., April 9th, 1865, 4.30 P.M.

HON. E. M. STANTON, Secretary of War, Washington.

General Lee surrendered the Army of Northern Virginia this afternoon on terms proposed by myself. The accompanying additional correspondence will show the conditions fully.

U. S. GRANT, Lieut.-General.

When news of the surrender first reached our lines our men commenced firing a salute of a hundred guns in honor of the victory. I at once sent word, however, to have it stopped. The Confederates were now our prisoners, and we did not want to exult over their downfall.

I determined to return to Washington at once, with a view to putting a stop to the purchase of supplies, and what I now deemed other useless outlay of money. Before leaving, however, I thought I would like to see General Lee again; so next morning I rode out beyond our lines towards his headquarters, preceded by a bugler and a staff-officer carrying a white flag.

Lee soon mounted his horse, seeing who it was, and met me. We had there between the lines, sitting on horseback, a very pleasant conversation of over half an hour, in the course of which Lee said to me that the South was a big country and that we might have to march over it three or four times before the war entirely ended, but that we would now be able to do it as they could no longer resist us. He expressed it as his earnest hope, however, that we would not be called upon to cause more loss and sacrifice of life; but he could not foretell the result. I then suggested to General Lee that there was not a man in the Confederacy whose influence with the soldiery and the whole people was as great as his, and that if he would now advise the surrender of all the armies I had no doubt his advice would be followed with alacrity. But Lee said, that he could not do that without consulting the President first. I knew there was no use to urge him to do anything against his ideas of what was right.

I was accompanied by my staff and other officers, some of whom seemed to have a great desire to go inside the Confederate lines. They finally asked permission of Lee to do so for the purpose of seeing some of their old army friends, and the permission was granted. They went over, had a very pleasant time with their old friends, and brought some of them back with them when they returned.

When Lee and I separated he went back to his lines and I returned to the house of Mr. McLean. Here the officers of both armies came in great numbers, and seemed to enjoy the meeting as much as though they had been friends separated for a long time while fighting battles under the same flag. For the time being it looked very much as if all thought of the war had escaped their minds. After an hour pleasantly passed in this way I set out on horseback, accompanied by my staff and a small escort, for Burkesville Junction, up to which point the railroad had by this time been repaired.

★ ★ ★

After I left General Lee at Appomattox Station, I went with my staff and a few others directly to Burkesville Station on my way to Washington. The road from Burkesville back having been newly repaired and the ground being soft, the train got off the track frequently, and, as a result, it was after midnight of the second day when I reached City Point. As soon as possible I took a dispatch-boat thence to Washington City.

While in Washington I was very busy for a time in preparing the necessary orders for the new state of affairs; communicating with my different commanders of separate departments, bodies of troops, etc. But by the 14th I was pretty well through with this work, so as to be able to visit my children, who were then in Burlington, New Jersey, attending school. Mrs. Grant was with me in Washington at the time, and we were invited by President and Mrs. Lincoln to accompany them to the theatre on the evening of that day. I replied to the President's verbal invitation to the effect, that if we were in the city we would take great pleasure in accompanying them; but that I was very anxious to get away and visit my children, and if I could get through my work during the day I should do so. I did get through and started by the evening train on the 14th, sending Mr. Lincoln word, of course, that I would not be at the theatre.

At that time the railroad to New York entered Philadelphia on Broad Street; passengers were conveyed in ambulances to the Delaware River, and then ferried to Camden, at which point they took the cars again. When I reached the ferry, on the east side of the City of Philadelphia, I found people awaiting my arrival there; and also dispatches informing me of the assassination of the President and Mr. Seward, and of the probable assassination of the Vice President, Mr. Johnson, and requesting my immediate return.

It would be impossible for me to describe the feeling that overcame me at the news of these assassinations, more especially the assassination of the President. I knew his goodness of heart, his generosity, his yielding disposition, his desire to have everybody happy, and above all his desire to see all the people of the United States enter again upon the full privileges of citizenship with equality among all. I knew also the feeling that Mr. Johnson had expressed in speeches and conversation against the Southern people, and I feared that his course towards them would be such as to repel, and make them unwilling citizens; and if they became such they would remain so for a long while. I felt that reconstruction had been set back, no telling how far.

I immediately arranged for getting a train to take me back to Washington City; but Mrs. Grant was with me; it was after midnight and Burlington was but an hour away. Finding that I could accompany her to our house and return about as soon as they would be ready to take me from the Philadelphia station, I went up with her and returned immediately by the same special train. The joy that I had witnessed among the people in the street and in public places in Washington when I left there, had been turned to grief; the city was in reality a city of mourning. I have stated what I believed then the effect of this would be, and my judgment now is that I was right. I believe the South would have been saved from very much of the hardness of feeling that was engendered by Mr. Johnson's course towards them during the first few months of his administration. Be this as it may, Mr. Lincoln's assassination was particularly unfortunate for the entire nation.

SOURCES

"Lincoln at War: Prominent Letters and Papers," by Abraham Lincoln, from *The Papers and Writings of Abraham Lincoln*, Volume Two, Constitutional Edition.

"O Captain! My Captain!," by Walt Whitman, was written in 1865 upon Lincoln's death and published in *The Saturday Press* and later collected in Whitman's *Leaves of Grass*. *Drum-Taps* is a volume of Whitman poetry republished in many collections.

"Facing Pickett's Charge," by Frank Aretas Haskell, is from his *The Battle of Gettysburg*, Wisconsin Military Commission, 1908.

"Catastrophe at Chancellorsville," by Colonel G. F. R. Henderson, is from his *Stonewall Jackson and the American Civil War*.

"The Wages of Fear: A Campfire Discussion," by George Cary Eggleston, is from *Southern Soldier Stories*, Macmillan Co., 1898.

"In the Ranks," by Reverend R. E. M'Bride, is from *In the Ranks: From the Wilderness to Appomattox CourtHouse*, 1883.

"A Confederate Soldier Speaks His Mind," by Carlton McCarthy, is from *Detailed Minutiae of Soldier Life in the Army of Northern Virginia*, 1882.

"America's Deadliest Day," by Frederick L. Hitchcock, is from *Antietam: One Officer's Story of America's Deadliest Day*, 1904.

"A Common Soldier," by Leander Stillwell, is from *The Story of a Common Soldier of Army Life in the Civil War, 1861–1865*.

"The Soldier's Life: A Confederate View," by Carlton McCarthy, is from *Detailed Minutiae of Soldier Life in the Army of Northern Virginia*, 1882.

"Slaughterhouse at Fredericksburg," by Frederick L. Hitchcock, is from *War from the Inside*, 1903.

"Among the Wounded," by Walt Whitman, is from *The Wound Dresser*, 1898.

"On Confederate Battlefields," by Carlton McCarthy, is from *Detailed Minutiae of Soldier Life in the Army of Northern Virginia*, 1882.

"The Truth About Gettysburg," by Helen D. Longstreet, is from *The Story of Gettysburg: Lee and Longstreet at High Tide*, 1904.

"The Flag Bearer," by Theodore Roosevelt, is from *Hero Tales from American History*, 1895.

"Love, Loss, and Army Life of the Common Soldier," by Leander Stillwell, is from *The Story of Common Soldier of Army Life in the Civil War, 1861–1865*, 1917.

"Army Life in a Black Regiment," by Thomas Wentworth Higginson, is from his book of the same title, 1869.

"Drummer Boy from Maine," by George T. Ulmer, is from *Adventurers and Reminiscences of a Volunteer Drummer Boy from Maine*, 1892.

"Vermont Sharpshooters," by William Y. W. Ripley, is from his book of the same title, 1892.

"Vicksburg During the Trouble," by Mark Twain, is from *Life on the Mississippi*, 1883.

"The Rebel Army Life," by Carlton McCarthy, is from *Detailed Minutiae of Soldier Life in the Army of Northern Virginia*, 1882.

"Appomattox: How the War Ended," by Ulysses S. Grant, is from *Personal Memoirs of U. S. Grant*, Volume 11.

ABOUT THE EDITOR

Lamar Underwood's longtime editing and writing career includes fifteen anthologies he has edited for Lyons Press. With titles ranging through such diverse subjects as survival, military history, aviation, and adventure, Lamar's anthologies also include his first mountain man book, *Tales of the Mountain Men*, published by Lyons in 2004. Books he has written include *The Quotable Soldier*, *The Quotable Warrior*, and *The Quotable Writer*—all Lyons Press—and the novel *On Dangerous Ground*, published by Doubleday in 1989. He is a former editor in chief of both *Sports Afield* and *Outdoor Life* magazines and has written numerous articles published in a wide list of magazines.